Learning Space

ADVANCE PRAISE FOR

Learning Space: Exploring Critical Pedagogy through Science Fiction

"*Learning Space: Exploring Critical Pedagogy through Science Fiction* offers an engaging, accessible path into a better understanding of critical pedagogy and science fiction, highlighting the role that both can play in forming a critical consciousness. Delamarter's welcoming prose invites readers into the conversation, using highly recognizable science fiction texts and scenarios to encourage a practical, thoughtful reimagining of critical pedagogy's ethos and praxis in today's classrooms. Science fiction's speculative vision provides fertile ground for understanding critical pedagogy's role in creating a more just world through education, and Delamarter brings this richness to life on the page with helpful, relatable examples and through clear, organized chapters."

Edward Ardeneaux IV
Associate Professor of English
University of the Ozarks

"*Learning Space: Exploring Critical Pedagogy through Science Fiction* is essential reading for pre-service teachers as well as the most seasoned veterans. Through his thorough and insightful exploration of the representation of learning spaces in science fiction ranging from *Star Trek* to *Fahrenheit 451*, Delamarter deftly articulates how applying critical pedagogy theory to such texts reveals the injustices and oppressions found in the real world, and in the real classroom."

Stephanie C. Fulcher
Distinguished Practitioner of English Education
Murray State University

"In an age where science fiction looks more and more like reality, the book *Learning Space: Exploring Critical Pedagogy through Science Fiction* by Jeremy Delamarter brings insights and thoughtful questions to light for both educators and learners. From epic franchises to Paulo Freire, Delamarter explains the benefits of understanding critical pedagogy in the age of artificial intelligence through the lens of science fiction. *Learning Space* allows fans and nonfans to enjoy the lessons and excellent examination of prevailing ideologies in a detailed and highly researched text."

Carey Millsap-Spears
Professor of Communications
Moraine Valley Community College and author of
Star Trek Discovery and the Female Gothic: Tell Fear No

Learning Space

Exploring Critical Pedagogy through Science Fiction

By Jeremy Delamarter

Myers Education Press

GORHAM, MAINE

Myers Education Press

Published by Myers Education Press, LLC
P.O. Box 424 Gorham, ME 04038

Myers Education Press is an academic publisher specializing in books, e-books, and digital content in the field of education. All of our books are subjected to a rigorous peer review process and produced in compliance with the standards of the Council on Library and Information Resources.

Library of Congress Cataloging-in-Publication Data available from Library of Congress.

13-digit ISBN 978-1-9755-0635-3 (paperback)
13-digit ISBN 978-1-9755-0636-0 (library networkable e-edition)
13-digit ISBN 978-1-9755-0637-7 (consumer e-edition)

Printed in the United States of America.

All first editions printed on acid-free paper that meets the American National Standards Institute Z39-48 standard.

Books published by Myers Education Press may be purchased at special quantity discount rates for groups, workshops, training organizations, and classroom usage. Please call our customer service department at 1-800-232-0223 for details.

Cover design by Teresa Lagrange.

Visit us on the web at **www.myersedpress.com** to browse our complete list of titles.

DEDICATION

THIS BOOK IS DEDICATED to my grandfather, Bob Green, who is the model of lifelong learning. I love you.

CONTENTS

ACKNOWLEDGMENTS

No book is born on its own. Instead, it comes to life through communal interaction. I may have done the writing, but make no mistake: this was a team effort. This book would not be possible without grace, insight, humor, and long-suffering patience from the following people: My Saint Martin's colleagues Karen Widdowson, Michele Bledsoe, Celeste Trimble, Julie Moon, Linda Maier, Jackie Clark, Johanna Powell, Ariah Hayes, McKenna Johnson, Katie Hancock, Shawn Ritter, Marley Redd, Jillian Abbe, and Tanya Smith Brice; my Twitter friend Liz Faber, who gave me the idea for this book in the first place, and my former colleague Jeremiah Webster, who helped me see literature in a new way; the administrators at my former university, who gave me a sabbatical to think this thing through; my family—Tracey, Rosy, Lucas, and Max—for listening to me yammer on during dinner; the authors, thinkers, and creators in this book, including George Lucas, Gene Roddenberry, Isaac Asimov, Ray Bradbury, and all the others whose stories captured my heart as a child and my mind as an adult; and, finally, all the students and teachers who fight every day for educational justice. You are all the true authors of this book.

FOREWORD

DEAR READERS, THIS BOOK is pretty much as old as my friendship with Dr. Delamarter. Three or four years ago, having just finished reading my own book, *The Computer's Voice: From Star Trek to Siri*, Dr. Delamarter messaged me on Twitter to bounce some ideas around about a monograph on science fiction and pedagogy. We wound up chatting for about an hour; and by chatting, I mostly mean nerding out about all our favorite sci-fi books, movies, and TV shows. As it turns out, we're sort of mirror images of each other—I am a science fiction scholar who loves pedagogy theory, and he is a pedagogy scholar who loves science fiction. (I'll leave it to the reader to decide who is the Federation version and who is the Terran version in this *Star Trek* mirror analogy.) Both our friendship and the book have grown enormously, though ironically, I will probably meet this book in person before I meet the author! I'm delighted to have been able to see the progress from that initial germ of an idea into what it is today—a set of essays that I hope you will find as intriguing, thought-provoking, and formative for your learning and teaching as I have found my friendship with Dr. Delamarter to be.

A few years ago, Dr. Delamarter invited me to sit in on one of his graduate education classes. We began with a painting, which we described in detail. From there, we reviewed key concepts from the day's reading about the Enlightenment and education, connected it back to the painting, and then shifted into a broader discussion about Enlightenment themes. It was a wonderfully collaborative experience, with Dr. Delamarter acting less as a lecturer and more as a weaver of the ideas we all brought to the table. The experience of reading this book is much like sitting in on one of Dr. Delamarter's classes. He begins each chapter/class with a text (in this case, a sci-fi book or film), then expertly connects our thoughts about the text to the subject at hand, leaving us with questions for discussion and a new excitement about both pop culture and pedagogy.

There are plenty of books out there about how to teach science fiction, of which this is *not* one. *Learning Space*, in the most delightfully meta sense, is itself a learning space where science fiction is the catalyst for a set of conversations about critical pedagogy. I hope you will share your thoughts and ideas with me and others, both in the classroom and on social media, as we build onto the discussion Dr. Delamarter and I began long ago on a Twitter far, far away.

Liz W. Faber, Ph.D.
Dean College
August 2024

PREFACE

THIS BOOK WAS BORN in a tent somewhere deep in the heart of Capitol Reef National Park. In the fall of 2021, I was on sabbatical, motorcycling my way across the western United States, setting up my camp for the night in whatever backcountry site I could find. Each night, I would crawl fully clothed into my sleeping bag and watch old episodes of *Star Trek: The Next Generation* until I fell asleep. On the night this book was born, I watched an episode called "New Ground" from Season Five. In the episode, Lieutenant Worf's son Alexander is suffering some psychological trauma related to the death of his mother. This trauma is manifesting in disruptive classroom behavior, and Worf, who has only recently taken custody of his son, doesn't know what to do. The episode ends with the ship's teacher, the ship's counselor, and the ship's entire administrative team providing wraparound care to both Alexander *and* Worf. I was struck by what an accurate portrayal of effective trauma-informed instruction it was, and I fell asleep thinking about how I might use this episode in some of my courses just as soon as my sabbatical was over.

You have a lot of time with your own thoughts when you're on a motorcycle, and by the time I pulled back into my driveway a few weeks later, I had drafted a rough outline of this book in my head. It had become clear to me that the story I needed to tell was bigger than a single episode of *Star Trek*. What I needed to write about was the relationship between science fiction and learning on a much grander scale. I needed to highlight the ways that sci-fi stories have the ability to confront us, to wake us from our slumber. As Kafka noted long ago, "a book must be an ice axe to break the sea frozen inside us."

For far too long, educational reform movements have focused on the technical. We fixate on reforming classroom instruction or revising the curriculum. We find new ways to train teachers. We introduce new tools, purchase new products, institute new policies. We spin our collective wheels trying to solve our educational woes, and yet, at the end of the day, we're no further along. Technical reform matters, but it almost always results in surface-level change. What almost never gets addressed is the need for philosophical reform. If you give a teacher shiny new tools but fail to address the tacit philosophy at work in the classroom and the school at large, the new tools will simply serve to reinforce the status quo. Reform efforts focus too often on the *how* of education, but they rarely, if ever, address the more fundamental *why*.

We are due for a philosophical reckoning. Well-intentioned educators at all levels go about the day-to-day work of teaching without necessarily being aware of the philosophical frameworks that undergird their pedagogy. They don't necessarily realize that they are caught in the gravity well of a philosophical black hole. They can't see it, and they might not even know it's there, and yet the mass and gravity of the underlying philosophy bend the space-time of education, drawing all learning toward its center. The teacher might fire the pedagogical thrusters, shifting learning slightly this way or that, but the ultimate result is the same. What students learn, what their education is steering them toward, is determined less by the individual action of the teacher and more by the unseen and often unacknowledged forces of educational philosophy. It's almost impossible to change direction if you're not aware of who—or what—is actually steering the ship.

It's interesting that the word *reckoning* has both accountability and nautical connotations. The coming reckoning will hold us to account for failing to act while inertial forces steer us toward disaster. But this same reckoning can also help us chart a new way forward, a new path to the stars. It is my hope that the critical awareness that the stories in this book might bring about will do both. As we begin to recognize our complicity in inequitable systems of learning, we might also finally, for perhaps the first time, identify new ways of thinking and being that will help us break orbit and set our sights on new worlds. This is, to borrow from Shakespeare, a reckoning "most devoutly to be wished" (Hamlet, III.i).

There is no such thing as an education free from philosophy. Belief systems and values are at the core of everything we do, whether we know it or not. It is my hope that the stories and strategies contained in this book help you recognize the philosophies at work in your learning. May they help you interrogate and, if necessary, break free from systems of inequity. May they provide you with new foundations upon which to ground your learning. And, most importantly, may they help you to do the same for others.

CHAPTER ONE

Worldbuilding: Sci-Fi, Justice, and Education

Introduction

TO THE EDUCATORS AND students who will be reading this book: It would be reasonable to assume that an exploration of the intersection between critical pedagogy and science fiction would focus primarily on technology and equity. One seeming hallmark of the science fiction classroom is the presence of some sort of human/machine interface that facilitates the learning process. For example, in Elizabeth Moon's (2003–2008) series *Vatta's War,* each student in the Space Force Academy is fitted with a neural implant, giving them real-time access to the databases and servers needed to command military spaceships. In *Star Trek: The Next Generation* (Roddenberry, 1987–1994), engineer Geordi LaForge wears a special set of goggles that link directly to his brain. These goggles not only allow him to see (he is blind), but they also provide him with additional information that the rest of the crew cannot access.

In other stories, however, the human/machine interface is separate from the person. Perhaps the most common form of this interface is the robot. Two of the most well-known science fiction robots—R2D2 and C3PO from *Star Wars* (Lucas, 1977)—are prime examples. As C3PO constantly reminds those around him, he is a protocol droid whose primary functions are to facilitate human-to-human and human-to-machine interactions. He translates millions of languages, including translating between human beings and a range of seemingly sentient computers (such as R2D2 or the hyperdrive computer on the *Millennium Falcon*). R2D2, meanwhile, uploads and downloads information directly from other computers and converts it into usable forms for the humans around him.

Science fiction has also explored the implications of using robotics in education, and there has been a long-standing fascination with the idea of robotic substitutes for human teachers. For example, Isaac Asimov's (1951) short story *The Fun They Had* recounts a conversation between a young boy and girl who are waiting for their robot teacher to be repaired. Similarly, Robert F. Young's (1957) short story *Thirty Days Had September* tells about a man who falls in love with the robotic schoolteacher that he bought for his son. Interestingly, both stories cast a suspicious eye on the robotic substitutes. In Asimov's story, the children are lamenting the isolation that comes from being taught alone by a robot. In Young's story, the robot lures the man away from his family. In both cases, the robot represents a technological impediment to human connection.

In many ways, the robotic teachers of science-fiction represent our concerns about the role of technology in education. For example, the robotic teacher has the capability to automate the undesirable elements of teaching, such as grading large numbers of essays, but it also has great capacity to harm. Robots freed from the moral and relational constraints of humanity might turn on their makers, as in James Cameron's (1984–2019) *Terminator* films or in 2014's *Ex Machina* (Garland). Faber (2021) notes that science-fictional portrayals of robot teachers often reflect both our societal unease about dehumanization and our wonder at the pedagogical potential of a more automated learning. This state of ambivalence, Faber claims, allows us to "consider the relationships among humanity, technology, and instructional design" (p. 59).

I take Faber's imperative seriously. As an ardent fan of science fiction, and as a scholar of educational thought, I marvel at the seeming prescience of science fiction authors, particularly in their ability to forecast the ever-increasing role of technology in our interpersonal and extra-personal interactions. From the TV walls of Bradbury's (1953) *Fahrenheit 451* to the tricorders of the myriad *Star Trek* (Roddenberry, 1966–present) films and TV shows, science fiction has shown us both the utopian and dystopian possibilities of a technologically mediated life. And, to be clear, this is not just the stuff of science fiction. As I write this introduction, in the early months of 2024, the United States and, indeed, most of the world, are still emerging from the throes of the COVID-19 pandemic. In the Puget Sound region of Washington State where I live, most K–12 schools and universities were forced to move to fully online education. Teacher/student interactions were mediated exclusively via Zoom or some other online conferencing software. Although it was a temporarily necessary move, this abrupt shift to virtual learning spaces highlights a great disparity in technological and economic resources. Students without reliable or broadband home Internet struggled to participate, and students with exceptional learning needs were often unable to access their mandated supports. One of the many lessons we have learned from the COVID shutdowns is that we are not yet ready to deliver large-scale, high-quality, and technologically-mediated instruction in an equitable fashion. Moving to Zoom exposed those fault lines.

But education is not only being increasingly mediated by technology, but in some cases, the machines are making the decisions. For example, the role of artificial intelligence in both instruction and assessment is on the rise, and it is not inconceivable that a teacher somewhere is using an AI bot to grade an essay that a student "wrote" using ChatGPT. Algorithms are being touted as the solution to large-scale educational problems. During the COVID-19 pandemic, for example, when students were unable to sit for their A Level exams, Great Britain turned to AI to assign scores based not on students' actual performance but rather on a complex combination of predictor variables (Office of Qualifications and Examinations Regulation, 2020). As you might imagine, this move was not well-received by the public, partly due to the fundamental lack of equity in the algorithmic process. Variables were weighted differently depending on students' class sizes, giving students from private schools an algorithmic advantage over students from public schools. Once again, the COVID-19 pandemic highlighted the deep, systemic inequities around technology and education.

But questions of equity and technology in education are not what this book is about, or at least not directly. An analysis of technology in the science fiction classroom is, in many ways, an analysis of instructional means. It is an analysis of pedagogical technique and of lesson design. In the real classroom, where many of these issues are playing out in real time, it is an analysis of algorithmically designed curricula, of learning via machine *and* of machine learning, which are two very different, albeit highly related, phenomena. In any case, our discourse regarding the relationship between learning and technology most often focuses on the how-tos. We debate (rightly) issues of access and equity, issues of funding, issues of modality, student engagement, and a host of other important topics. These are necessary conversations, and as I said earlier, it is reasonable to suppose that a book on education in science fiction would focus on a fairly straightforward question: What can science fiction tell us about *how* we can use technology equitably in the classroom?

This book, however, is not interested in *how*, per se, or at least not in isolation. Instead of focusing solely on the means of teaching and learning, I am interested in what the representations of teaching, learning, and knowing in popular science fiction reveal about our educational *ends*. I am interested in the *why*. What is the purpose of education? What does it mean to learn? What is knowledge, and how does one acquire it? Is *acquire* even the right word? What kinds of actions and responsibilities does knowledge entail? Whose interests does formal education serve? Whose interests *ought* it serve? Is education meant to preserve existing systems or to bring about new ones? Is there a difference between education and learning?

These are not new questions, but I believe they are the right ones. The decades-long narrative of a failing American educational system has brought about countless reform movements all aimed at fixing what is "broken." Some of these efforts have been well-intended; others have not. What they mostly have in common, however, is a focus on reforming the *means* of education. New curricula, smaller class sizes, improved teacher training, standards-based accountability—these are all important, and they merit our attention. They are, however, not the core of what ails American education. Our problems are problems of ends, not of means. The only coherent "reform" effort addressing questions of educational purpose is the amorphous neoliberal movement that essentially reduces and constricts the purpose of education thusly: to serve corporate interests.

This book is not a screed against a neoliberal agenda, however. Others far more articulate than I have written exceedingly well on this very topic (see, for example, Bowl, 2017; Brecher, 2019; De Lissovoy, 2014), and I leave it to them to fight that fight. Furthermore, this book is not a manifesto in which I soapbox about my own educational beliefs and rant about how schools are failing to do things the way I think they should. Although there is a long and unfortunate tradition of mostly white male professors pontificating on the "proper" aims of education, this book is not intended to be part of that tradition. Instead, this book has the relatively humble goal of teaching you something. *Quite simply, the purpose of this book is to intro-*

duce you to the features, vocabulary, tools, and goals of critical pedagogy so that you can recognize and change inequitable educational systems.

So why science fiction? Why not just write a more standard textbook about critical pedagogy? First and foremost, I am an ardent science fiction fan, and there is simply a great joy in researching and writing about a genre that I love. Second, science fiction is an exceedingly popular genre, both in print and on screen (Ames, 2013), and there is emerging quantitative evidence that science fiction literacy correlates with real world actions, such as voting and supporting proposed legislation related to AI (e.g., Young & Carpenter, 2018). Given its increasing popularity and its ability to impact cultural attitudes, perceptions, and actions, science fiction is, quite simply, important.

Finally, and most importantly, I have chosen to use science fiction as an introduction to critical pedagogy because of its literary and humanistic richness. While once considered a fringe pursuit, science fiction studies have grown both in popularity and acceptance in the modern academy. The formal and aesthetic qualities of the genre have grown far beyond the space operas of the early 20th century, and some now consider it the preeminent genre for literary and critical analysis (e.g., Freedman, 2020). Furthermore, as I will discuss, science fiction is, perhaps due to its speculative nature, uniquely positioned to examine the implications and boundaries of power, gender, biological determinism, climate change, sentience, and nearly every other scientific and [trans]humanistic concern confronting us in the 21st century. In this way, science fiction is perhaps the most focused of lenses through which to analyze our cultural assumptions about the relationship between education and power. In short, science fiction is a wonderful tool both for learning about and for engaging in critical pedagogy.

As will be discussed at length later in this chapter, these assumptions are embodied in *learning spaces*, which are the sometimes physical, always relational, philosophically laden locations where learning takes place. We will be examining the learning spaces in science fiction films, books, and other media from the mid-20th century to the present day in order to uncover the presuppositions about education and power that are sometimes explicit but that are more often tacit, buried in the in-between and the unstated. We will be highlighting the major features of critical pedagogy that these narratives embody, and we will occasionally delve into historical accounts of how these beliefs came to be, particularly in educational settings. I say "we," because my own educational presuppositions recognize the acts of learning and teaching as communal endeavors. In the words of Lave & Wenger (1991), learning is always situated, and in this case, it is situated in the interaction between you, me, and the words printed on this page. I see you as my co-laborer in this work, and I hope you see yourself the same way.

Mostly, I hope that my deep love for both science-fiction and education comes through on the page. I write this book as neither a critique of the genre nor a critique of educational practices. Instead, this is a love letter to the truth-telling power of good art and the life-altering power of learning.

A few notes about the style of this book are warranted at this point. As you may already have noticed, the tone of this book will alternate between that which is familiar in serious academic scholarship and that of an unrepentant fanboy. I cannot hide my love for science fiction, nor do I want to. Likewise, I cannot hide my commitment to rigorous scholarship. Passion and intellect are not mutually exclusive, and I hope you approach your own teaching and learning with the same mix of heart and mind.

Whenever possible, I alternate between *he, she*, and *they* pronouns when talking about teachers and students. I do need to note, though, that some of the texts we will be analyzing represent unfortunate patriarchal norms. When quoting from those texts, I will retain the original language. In my analysis, however, I will extend the pronouns to include all readers and all teachers.

Furthermore, I invite you to extend my own analysis to your specific situation. This book is meant to introduce critical pedagogy through science fiction, but it is not intended to be the final word on the subject. On the contrary, my hope is that this book will be a catalyst for you to seek out and embrace the *novum* in your own learning spaces.

So let's dig in.

What is Critical Pedagogy?

Although the tenets, features, and nuances of critical pedagogy will be unpacked and demonstrated over the course of this book, a working definition will help the rest of this introduction pop into focus. Please note that this brief introduction to critical pedagogy is far from complete. The upcoming chapters will provide much more detail. For now, though, a short overview:

Critical pedagogy is both a philosophy and a practice. Philosophically, critical pedagogy is the belief that "*all* education is political [and that] teaching is never a neutral act" (Friere, 1970, p. 19). In this case, *political* does not refer to Democrat or Republican political parties but rather to the formal and informal civil and social power structures and ideologies at work in a given society. If teaching is never neutral, then every act of schooling must therefore be working to either maintain or subvert existing power structures. Curricula, teacher/student interactions, school schedules, classroom architecture—all of these (and more!) serve to reinforce social structures and dominant ideologies or to push back against them. For example, critical pedagogy insists that the arrangement of desks in a classroom is as politically charged as any other element of school. The "traditional" classroom set-up of students in individual desks and the teacher standing at the front of the classroom reinforces a hierarchical authority structure, *regardless of the teacher's intent*. Such an arrangement operates on the perhaps unspoken assumption that students are to work individually, not collectively. Furthermore, the teacher and the students locate themselves at opposite ends of the room, much like a priest and a congregation might be separated in a church building. The kind of pedagogy compelled by this kind of classroom arrangement might focus on direct lecture. Students may work silently at their desks, completing worksheets.

These are not neutral endeavors, according to critical pedagogy. They are power laden, assuming a specific type of relationship between students and teachers, students and knowledge, and students and one another. A critical *pedagogue*—that is, a practitioner of critical pedagogy—might highlight that a classroom like this frees the teacher to move about the room, while students are expected *not* to move. Questions of bodily autonomy begin to arise. Who is allowed to speak? Who is expected to remain silent unless given permission? Who is allowed to go outside? Who is not? Who is allowed to meet their basic biological needs? Who must ask permission to use the restroom? Critical pedagogy highlights the simple fact that every aspect of the educational setting, just like every aspect of educational practice, is political. There is no such thing as neutral education, and the "exploration of the inextricable relationship among knowledge, ideology, and power . . . [is] essential to any critical pedagogy" (Leistyna et al., 2004, p. 9).

If the philosophy of critical pedagogy is the claim that "all education is political," then the practice of critical pedagogy lies in exposing and evaluating the political nature of education. If all education is ideological, the critical pedagogue should ask: Whose ideology is being taught (Leistyna & Woodrum, 1996)? More specifically, critical pedagogy in action involves a "commitment to the unwavering liberation of oppressed populations and a belief in the historical possibility of change" (Darder et al., 2003, p. 113). Just as civic and social power structures often serve to disenfranchise and marginalize segments of the population, and just as these same structures seek to maintain the systems of power that keep the elite ruling class in charge, so too do our educational practices serve to maintain and reinforce inequality. The practice of critical pedagogy, then, is both to *expose* the inequalities inherent in educational practice and to *resist* them.

A critical pedagogue, for example, might expose a school's racially inequitable suspension practices by highlighting how Black students are suspended at far higher rates than white students for similar offenses (read more about this phenomenon in Chapter Five). She might then resist the inequity by leading a series of professional development activities aimed at implementing non-punitive, reconciliation-based strategies. Similarly, a critical pedagogue might *expose* the casual sexism in a math teacher's practices by highlighting how often the teacher responds differently to male and female students when they struggle. She might then *resist* in any number of ways, such as a short conversation, a suggestion for PD, or even a reevaluation of her own classroom practices.

At its most basic level, critical pedagogy is the process of exposing and seeking to change inequitable educational practices. Critical pedagogy often overlaps with other critical philosophies, such as Marxism, feminism, queer studies, race studies, and disability criticism. These critical lenses share both the belief that inequities exist and the conviction to do something about them. And although critical pedagogy may certainly examine the roles of economics, race, gender, ability, sexual orientation, and a host of other factors in perpetuating inequalities, it will do so by focusing on the educational sphere.

The process of engaging in critical pedagogy involves examining one's own beliefs and practices just as much as examining those of the educational system. It involves enabling teachers and students alike to become conscious of the hidden structures and belief systems with which they are surrounded (Bartolomé, 2004; Rautins & Ibrahim, 2011), and it involves equipping them with the critical tools and political acumen both to emancipate themselves from oppressive structures and to transform their educational settings (Bercaw & Stooksberry, 2005). In short, critical pedagogy enables both educators and students to see educational inequities that were previously hidden and, perhaps more importantly, to free themselves and others.

If critical pedagogy is the practice of exposing and resisting the power structures and ideologies hidden in education, how does science fiction fit with these goals? How does science fiction aid in developing a deeper consciousness of the world around us? To answer these questions, we must first define what we mean by *science fiction*.

What is Science Fiction?

Although the Oxford English Dictionary defines *science fiction* as "fiction in which the setting and story feature hypothetical scientific or technological advances, the existence of alien life, space or time travel, etc., *esp.* such fiction set in the future, or an imagined alternative universe" (Science Fiction, n.d.), the notion of what is and what is not science fiction is hotly contested (Roberts, 2016). In general, definitions of science fiction fall into one of three categories: instrumentalism, reader-response, or formalism.

Instrumentalism

For many, science fiction is defined by its utility (that is, its usefulness at bringing about a specific goal). In this sense, science fiction is an "instrument" or a "tool" that we can use to achieve a desired result. For example, some recent literature has defined science fiction as a popular mode for "thinking about life in a modern technoscientific world" (Weiner et al., 2018, p. 7), a tool for exploring new and future energy sources (Raven, 2017), a space for exploring public expectations of urban space (Collie, 2011), and a conduit through which individuals can reflect on career choices (Orthia, 2019).

Science fiction is also increasingly being used as a tool for science communication (Menadue & Cheer, 2017). The genre is particularly useful for the *teaching* of science, especially in secondary and post-secondary settings. A brief and admittedly unscientific Google Scholar search reveals that science fiction is used for teaching such disparate STEM topics as accounting (e.g., Persson & Fafatas, 2018), astronomy (e.g., Fraknoi, 2002), climate change (e.g., Whyte, 2018), computer ethics (e.g., Burton et al., 2018), engineering (e.g., Segall, 2002), evolution (e.g., Bixler, 2007), petrochemicals (e.g., Aisyah et al., 2017), physics (e.g., Dark, 2005), nanotechnology (e.g., Berne & Schummer, 2005), robotics (e.g., Gonzales-Jiminez, 2018), and thermodynamics (e.g., Liberko, 2004). In addition to its role in STEM education, science fiction is also used to teach such social science subjects as child development (e.g., Kirsh, 1998), classroom management (e.g., Fernández-Llamas et al., 2018), gender and sex psychology (e.g., Lips, 1990), human ethics (e.g., Blackford, 2017), literary analysis (e.g., Fife, 1999), narrative structure (e.g., Bengels, 2005), and political science (e.g., Barton-Kreise, 1993). Furthermore, there is empirical reason to suspect that science fiction may, in fact, be an effective tool for teaching scientific facts, principles, and concepts (e.g., Laprise & Winrich, 2010; Menadue & Jacups, 2018).

Reader-Response

In contrast to the utilitarianism that I have just described, other definitions locate science fiction's essence in the interaction between the world of the text and the world of the reader. To quote prolific author Philip K. Dick (1981/1997), a science fiction text consists of

> a fictitious world; that is the first step . . . It is our world dislocated by some kind of mental effort on the part of the author, our world transformed into that which it is not or not yet . . . [this] dislocation must be a conceptual one, not merely a trivial or bizarre one—*this* is the essence of science fiction, the conceptual dislocation within the society so that as a result a new society is generated in the author's mind, transferred to paper, and from paper it occurs as a convulsive shock in the reader's mind, *the shock of dysrecognition*. He knows that it is not his actual world that he is reading about. (preface)

In Dick's formulation, the essence of science fiction resides in the intersection between the author's text and the reader's cognitive facilities. This interpretive middle space (Rosenblatt, 1993) highlights the relationship between the reader and the text and rejects the binary or dualistic notion that meaning or definition resides in either. Without delving into the intricacies of reader-response theory, however, I must acknowledge the reader's role in meaning-making while simultaneously rejecting Dick's definition of science fiction, at least for our purposes here. A solely utilitarian or reader-response-based definition of the genre is of little value for this book, although

I do not deny that science fiction may, indeed, possess the powers just described. Probing or proving such claims, however, is far beyond the scope of this book, if for no other reason than that this book is not an exploration of the minds of science fiction readers but rather an exploration of the texts themselves.

Formalism

For a number of science fiction authors and theorists, science fiction should be defined according to the forms and structures of the literature itself. In other words, formalists claim that there's something in the structure of science fiction that sets it apart from other genres, regardless of how it is used or received. Celebrated author Robert Heinlein (1991) conceives of science fiction narratives as encounters with the "new:"

> In the speculative science fiction story accepted science and established fiefs are extrapolated to produce a new situation, a new framework for human action. As a result of this new situation, new human problems are created—and our story is about how human beings cope with those new problems. (p. 5)

By this definition, science fiction is a narrative form in which the protagonist encounters a newness that has been occasioned or brought about by scientific development. This newness is often referred to as a "novum" that results in "estrangement" (Suvin, 1988). Of course, the novum as an integral element of narrative development is not unique to science fiction. Campbell (1949) famously highlighted the general narrative structure of the hero's quest, in which the protagonist is compelled to leave the known world, cross the threshold, and enter the special world. This narrative structure is shared by all human cultures and is so prevalent as to be considered archetypal. Indeed, many of our most popular science fiction stories are built upon this structure, a narrative structure most famously codified in the *U.S.S. Enterprise*'s mission to "boldly go where no one has gone before" (Roddenberry, 1987–1994).

To be sure, it could be compellingly argued that *all* narratives involve encounters with the unknown, albeit not on a stellar scale. Something must disturb the equilibrium of the textual world, forcing protagonists into unfamiliar spaces, be they relational, psychological, or physical. In this sense, stories of all types and genres require a novum as a catalyst to begin the action. The *novum* of science fiction, however, differs from this generalized narrative novum. The difference lies in the novum's source: namely, in science. Broderick (1995) explains science fiction thusly: "SF [science fiction] is that species of storytelling native to a culture undergoing the epistemic changes implicated in the rise and supercession of technical-industrial modes of production, distribution, consumption, and disposal" (p. 155). The term *epistemic* refers to the way that we know things (a topic we will cover in greater depth in Chapter Seven). Broderick's definition highlights the relationship between epistemic changes (Suvin's *estrangement*) resulting from the ascendency of new technologies and/or scientific understandings.

For example, whereas the narratives of both the Harlequin Romance and the science fiction story may both focus on the disruption of long-cherished relationships, the novum of the romance story may be due to regular and understood phenomena, such as sexual attraction, changes in economic status, etc., while the novum of the science fiction story, by contrast, will arise as the result of scientific/technological development. Though the story of a woman and her robot lover, such as Asimov's (1957) *The Naked Sun*, may share many narrative and formal elements with a Harlequin Romance, (e.g., unrequited love, rebellion against sexual mores, exaggerated descriptions of sexual arousal), the robot story is predicated upon a novum that is foreign to and incongruent with the world of the Harlequin text: science as disruptor.

The disruptive potential of science manifests not only through the development of new technologies but also through the new understandings of the universe that these technologies make possible. New and improved telescopes lead to radical revisions in the understanding of the cosmos. Large particle colliders reveal quantum entanglements that defy our most basic assumptions about cause and effect. The steam engine, the assembly line, the cell phone, the nuclear weapon: each of these is a novum not because it is a new technology per se but rather because it is a new technology that occasioned a new understanding of human beings in relation to themselves, to one another, and to the material world that they inhabit. In many ways, the novum of science fiction may be conceived of as a technologically/scientifically induced recalibration of humanity's relationship to the material order, a recalibration in which "what had been seemingly clear and unremarkable comes to stand out as something worth asking about" (Gunkel, 2018, p. 14). Rhee (2018) refers to this as the *robotic imaginary*, in which technology and human relational understanding "do not exist in vacuums, but are intractably tied to discourse and worlds beyond their immediately perceptible parameters" (introduction).

The notion of "worlds beyond . . . parameters" (introduction) is fitting, because, as the next section discusses, science fiction has its roots in changing understandings of the spatial and temporal scale of the cosmos. In a quite literal sense, science fiction is a literary form that questions humanity's place in the universe.

A cosmological and material novum

Prior to the development of telescope technologies that allowed for observation across astronomical distances, the universe was conceived of in primarily theological terms, at least by those in the West. In the mid-2nd century AD, Roman astronomer Ptolemy created a mathematical model of the solar system that put the Earth squarely in the center of the physical universe with all observable planets, stars, moons, and other celestial bodies orbiting around it. But Earth was not just the center of the physical universe: it was the center of the spiritual universe, as well. It was also the focal point of the Christian God's creativity and salvation. In this model of the universe, the relationship between the planets, the stars, and everything else in the heavens was understood purely in spiritual terms or theological terms, and the "science fiction" of the day echoed this spiritual understanding (Roberts, 2016). For example, although there is literature from this time period that tells of voyages to the moon or to the spheres beyond, these voyages are almost exclusively allegorical or spiritual. The geocentric, or earth-centered, structure of the cosmos reflected the spiritual nature of God and of God's special relationship with humanity. A literary trip to the moon, therefore, could tell us nothing other than theological truths and could serve no purpose other than to reinforce what was already understood about the nature of God and creation. Most importantly, the *voyage extraordinaire* was a spiritual journey, not a material journey. Roberts (2016) notes that even the mode of travel to and from the heavens was spiritualized, with travelers often being borne on the backs of angels or being accompanied by saints, much akin to Virgil guiding Dante through hell in the *Inferno*. Just as Dante's descent was understood in spiritual and not literal subterranean terms, voyages into the (quite limited) cosmos were similarly non-material.

However, the invention of more powerful telescopes led to both the discovery of worlds beyond the boundaries of our solar system (thanks, Galileo!), and, most importantly, new mathematical models and scientific evidence that placed the *sun*, not the Earth, at the center of our solar system (and thanks, Copernicus!). These discoveries had a radical impact on both European theological understandings and on the literary accounts of traveling to the heavens. As the true scale of the universe began to be understood, questions and doubts about a geocentric theology began to infiltrate the literature of what we would today call "space travel." Literary encounters with beings on other planets became occasions to speculate about the extent to which God's salvation might extend to non-human sentient races (e.g., Godwin, 1995/1638; Wilkins, 1973/1638). As the material conditions of the moon became more fully understood, two authors even speculated that aliens living on the moon must live in an unsanctified state, because it is not possible to grow grapes in an airless vacuum, rendering sacramental wine and holy communion quite literally out of reach (Schmidt & Layritz, 1679).

All this is to say that location matters, and when trying to classify and define science fiction, it is helpful to consider the locus of cognitive estrangement. One immediate effect of Copernican revelations was the collapse of cosmological borders and boundaries. The realization that the planets orbit the sun, not the Earth, and the even greater realization of a vast universe beyond the boundaries of our solar system, led to a radical reconceptualization of space—a reconceptualization that continues to be explored in science fiction today. By *space*, I do not mean merely mean *outer space* or that which exists beyond Earth's atmosphere. I refer instead to *spatial scale*. As 16th and 17th-century Europe began to grapple with the sheer size of the material universe, questions of physical distance gave rise to questions of theological distance. A universe that does not rotate around God's salvation of humanity allows for the possibility that human beings are neither unique nor special and are instead just one among perhaps untold numbers of sentient species inhabiting countless worlds circling countless stars. The question of humanity's place in an increasingly large and ever-expanding material universe became at once a question of cosmological location *and* a question of spiritual importance.

Indeed, this new understanding of humanity's scale in relation to the material universe was being propelled by new *micro*scopic technology, as well. As Roberts (2016) notes:

> A great many Enlightenment [and proto science fiction] works find the macroscopic and the microscopic to be new imaginative resources of wondrous possibility. . . . [F]irst, various new scientific discoveries and inventions had revealed that the universe is incomparably huger than previously thought. It also revealed that whole ecosystems existed far too small for the unaided eye to see. But there is both a metaphorical and an empirical dimension to this new fascination with scale; knowledge itself, the cornerstone of Enlightenment praxis, had be reconceptualized as something simultaneously very large and very small. (p. 87)

To be sure, science fiction authors have explored the *minute* with a fervor almost as great as that with which they have explored the colossal. Asimov's (1966) *Fantastic Voyage*, for example, tells of doctors and scientists who, having been miniaturized, enter a patient's body in an attempt to save him. They encounter wonder upon wonder, much as if they were exploring the cosmos. Indeed, the publisher's own description of the book refers to this miniaturized voyage as "the last frontier of man" (About Fantastic Voyage, 2024). *Star Wars* (Lucas, 1977), perhaps the most famous and commercially successful collection of science fiction stories ever told, explores the material universe at both the micro and macro levels. On one hand, the characters fly about the galaxy, jumping from star system to star system with a faster-than-light hyperdrive. At the same time, the films explain that the Force, the quasi-magical energy that gives Jedi their powers and binds all living things together, is actually a function of *midichlorian*, sub-cellular structures that are abundant in Jedi and that presumably operate according to known laws of genetics. (Indeed, Force powers do seem to be passed down from parent to child.) Thus, the cognitive estrangement in science fiction is located in both the very large and the very small. It is also important to note that although the Force looks very much like magic, and although it is discussed in spiritual and religious terms within the world of the films, the same films go to great and sometimes inconsistent lengths to assure us that the Force is, in fact, *material*, not spiritual.

The rejection of spiritualism in favor of a materialism, which began in earnest in the 16th century and continues to this day, is the genesis of what we now call science fiction. Roberts (2016) asserts—and I agree—that the cognitive estrangement that characterizes science fiction emerged from the collapse of the Ptolemaic cosmos, which was built on the belief that the

Earth was the center of the solar system and, indeed, the entire universe. As this old model of the cosmos passed away, a new genre of literature emerged that explored human beings' relationship to an infinite and material cosmos. Whereas pre-Copernican literature wrestled with questions of humanity's place and role in the created order, these questions were framed spiritually. In contrast, although the science fiction that emerged from the ashes of the Ptolemaic cosmos wrestled (and still wrestles) with similar questions, these questions are often framed materially. In the Ptolemaic cosmos, the question "what does it mean to be human?" dealt with issues of sin and redemption, of being made in the image of God, of the lower elements of the created order, and of other theological queries. In a post-Copernican cosmos, however, the question "what does it mean to be human?" confronts and interrogates issues of biology, of artificial intelligence, of genetic manipulation, of extra-terrestrial sentience, and of a thousand other fantastic and yet material concerns. In the former, wonder and humility arise out of humanity's relationship with a spiritual deity who is far greater than the limits of human comprehension; in the latter, the same wonder and humility arise out of humanity's relationship to a material universe that far exceeds the capacities of human imagination. Consequently, these new material understandings of the cosmos, and the scientific process and technological advances that were both their cause and effect, led European society to reform and reimagine humanity's relationship with the cosmos, and it is in this nebular dust of an exploded cosmology that the star of science fiction was born.

Of course, *spatial estrangement* is not the only novum at work in science fiction. For example, *temporal estrangement* is considered by many to be *the* hallmark of the genre. The time travel paradoxes of James Cameron's (1984–2019) *Terminator* films, the yet-to-be empires of Asimov's (1951–1953) *Foundation* trilogy, the relativity effects of Poul Anderson's (1970) monumental *Tao Zero* and Joe Halderman's (1974) terrifying *The Forever War*, the extended lives of Richard Morgan's (2002) *Altered Carbon*, the past and future dystopias of Octavia Butler's *Kindred* (1979) and *The Parable of the Sower* (1993), or the "long time ago" tales of George Lucas's (1977–present) *Star Wars* universe—these are but a small sampling of the texts in which temporal dislocation serves as the novum. Still other, newer nova exist. We might look to the virtual nova of William Gibson's (1984) *Neuromancer* or Dan Simmons' (1989–1997) *Hyperion Cantos*, in which the principal disruption is neither time nor space but rather a new, digital, binary frontier in which the rules of the universe as we understand them simply do not apply. A similar description could perhaps be used in regard to a synthetic novum, in which the locus of estrangement is the built human, the manufactured man of Asimov's (1950) *I, Robot*, of Paolo Bacigalupi's (2009) *The Windup Girl*, Philip K. Dick's (1968) *Do Androids Dream of Electric Sheep* and the film *Bladerunner* (Scott, 1982) that it inspired, or even, to an extent, N.K. Jemisin's (2015–2017) astounding *Broken Earth* trilogy.

These are wildly disparate texts, and yet they share common features. The time is out of joint. Space has been stretched and squeezed. Bodies have been broken and built anew, man merged with machine to the point that we cannot tell where one ends and the other begins. The virtual has bled into the actual, blurring the borders between the quasi and the real. These, in a nutshell, are the calling cards of the genre. The material and scientifically-induced novum is the essence of science fiction, at least as we are defining it for the purposes of this book. In summary, science fiction is simply that type of story in which the rules for engaging with a material cosmos are called into question by an equally material disruption.

But this is not a book about science fiction, per se. It is a book about how science fiction can help us understand critical pedagogy. In order to reach that understanding, we will be analyzing science fiction texts with a particular focus in mind. In short, we are going to cast a critical eye on the learning spaces within each text.

What is a Learning Space?

If we are to approach critical pedagogy through the medium of science fiction texts, it would be reasonable to assume that the texts we are looking at contain classrooms or other formal learning spaces. This is rarely the case, however. As noted above, the term *space* denotes much more than location: it involves relationships between beings and objects, belief systems about the value and nature of those relationships, and a host of other embedded assumptions. While learning spaces can, indeed, be conceived of as shared physical locations, they can also be treated as relational, ecological, and even political phenomena. They can be designed, or they can emerge spontaneously. They can be built upon fixed and well-defined power structures, or they can arise organically among peers. Finally, and perhaps most importantly, learning spaces embody the philosophical and pedagogical beliefs of their creators and/or inhabitants. It is this last point that is of greatest interest for our work here.

To explain exactly what we mean by *learning space*, we must begin with what is perhaps the best known and most familiar learning space of all: the classroom.

The Classroom as Learning Space

I have used the phrase "the science fiction classroom" repeatedly in this introduction, and I must admit that this phrase is, in the context of this book, somewhat misleading. While some of the texts we will analyze do feature formal learning spaces, such as classrooms and other official settings, the great majority of them do not. Indeed, this book is less concerned with *schooling* and more concerned with the educational processes and beliefs that are portrayed in the texts, regardless of where they take place within the world of the text.

Still, it is worth defining our terms. For the purposes of this book, *classroom* might best be understood as a specific space located within a larger institution that is devoted to learning. This broad definition allows for the science fiction classroom to be set nearly anywhere in time and space, so long as it is contained within the boundaries of a larger educational institution. Such a classroom might be part of a physical institution, such as a 21st century school building. Conversely, the classroom space might just as easily be virtual, bounded not by bricks and mortar but rather by shared presence in online space. To be sure, classrooms today are defined less by their physical structures and more by their function as shared spaces devoted exclusively to "influencing pupils' learning, development, . . . [and behavior]" (Jedeskog, 2003). Despite the functional similarities between brick-and-mortar classrooms and their virtual counterparts (e.g., Williams, 2001), the social and procedural differences between physical and virtual classrooms are profound (Heymann, 2020). Still, both physical and virtual classrooms are marked by the exclusivity of their functions. The shared space of the virtual classroom is functionally bounded in that it is limited to the learning activities determined by the educational institution of which it is a part. Although a student may sit at the same desk and use the same computer for both her virtual classes and her online social media activity, for example, the space she enters is different in each case. Lammers (2016) highlights online gaming forums, for example, as "affinity spaces" in which participants' interactions are voluntary and formed around shared interest. Although these spaces do not share a function with classroom spaces, they are, in fact, *learning* spaces, in that participants adopt and master communal norms as a result of peer influence. Similarly, Hagel & Armstrong (1996) divided online spaces into four general categories of interest (similar to affinity spaces), relationship, fantasy, and transaction, each of which is marked by a different function. Although the online world has changed a great deal since the close of the 20th century, and although contemporary online spaces certainly involve a much wider range of functions than the four listed by Hagel & Armstrong, the basic premise remains: different online spaces serve different functions, regardless of whether the participant accesses them with the same hardware and in the same physical location.

A classroom, then, is a learning space devoted solely to the interactions between teacher and students that are designed to facilitate students' academic learning within the context of an educational institution. Whether physical or virtual, they are discrete spaces dedicated to fostering students' academic learning and marked by institutionally sanctioned teacher/student interactions. In short, a classroom is a space officially and formally devoted to learning.

However, although a classroom is a learning space, not all learning spaces are classrooms. Indeed, most learning takes place *outside* formally designated learning spaces (i.e., classrooms). As will be discussed next, most learning spaces facilitate a different type of learning than that facilitated by a classroom. Furthermore, the type of space in which learning happens dictates to a degree the type of learning that *can* take place. Or, more accurately, a learning space facilitates the type of learning that its designers and/or users believe *should* take place. A central tenet of this book, and one that will be fleshed out over the upcoming chapters, is that the ways that science fiction texts portray learning spaces reveal a great deal about the texts' pedagogical and philosophical presuppositions. In other words, the ways that a text depicts learning spaces, broadly conceived, reveal the text's underlying beliefs about the nature and purpose of teaching and learning, particularly as teaching and learning relate to power.

Designed Learning Spaces

As a type of learning space, a classroom (virtual or physical) reflects the learning beliefs of those who designed it, but it may not reflect the beliefs of those who will actually use it (Thomas, 2010), a situation that "constrain[s] the kinds of learning that [classrooms] make possible via the limited affordances that characterise them" (p. 503). In this sense, a classroom is the "architectural embodiment of educational philosophies" (Monahan, 2002). This embodiment not only reflects the designers' beliefs about learning, but it actively facilitates learning in accordance with those beliefs (Van Note Chism, 2006). Conversely, the same classroom renders learning outside the embodied philosophy much less probable (Strange & Banning, 2002).

As a static embodiment of the designers' educational philosophies, a classroom exerts a more or less unidirectional influence on learning. Bennett (2007) differentiates between classrooms and learning spaces by noting that the latter are characterized by student agency in their own learning, whereas the learning in the former is controlled by someone "other than the student" (p. 14). This is not an issue of teacher/student interaction, per se, but rather an issue of design:

> In thinking about the design of learning spaces, the most important aspect of this stratification of academic life is the way that claims to authority over knowledge are asserted and upheld. The archetypal behavior for asserting authority over knowledge is the faculty member's lecture; the archetypal space designed to reinforce that authority is the classroom, with the teacher standing in front and in command of the chalk board and other teaching technologies, while students are seated attentively facing their instructor. There are many other ways we design spaces to reinforce claims to authority over knowledge. (p. 19)

As designed learning spaces, classrooms reinforce the relationships and epistemological assumptions inherent in the designers' philosophies about teaching, learning, and knowing. These reinforcements serve to "contain" learners' work within the boundaries of the designers' pedagogical intent (Bligh & Cook, 2017, p. 74).

Emergent Learning Spaces

In contrast to designed learning spaces, which may be more or less static and less amenable to easy alteration, emergent learning spaces are, by nature, responsive and evolving. Damşa et al. (2019) view emergent learning spaces through an ecological lens:

> [an ecological view of learning spaces] emphasizes a core premise that is strongly at variance with ideas that still dominate mainstream perspectives on learning: namely, that learning is not a confined, internal process but instead involves mutually constitutive relationships between individuals and their (social, intellectual and . . . material) environments, where both person and environment are transformed. (pp. 2077–2078)

As ecologies, emergent learning spaces allow for bi-directional influence over both the nature of the space itself but also over the learning values and beliefs embedded within that space. Instead of inhabiting a previously designed and constructed space that embodies a fixed philosophy, learners become co-constructors of both knowledge and, indeed, the space itself, even if the space has been "pre-configured" by teachers (p. 2078).

A critical element of learning ecologies is the availability of and access to interrelated learning resources (Luckin, 2008). These resources may include individual and communal relationships, digital tools, cultural assets, social contexts, existing knowledge bases, and discipline-specific practices. The learner asserts her own agency to "assemble a learning space" (Markauskaite & Goodyear, 2017), (re)negotiating both learning practices and purposes within the relational bounds of the ecology (Ellis & Goodyear, 2016).

These ecological bounds are important, because although the emergent learning space affords the learner a degree of agency not typically found (or perhaps, possible) in the designed learning space, this agency is not absolute. Instead, it exists and is enacted within a web of social, physical, and practical relationships. Although the learner gathers resources for their own learning, many of those resources possess their own agency and may exist in overlapping ecologies of their own (Damşa et al., 2019). Thus, the emergent learning space *is* bounded, though its boundaries may be permeable (Akkerman & Bakker, 2018). A science fiction example of this bounded agency within a learning space might be Luke Skywalker's discovery that the Force "controls [his] actions" but it also "obeys [his] commands" (Lucas, 1977).[1]

In addition to learner agency, emergent learning spaces are also marked by their socio-relational nature. In contrast to "built" learning spaces, which focus on the physical or structural arrangement of the space (Blackmore et al., 2011), emergent learning spaces are often defined relationally, focusing less on the interaction between the learner and the physical/virtual environment and more on the learning interactions that take place within environments that are socially constructed. Tschakert, et al. (2016), for example, highlighted the intertwined roles of community practices, hierarchical organizational structures, and individual relationships in facilitating co-learning spaces within a larger political context. Access to and agency within the learning process depended less on physical or virtual access to a fixed space (e.g., classroom or database of information) and more on *relational* access and agency within the constraints of the organization and the community.

Others reject the notion of a dualistic approach to learning spaces (as either socio-relational or built) and focus instead on emergent learning spaces as sociomaterial in nature (e.g., Mulcahy et al., 2015):

> A learning space is the product of heterogeneous relations: (i) a vision or a discursive dynamic such as twenty-first century learning, student-centred learning or personalised learning; (ii) a design or a material dynamic such as a traditional classroom or a newly built open space or a mix of each; and (iii) a shared structure or a social dynamic such as the organisational set up of the school. . . . (p. 590)

In a sociomaterial space, the learner draws upon relational and structural resources in order to facilitate learning. However, as previously noted, the physical and social structures of the space both enable and constrain learning. In this sense, learning is bound within and bounded by the relational and material spaces in which it takes place, but it also creates and shapes the very space within which it is bound. It is simultaneously cause and effect, process and product, designer and designed.

Whether designed or emergent, sociomaterial or static, learning spaces both reflect and embody their creators' and/or inhabitants' beliefs about learning and knowing. Just as an analysis of real-world learning spaces can reveal the pedagogical and epistemological assumptions of the institutions and cultures in which these spaces are embedded, so too might an analysis of fictional learning spaces serve to reveal the pedagogical and epistemological beliefs around which the world of the text has been built.

How Do Critical Pedagogy and Science Fiction Work Together?

And now we reach the heart of the matter: how representations of learning spaces in popular science fiction both demonstrate the tenets of critical pedagogy *and* enable current and future educators to cast a critical lens on their own learning spaces. Examining the power structures embedded in a fictional learning space will enable you to recognize the same dynamics at play in the real world.

Let me give a brief example: An analysis of the Starfleet Academy, which is the official educational institution for all Starfleet officers in the world of *Star Trek*, might reveal a disconnect between Starfleet's stated mission to seek out "newness" and the hierarchical, bureaucratic, and liminal spaces in which Starfleet officers are trained. Indeed, the quasi-militaristic service academy reinforces rigid power structures that are seemingly at odds with its ostensible desire to push beyond known boundaries of knowledge. In the world of *Star Trek*, Starfleet learning spaces consist of officially sanctioned activities that take place within officially sanctioned buildings, suggesting that learning itself consists of the reiteration of officially sanctioned knowledge in officially sanctioned ways. Furthermore, the Academy's ways of knowing privilege Western rationalism and empiricism. The fact that Mr. Spock, a humanoid alien, becomes a Starfleet instructor is perhaps attributable to his race's preexisting commitment to Western positivism, in which scientific inquiry and quantitative fact are the ultimate—and, indeed, *only*—ways of knowing. Alternate ways of knowing are conspicuously absent from Starfleet's educational practices, despite the wide range of races and sentient beings that make up its ranks, not to mention the wide range of human cultures that it is supposed to represent. The Academy is devoted to the exploration of "newness" via educational means that are, in fact, centuries old and rooted in Western colonial practices, in that Western ways of knowing form the basis for both military and political power, which is the same power used to expand Starfleet's dominion/territory. In short, although Starfleet claims to embrace "newness," its educational practices suggest that the opposite may, in fact, be true.

The same critical lens that exposes the disparity between Starfleet's stated values and its actual practices can be turned on American schools. It is difficult to imagine a public school or university in America that does not have a stated commitment to equitable instruction for all students, and yet the so-called achievement gap persists. Black students are suspended at significantly higher rates than their white counterparts, often for the same offenses. Furthermore, in contrast to a rapidly diversifying student demographic, the education workforce remains almost exclusively white. Despite mission statements and diversity initiatives, the simple and troubling fact is that education in America remains profoundly inequitable. There is a disconnect between the system's stated values and the system's actual practices.

Casting a critical eye on *any* learning space, whether fictional or real, will highlight the extent to which the learning space seeks to maintain the status quo. Many learning spaces preserve old understandings, maintain existing power structures and hierarchies, and reinforce already-established relationships between people and the material world. These spaces discourage questioning and instead serve to enclose or limit the learner's cognitive estrangement. As we will discover, these learning spaces are often purposefully designed, and they often represent institutional interests with clearly codified and predetermined outcomes. Freire (1970) famously referred to these spaces as being part of "the banking concept" (p. 72) of education, in which the power structures that marginalize the dispossessed are maintained and even strengthened. Formal learning spaces, he claimed, are primarily places of power that neither encourage nor allow for boundary-breaking thought or action. Giroux (2001), too, critically highlights the constrictive function of learning spaces in "legitimate[ing] the existing society" (p. 36). As will become clear, the learning spaces in science fiction often serve to maintain the existing and accepted boundaries of knowledge, relationship, and power.

In contrast, other learning spaces transgress the same boundaries that constrictive learning spaces seek to maintain. By *transgress*, I mean that these learning spaces promote learning that extends beyond the generally accepted sociomaterial borders. These learning spaces may reject a homocentric cosmos or call into question the ways of being and knowing that dominate the world of the text. The word *transgress* is carefully chosen, because it carries with it hints of subversion and of defiance. I have borrowed this word from bell hooks (1994), whose critical feminist educational theories crystallize the transgressive potential of learning spaces far better than I can:

> The classroom [learning space] remains the most radical space of possibility . . . for years it has been a place where education has been undermined by teachers and students alike who seek to use it as a platform for opportu-

> nistic concerns rather than as a place to learn. Urging all of us to open our minds and hearts so that we can know beyond the boundaries of what is acceptable, so that we can think and rethink, so that we can create new visions, I celebrate teaching that enables transgressions—a movement against and beyond boundaries. (p. 12)

Transgressive learning spaces are those that not only allow for learners to reevaluate their understandings of the sociomaterial cosmos but that actually encourage and foster such reevaluations.

Although this text does not generally deal with real people, it does directly address real and actual systems of power and injustice that are inherent in actual educational practices and learning spaces. It is true that our analysis will be applied primarily to fictional worlds and imaginary learning spaces. However, when applied to science fiction, critical pedagogy theory can reveal a great deal about the relationships among power, knowledge, and oppression *within the world of the text*, which are often analogous to those that exist in our experienced world. This critical approach can reveal the extent to which learning spaces shun or welcome the cognitive estrangement that leads to new ways of thinking and being. In the words of Giroux (2001),

> critical theory points educators toward a mode of analysis that stresses the breaks, discontinuities, and tensions in history, all of which become valuable in that they highlight the centrality of [learner] agency and struggle while simultaneously revealing the gap between society as it presently exists and society as it might be. (p. 36)

What is a "Popular" Science Fiction Text?

Choosing texts for analysis in this book was difficult, if for no reason other than the fact that science fiction as a genre constitutes an enormous corpus drawn from an ever-growing range of modalities. For the purposes of this book, I have chosen to limit my analysis to popular culture texts. That is, I will be analyzing texts that have escaped the gravity well of the science fiction community and have entered the general public consciousness. For example, although Peter Watts' (2009) short story *The Island* depicts a haunting and nearly dehumanized constrictive learning space that practically begs to be analyzed, few people outside of a die-hard core of sci-fi enthusiasts have ever heard of it. In contrast, Ray Bradbury's (1953) equally haunting novella *Fahrenheit 451* is required reading at high schools across the country. It is a text with language, images, and basic plot points that have seeped into the culture at large. This same cultural seepage can be applied to the films, television shows, and other media of both *Star Wars* (Lucas, 1977–present) and *Star Trek* (Roddenberry, 1966–present), each of which will be analyzed in this volume.

The rhetorical power of popular texts must be acknowledged. As a coherent set of cultural signs, a text is inherently ideological, serving as a rhetorical nexus in which cultural ideologies might be confirmed or disconfirmed (Brummett, 2017). A *popular* text, then, is one that facilitates this rhetorical argument through the use of signs drawn from "everyday objects, actions, and events" (Sellnow & Endres, 2024, p. 6). The texts analyzed in this book are popular in the sense that they have entered into the "everyday" lexicon of American culture. Consider *Star Trek:* Spock's imperative to "live long and prosper" (Roddenberry, 1966–present), the process of being beamed up, the notion of faster than light travel being "warp speed" (not to mention the accompanying folding of space/time that undergirds warp theory), Klingons, the imminent death of a red shirted character, etc.—all these have entered mainstream consciousness to the point that people who have never seen an iteration of *Star Trek* understand the references. Consequently, these references and allusions are found in television commercials for cars, cell phones, computers, public utilities, and over-the-counter medicines (Martin, 2013); rap albums from mainstream artists such as The Beastie Boys, The Wu-Tang Clan, Jay Z, Lil Wayne, and Tupac Shakur (Rys, 2015); and even in interviews with President Barack Obama (Romano, 2008, WIRED, 2016). Officially licensed Star Trek-themed lunch boxes, pizza cutters, silverware, place settings, calculators, Silly Putty, and Barbie dolls have all been available for purchase at mainstream stores over the years (Smith, 2020).

References and allusions to Star Trek can be found in nearly every aspect of the "everyday," and Star Trek may reasonably be considered a popular text (or corpus), because it has infiltrated mainstream society to the point that its signs are recognizable and understood by the general population, rendering them viable units both for rhetorical persuasion *and* analysis.

My identification of popular science fiction texts comes with this caveat, however: I have not used a predetermined standard of book sales or box office performance when selecting texts, nor have I conducted or relied upon public surveys of recognizable science fiction texts. Instead, I have based my decision to include texts solely on my general and educated sense of a text's entry into the public consciousness. While each of the texts I have chosen to analyze has enjoyed both critical and commercial success, my determination of what is and what is not *popular* science fiction is ultimately mine and mine alone. It is likely—indeed, even probable—that you will disagree with some of my choices in this regard.

The other determining factor for a text's inclusion had to do with the nature of the term *text* itself. Digressing into a lengthy dissertation about which media do and do not constitute a "text" is far beyond this book's goals or even interests. Instead, I sought merely to provide a balance between various media types. The texts analyzed in this book include movies, TV episodes, books, and short stories. When a text exists in two or more types of media, such as, for example, Michael Crichton's (1990) book *Jurassic Park* and Steven Spielberg's (1993) movie of the same name, I have chosen to analyze the version with which the general public is most likely more familiar. Furthermore, I have chosen *not* to analyze comic books, graphic novels, or video games, not because these are not texts, but rather because they are sophisticated enough texts to merit their own fields of study and to be beyond the borders of my own expertise. In short, I fear I could not do them justice.

Although I presume that the reader will have a general familiarity with most of the texts examined in this book, my intent is to provide enough context and summary within each chapter that a reader unfamiliar with the text in question will be able to follow the argument.

Chapter Summaries

The chapters in this book are, to a degree, coherent. For example, each chapter will include the same basic information:

- a brief summary of the chapter's main argument and relevant theories
- a highlighted list of relevant vocabulary
- a summary/synopsis of the science fiction text
- a more detailed description of the relevant critical ideas

- an analysis of the text through the critical pedagogy lens
- an application of the analysis to real-world learning spaces
- reflections/activities for deepening understanding.

At the same time, each chapter can stand alone. In that sense, this book is more like a collection of related essays than it is a "traditional" textbook with a rigid, sequential reading order. With the exception of the chapter you are reading now, you can read or assign these chapters in any order. Of course, this means that many of the ideas, terms, and key understandings will be repeated from chapter to chapter, because certain ideas and terms are fundamental to all of critical pedagogy. Endnotes in each chapter will refer you to other chapters for additional reading if the topics are related. Please consider repeated terms and ideas to be an opportunity to deepen your understanding via a spiraling curriculum.

Finally, the chapters that follow are intended to be *used*. That is, they are not meant to stay locked inside the pages of this book. Instead, they are meant to change the way you think and see. They are meant to impact the way you interact with the learners in your own learning spaces. They are meant to provide you with both the tools and the desire to question the cosmos of your own classroom. If this book is nothing more than an interesting intellectual exercise, then we both will have failed, because the study of critical pedagogy is meant to lead to equitable and life-giving practice. This is, perhaps, the most important rationale for approaching critical pedagogy via science fiction: stories have the power to change and transform those who hear them.

Chapter Two, Fuel for the Fire: Canon and Cultural Literacy in Fahrenheit 451

Chapter Two begins by exploring the nuances of canon theory, exposing the mythical nature of the Western Canon and the books that we "should" read. Literary canons are often used to enforce a sort of literary orthodoxy, reinforcing essentialist notions of which stories are necessary for maintaining social and cultural cohesion. On paper, the pedagogical canon promotes cultural literacy, which helps us maintain a common cultural identity. Theoretically, this is an inclusive endeavor. But more often than not, canons—particularly pedagogical canons—are used to exclude and divide, preserving one culture by destroying another. Today, books have become sites of both attack and resistance, the latest weapons in our ongoing canon wars.

Chapter Three, Calculating the Future: Algorithms, Agency, and Oppression in Asimov's *Foundation* Trilogy

As outlined in Chapter Three, Isaac Asimov's (1951–1953) *Foundation* trilogy paints a chilling picture of a world in which algorithmic modeling not only predicts what *might* happen but is allowed to determine what *should* happen. This is strikingly similar to the world of 21st century education, in which decision-making processes are increasingly being ceded to the machines. What were once predictor variables are swiftly becoming deterministic, used not to calculate the likelihood of student performance but instead to limit student choice and constrict student agency to the point that the predicted future becomes the necessary future. Unfortunately, algorithmic feedback loops present learners with ever-narrowing options, and even more unfortunately, most learners and educators remain blind to the ways that algorithmic processes can limit and diminish potential futures. As the *Foundation* trilogy so clearly demonstrates, the fight for algorithmic justice is a fight for human agency. It is the fight to present learners with the fullness of their potential futures instead of a mathematically curated sliver of reality that masquerades itself as natural and unbiased. Algorithmic justice provides learners the awareness necessary to use algorithms as helpful tools without giving up their own human agency, working toward an equitable world in which the future is not determined by the past.

Chapter Four, Stepping into a Larger World: Knowledge and Community in *Star Wars*

Chapter Four examines the roles of knowledge, community, and relationships in *Star Wars* by examining the ways that Obi-Wan Kenobi introduces Luke Skywalker to the Force. Drawing on Romantic educational philosophy and the ecological understandings of agricultural activist Wendell Berry, this chapter highlights the relational nature of both learning and knowledge. Contrasting the Galactic Empire's use of technical knowledge for dominion with Obi-Wan's use of relational knowledge that both responds to and guides the individual, the chapter foregrounds the ways that formal education devalues and destroys "other" ways of knowing.

Chapter Five, The Hidden Curriculum Strikes Back: Crime, Punishment, and Privilege in *Star Trek*

Cheating is often a form of academic rule breaking, and the consequences for cheating are often punitive. After all, if you break the rules, you should be punished. However, the "rules" are not always clear, and learning spaces are rife with examples of students breaking rules with no consequences applied. The differentiated enforcement of rules-based school discipline is sometimes a matter of the "hidden curriculum"—the unwritten rules about school behavior and school values. Too often, these unwritten rules reinforce the norms of the dominant group, and students from minority groups are punished in grotesquely disproportionate numbers for engaging in the same behavior as their white peers. An education focused on learning instead of compliance exposes the unwritten rules and either applies them equitably or does away with them altogether.

Chapter Six, There is No Try: Deficit Models and the Banking Concept in *The Empire Strikes Back*

Chapter Six explores the metaphor of knowledge as a form of wealth, which is deeply entrenched in our contemporary school systems. The "banking concept" of education assumes that students are empty vessels to be filled with knowledge. The more passively a student submits to being filled, the better student they are. Paulo Freire and other critical pedagogues highlight the ways that the banking concept of education serves both to maintain inequitable social power structures and to systematically disempower students all in the name of "opportunity." Under the banking concept, education is not actually freeing; instead, the more "official knowledge" a student accrues, the deeper in debt they actually become. An education aimed at emancipating students focuses not on the accumulation of intellectual currency but rather on helping students build social and cultural capital for them and their communities.

Chapter Seven, War of the Words: Weaponization and Linguistic Justice in *Arrival*

Chapter Seven explores the ways language and culture are inextricably bound to each other and how policing and politicizing of language in education have an enormous impact not only on the individuals involved but also on the communities of which they are part. The weaponization of language is used to divide people and (re)establish the dominance of one group over another. The push for "standard" or "academic English" in classrooms is one iteration of this weaponization, casting doubt on the legitimacy of other ways of knowing and perpetuating centuries of eradication practices. An education focused on linguistic justice acknowledges the cultural impact of standard English policies and practices, and it seeks to reaffirm the value, legitimacy, and necessity of "other" ways of speaking and being.

Notes

1. Luke's agency in learning the ways of the Force will be discussed in detail in Chapters Four and Six.

References

About Fantastic Voyage. (2024). https://www.penguinrandomhouse.com/books/5649/fantastic-voyage-by-isaac-asimov/

Aisyah, R., Zakiyah, I. A., Farida, I., & Ramdhani, M. A. (2017). Learning crude oil by using scientific literacy comics. In *Journal of Physics: Conference Series* (Vol. 895(1), 0122011.). IOP Publishing. https://doi.org/10.1088/1742-6596/895/1/012011

Akkerman, S. F., & Bakker, A. (2018). Persons pursuing multiple objects of interest in multiple contexts. *European Journal of Psychology of Education, 34*(1), 1–24. https://doi.org/10.1007/s10212-018-0400-2

Ames, M. (2013). Engaging "apolitical" adolescents: Analyzing the popularity and educational potential of dystopian literature post-9/11. *The High School Journal, 97*(1), 3–20. https://doi.org/10.1353/hsj.2013.0023

Anderson, P. (1970). *Tao zero.* New York, NY: Doubleday.

Asimov, I. (1950). *I, robot.* New York, NY: Gnome Press.

Asimov, I. (1951, December 1). The fun they had. *Boys and Girls Page.*

Asimov, I. (1951–1953). The foundation trilogy. New York, NY: Gnome Press.

Asimov, I. (1957). *The naked sun.* New York, NY: Doubleday.

Asimov, I. (1966). *Fantastic voyage.* New York, NY: Bantam Dell.

Bacigalupi, P. (2009). *The windup girl.* San Francisco, CA: Night Shade Books.

Bartolomé, L. I. (2004). Critical pedagogy and teacher education: Radicalizing prospective teachers. *Teacher Education Quarterly, 31*(1), 97–122. https://www.jstor.org/stable/23478420

Barton-Kriese, P. (1993). Exploring divergent realities: Using science fiction to teach introductory political science. *Extrapolation, 34*(3), 209.

Bengels, B. (2005). Using science fiction to teach point of view. *Extrapolation, 46*(2), 259.

Bennett, S. (2007). First questions for designing higher education learning spaces. *The Journal of Academic Librarianship, 33*(1), 14–26. https://doi.org/10.1016/j.acalib.2006.08.015

Bercaw, L., and Stooksberry, L. (2005). Teacher education, critical pedagogy, and standards: An exploration of theory and practice. *Essays in Education, 12*(1), Article 2. https://openriver.winona.edu/eie/vol12/iss1/2

Berne, R. W., & Schummer, J. (2005). Teaching societal and ethical implications of nanotechnology to engineering students through science fiction. *Bulletin of Science, Technology & Society, 25*(6), 459–468. https://doi.org/10.1177/02704676052830

Bixler, A. (2007). Teaching evolution with the aid of science fiction. *The American Biology Teacher, 69*(6), 337–340. https://doi.org/10.1662/0002-7685(2007)69[337:TEWTAO] 2.0.CO;2

Blackford, R. (2017). *Science fiction and the moral imagination: Visions, minds, ethics.* Germany: Springer International Publishing. https://doi.org/10.1007/978-3-319-61685-8

Blackmore, J., Bateman, D., Loughlin, J., O'Mara, J., & Aranda, G. (2011). Research into the connection between built learning spaces and student outcomes (Version 1). Deakin University. https://hdl.handle.net/10536/DRO/DU:30036968

Bligh, B., & Crook, C. (2017). Learning spaces. In E. Duval, M. Sharples, & R. Sutherland (Eds.), *Technology enhanced learning* (pp. 69–87). Cham, Switzerland: Springer. https://doi.org/10.1007/9783-312-02600-8

Bowl, M. (2017). *Adult education in neoliberal times: Policies, philosophies, and professionalism.* New York, NY: Palgrave Macmillan. https://doi.org/10.1007/978-3-319-50883-12

Bradbury, R. (1953). *Fahrenheit 451.* New York, NY: Ballantine Books

Brecher, B. (2019). Universities: The neoliberal agenda. In Clack, B. and Paule, M. (Eds.), *Interrogating the neoliberal lifecycle: The limits of success* (pp. 127–142). New York, NY: Palgrave Macmillan. https://doi.org/10.1007/978-3-030-07700-6

Broderick, D. (1995). *Reading by starlight: Postmodern science fiction.* London, UK: Routledge.

Brummett, B. S. (2017). *Rhetoric in popular culture.* United States: SAGE Publications.

Burton, E., Goldsmith, J., & Mattei, N. (2018). How to teach computer ethics through science fiction. *Communications of the ACM, 61*(8), 54–64. https://doi.org/10.1145/3154485

Butler, O. (1979). *Kindred.* New York, NY: Doubleday.

Butler, O. (1993). *Parable of the sower.* New York, NY: Four Walls Eight Windows.

Cameron, J. (Director). (1984–2019). *Terminator.* Studio Canal.

Campbell, J. (1949). *The hero with a thousand faces.* New York, NY: Pantheon Books.

Collie, N. (2011). Cities of the imagination: Science fiction, urban space, and community engagement in urban planning. *Futures, 43*(4), 424–431. https://doi.org/10.1016/j.futures.2011.01.005

Crichton, M. (1990). *Jurassic park.* New York, NY: Alfred A. Knopf.

Damşa, C., Nerland, M., & Andreadakis, Z. E. (2019). An ecological perspective on learner-constructed learning spaces. *British Journal of Educational Technology, 50*(5), 2075–2089.

Darder, A., Baltodano, M., & Torres, R. D. (2003). Critical pedagogy: An introduction. In A. Darder, M. Baltodano, & R. D. Torres (Eds.), *The Critical Pedagogy Reader.* New York: Routledge.

Dark, M. (2005). Using science fiction movies in Introductory Physics. *The Physics Teacher, 43*(7), 463–465. https://doi.org/10.1119/1.2060648

De Lissovoy, N. (2014). *Education and emancipation in the neoliberal era: Being, teaching, and power.* United Kingdom: Palgrave Macmillan.

Dick, P.K. (1968). *Do androids dream of electric sheep?* New York, NY: Doubleday.

Dick, P.K. (1981/1997). *Paycheck and other classic stories.* New York: Citadel Press.

Ellis, R. A., & Goodyear, P. (2016). Models of learning space: Integrating research on space, place and learning in higher education. *Review of Education,* 4(2), 149–191. https://doi.org/10.1002/rev3.3056

Faber, L. (2021). Augmenting human pedagogy: A cultural history of automation in teaching. *Popular Culture Studies Journal,* 9(1), 44–62.

Fernández-Llamas, C., Conde, M. A., Rodríguez-Lera, F. J., Rodríguez-Sedano, F. J., & García, F. (2018). May I teach you? Students' behavior when lectured by robotic vs. human teachers. *Computers in Human Behavior, 80,* 460–469. https://doi.org/10.1016/j.chb.2017.09.028

Fife, E. (1999). *Using science fiction to teach mainstream literature [microform] / Ernelle Fife.* [Washington, D.C.]: Distributed by ERIC Clearinghouse https://eric.ed.gov/?id=ED438545

Fraknoi, A. (2002). Teaching astronomy with science fiction: a resource guide. *Astronomy Education Review,* 1(2), 112–119.

Freedman, C. (2020). *Critical theory and science fiction.* Middletown, CT: Wesleyan University Press.

Friere, P. (1970). *Pedagogy of the oppressed.* New York, NY: Bloomsbury.

Garland, A. (2014). *Ex Machina* [film]. Universal.

Gibson, W. (1984). *Neuromancer.* New York, NY: Ace.

Giroux, H.A. (2001). *Theory and resistance in education: Towards a pedagogy for the opposition.* Westport, CT: Bergin & Garvey.

Godwin, W. (1995, 1638). The Man in the moone: Or, a discourse of a voyage thither by Domingo Gonsales, the Speedy Messenger. In Butler's (Ed.), *Publication of the Barnaby Riche Society No. 3.* Ottowa: Dovehouse Editions.

Gonzalez-Jimenez, H. (2018). Taking the fiction out of science fiction: (Self-aware) robots and what they mean for society, retailers and marketers. *Futures, 98,* 49–56. https://doi.org/10.1016/j.futures.2018.01.004

Gunkel, D.J. (2018). *Robot rights.* Cambridge, MA: The MIT Press.

Halderman, J. (1974). *The forever war.* New York, NY: St. Martin's Press.

Armstrong, A, & Hagel, J. (1996), The Real Value of Online Communities. *Harvard Business Review,* 74, pp. 134–140.

Heinlein, R. A. (1991). On the writing of speculative fiction. In G. R. Dozois (Ed.), *Writing science fiction & fantasy, by the editors of analog and Isaac Asimov's science fiction magazine* (pp. 5–11). Davis.

Heymann, L. A. (2020). Together and apart in an online classroom. *Popular Media, 534.* https://scholarship.law.wm.edu/popular_media/534

hooks, b. (1994). *Teaching to transgress: Education as the practice of freedom.* New York, NY: Routledge.

Jedeskog, G. (2003). The stage design of a classroom. Presented at the *European Conference on Educational Research, University of Hamburg, September 17–20.*

Jemesin, N.K. (2015-2017). Broken Earth Trilogy. London, UK: Orbit.

Kirsh, S. J. (1998). Ender's Game: Using science fiction to teach child development. *Journal on Excellence in College Teaching, 9*, 47–53.

Lammers, J. C. (2016). "The hangout was serious business": Leveraging participation in an online space to design Sims fanfiction. *Research in the Teaching of English*, 309–332. https://doi.org/10.58680/rte201728162

Laprise, S., & Winrich, C. (2010). The impact of science fiction films on student interest in science. *Journal of College Science Teaching, 40*(2), 45.

Lave, J. & Wenger, E. (1991). *Situated learning: Legitimate peripheral participation.* Cambridge, UK: Cambridge University Press.

Leistyna, P. & Woodrum, A. (1996). Context and Culture: What is critical pedagogy? In *Breaking Free: The Transformative Power of Critical Pedagogy.* (Eds.) P. Leistyna, A.Woodrum & S. Sherblom. Cambridge, MA: Harvard Education Publishing.

Leistyna, P., Lavandez, M., & Nelson, T. (2004). Introduction—Critical pedagogy: Revitalizing and democratizing teacher education. *Teacher Education Quarterly*, 3–15. https://www.jstor.org/stable/23478408

Liberko, C. A. (2004). Using science fiction to teach thermodynamics: Vonnegut, ice-nine, and global warming. *Journal of Chemical Education, 81*(4), 509. https://doi.org/10.1021/ed081p509

Lips, H. M. (1990). Using science fiction to teach the psychology of sex and gender. *Teaching of Psychology, 17*(3), 197–198. https://doi.org/10.1207/s15328023top1703_17

Lucas, G. (Director). (1977). *Star wars episode IV: A new hope* [Film]. Lucasfilm.

Lucas, G. (1977–present). The Star Wars Universe. Lucasfilm.

Luckin, R. (2008). The learner centric ecology of resources: A framework for using technology to scaffold learning. *Computers & Education, 50*, 449–462. https://doi.org/10.1016/j.compedu.2007.09.018

Markauskaite, L., & Goodyear, P. (2017). *Epistemic fluency and professional education: Innovation, knowledgeable action and actionable knowledge.* Dordrecht, The Netherlands: Springer. https://doi.org/10.1007/978-94-007-4369-4

Martin, J. (2013). 11 Ads Featuring 'Star Trek' Stars. *cnet.com.* https://www.cnet.com/pictures/11-ads-featuring-star-trek-stars-pictures/

Menadue, C. B., & Cheer, K. D. (2017). Human culture and science fiction: A review of the literature, 1980–2016. *SAGE Open, 7*(3), 1–15. https://doi.org/10.1177/2158244017723690

Menadue, C. B., & Jacups, S. (2018). Who reads science fiction and fantasy, and how do they feel about science? Preliminary findings from an online survey. *SAGE Open, 8*(2), Article 2158244018780946. https://doi.org/10.1177/2158244018780946

Moon, E. (2003–2008). *Vatta's war.* New York, NY: Del Rey Books.

Morgan, R. (2002). *Altered carbon.* London, United Kingdom: Victor Gollancz Ltd.

Monahan, T. (2002). Flexible space and built pedagogy: Emerging IT embodiments. *Inventio, (4)*, 1. https://doi.org/10.17615/dgar-4g85

Mulcahy, D., Cleveland, B., & Aberton, H. (2015). Learning spaces and pedagogic change: Envisioned, enacted and experienced. *Pedagogy, Culture & Society, 23*(4), 575–595. https://doi.org/10.1080/14681366.2015.1055128

Office of Qualifications and Examinations Regulation. (2020). *Guide to AS and A level results for England, 2020*. https://www.gov.uk/government/news/guide-to-as-and-a-level-results-for-england-2020

Orthia, L. A. (2019). How does science fiction television shape fans' relationships to science? Results from a survey of 575 "Doctor Who" viewers. *JCOM: Journal of Science Communication, 18*, Article A08. https://doi.org/10.22323/2.18040208

Persson, M. E., & Fafatas, S. (2018). Accounting measurements, profit, and loss: a science fiction play in one act by Harold C. Edey. *Accounting History Review, 28*(1–2), 31–60. https://doi.org/10.1080/21552851.2018.1469419

Rautins, C., & Ibrahim, A. (2011). Wide-awakeness: Toward a critical pedagogy of imagination, humanism, agency, and becoming. *The International Journal of Critical Pedagogy, 3*(3).

Raven, P. G. (2017). Telling tomorrows: Science fiction as an energy futures research tool. *Energy Research & Social Science, 31*, 164–169. https://doi.org/10.1016/j.erss.2017.05.034

Rhee, J. (2018). *The robotic imaginary: The human & the price of dehumanized labor*. Minneapolis, MN: University of Minnesota Press.

Roberts, A. (2016). *The history of science fiction*. (2nd ed.). London, UK: Palgrave Macmillan.

Roddenberry, G. (1966–present). *Star Trek*. Paramount Global.

Roddenberry, G. (1987–1994). *Star Trek: The Next Generation*. Paramount Domestic Television.

Romano, A. (2008). The best of NEWSWEEK's top-secret election project, Vols. II, III and IV. *newsweek.com*. https://www.newsweek.com/best-newsweeks-top-secret-election-project-vols-ii-iii-and-iv-217862

Rosenblatt, L. M. (1993). The transactional theory: Against dualisms. *College English, 55*(4), 377. https://doi.org/10.2307/378648

Rys, D. (2015). 16 Hip Hop songs that shout out Spock from 'Star Trek." *xxlmag.com*. https://www.xxlmag.com/spock-16-hip-hop-songs-star-trek/

Schmidt, J.A., & Layritz, J.C. (1679). *Selenitas e luna proscriptos divini numinis gratia*.

Scott, R. (Director). (1982). *Bladerunner*. The Ladd Company.

Science fiction. (n.d.). In *Oxford English Dictionary*. Retrieved March 10, 2021, from https://www.oed.com/view/Entry/172674?redirectedFrom=%22science+fiction%22#eid

Segall, A. E. (2002). Science fiction in the engineering classroom to help teach basic concepts and promote the profession. *Journal of Engineering Education, 91*(4), 419–423. https://doi.org/10.1002/j.2168-9830.2002.tb00727.x

Sellnow, D. D., & Endres, T. G. (2024). *The rhetorical power of popular culture: Considering mediated texts*. Thousand Oaks, CA: Sage Publications.

Simmons, D. (1989–1997). The hyperion cantos. New York, NY: Doubleday.

Smith, D. (2020). Star Trek: The 10 weirdest official merch you can buy. *screenrant.com*. https://screenrant.com/star-trek-weirdest-official-merch/

Spielberg, S. (1993). *Jurassic Park*. [Film]. Universal Pictures.

Strange, C.C., & and Banning, J.H. (2002). *Educating by design: Creating campus learning environments that work*. San Francisco, CA: Jossey-Bass, 2002.

Suvin, D. (1988). *Positions and presuppositions in science fiction.* London, UK: Palgrave Macmillan.

Thomas, H. (2010). Learning spaces, learning environments and the dis'placement' of learning. *British Journal of Educational Technology, 41*(3), 502–511. https://doi.org/10.1111/j.1467-8535.2009.00974.x

Tschakert, P., Das, P. J., Pradhan, N. S., Machado, M., Lamadrid, A., Buragohain, M., & Hazarika, M. A. (2016). Micropolitics in collective learning spaces for adaptive decision making. *Global Environmental Change*, 40, 182–194. https://doi.org/10.1016/j.gloenvcha.2016.07.004

Van Note Chism, N. (2006). Challenging traditional assumptions and rethinking learning spaces. In Oblinger, D.G. (Ed.), *Learning Spaces*, chapter 2. Educause.

Watts, P. (2009). *The Island*. In Doziois & Strahan (Eds.), The new space opera 2. New York, NY: HarperVoyager

Weiner, J., Stevens, B. E., & Rogers, B. M. (2018). *Frankenstein and its classics: The modern Prometheus from antiquity to science fiction*. London, UK: Bloomsbury Academic.

Whyte, K. P. (2018). Indigenous science (fiction) for the Anthropocene: Ancestral dystopias and fantasies of climate change crises. *Environment and Planning E: Nature and Space, 1*(1–2), 224–242. https://doi.org/10.1177/2514848618777621

Wilkins, J. (1973, 1638). The discovery of a world in the Moone, or, a discourse tending to prove that 'tis probable there may be another habitable world in that planet. Delmar: Scholar's Facsimiles and Reprints.

Williams, D. L. (2001). The virtual classroom in relation to educational models. *International Journal of Educational Telecommunications, 7*(1), 23–32.

WIRED. (2016). President Obama speaks about the 'true meaning' of Star Trek. *trekcore.com.* https://blog.trekcore.com/2016/10/president-obama-speaks-about-the-true-meaning-of-star-trek/

Young, R.F. (1957, October). Thirty days had September. *The Magazine of Fantasy and Science Fiction.*

Young, K. L., & Carpenter, C. (2018). Does science fiction affect political fact? Yes and no: A survey experiment on "Killer Robots". *International Studies Quarterly, 62*(3), 562–576. https://doi.org/10.1093/isq/sqy028

CHAPTER TWO

Fuel for the Fire: Canons and Cultural Literacy in *Fahrenheit 451*

The Text: *Fahrenheit 451* (Bradbury, 1953). Book.

A Brief Disclaimer

A QUICK WARNING ABOUT this chapter: we are going to take a long and, I hope, not-too-arduous journey though the history of the "canon wars" in the 1990s, not to mention a brief excursion into the history of the Western Canon, itself. Though it might seem like we are spending far too much time dwelling in the past, I urge you to push through to the end, because the wars we are fighting over books in the classroom today are little more than continuations of those we have fought in the past. The players are different, and the stakes (I believe) are now higher, but the fundamental battle lines are the same.

I will warn you, too, that while this chapter interrogates the role of the literary canon in both creating cultural cohesion and inciting cultural division, it does not propose a solution to the problem of which books ought to fill our schools and classrooms. Although this chapter will raise a number of questions about inequality in canons and biased notions of literacy, it does not provide answers to those questions—at least, not in the positive sense. There are a number of solutions that do *not* work, and those will be addressed. But the "right" path forward is unclear to me. Or, more precisely, the theoretical path is clear and well lit, but the practical path—the path that would let us actually put the theories into practice—is rocky and hard to follow. It disappears, lost in the undergrowth ahead. Someone smarter than I will have to beat back the branches and forge a new way forward. Maybe that person is you.

Introduction

Fahrenheit 451 (Bradbury, 1953) is perhaps the most "popular" science fiction story that we are examining in this book. In this case, "popular" does not necessarily mean "beloved." Instead, it means that it might just be the story to which the most Americans have been exposed. This widespread exposure is due, of course, to the fact that *Fahrenheit 451* has been required reading in most public high school English classes for the last 50 years. As recently as 2010, *Fahrenheit* remained in the top 15 most frequently assigned books in 9th and 10th grade English classes (Stotsky et al., 2010). Research on how to best incorporate *Fahrenheit* into high school coursework dates back to at least the 1960s (Hamblin, 1968) and has continued unabated to the present day (e.g., Beach & O'Brien, 2005; Ebbers, 1991; Emmons, 2014; Kelley, 2024; Sisario, 1970; Wagner & Novak, 1981). All this is to say that most Americans who have graduated from public schools in the last half-century will most likely have read (or, at the very least, will have been assigned to read) *Fahrenheit 451*.

And this is where things get interesting, because *Fahrenheit 451* is a book in part about the importance of common reading, and yet it is, itself, a common read. Most high school graduates probably remain familiar with its basic premise: in a world where screens are everywhere and a mindless conformity trumps all, one man dares to fight back against intellectual lethargy by *reading*, protecting and cherishing the very books that, until yesterday, it had been his job to burn.

More scholars, journalists, and public commentators than I can count have marveled at Bradbury's ability to predict the disconnected and isolated nature of 21st century life. For example, his descriptions of 24/7 entertainment being delivered by ever-present screens foretold the "addictive" nature of hand-held social media and the death of the book (Hajiyeva, 2024), the rise of "fake news" as a means of media manipulation (Owsianik, n.d), technologies such as wireless ear buds, flat screen TVs, and ATMs (Rundle, 2012), and even an American societal swing toward a preference for authoritarianism (Brownstein, 2020). Entire books could be (and have been) written about Bradbury's prescience and ability to foresee the general thrust of American civil and social life.

But that is not what this chapter is about, or at least not directly. Instead, we are casting a critical eye on the role of books and stories in maintaining a cohesive society. In this sense, Bradbury was, indeed, looking into the future as he wrote, for the battles over books in *Fahrenheit 451* are the same ones we are fighting today.

The Story

It's a good day to burn books. Heck—*every* day is a good day to burn books. At least, this is what fireman Guy Montag tells himself as he goes to work each day. A fireman's work is honest work: catching lawbreakers in the act of reading or even having reading materials, and then burning the books, the houses, and sometimes even the lawbreakers themselves, to the ground. Montag has never seriously questioned the rightness of his actions, and he has always toed the party line. Sure, he is hiding books of his own, but that is just idle curiosity, right? He hasn't actually *read* them. He is not a common criminal.

Yes, Montag is happy. So is his wife. She is so happy that she intentionally overdoses on sleeping pills. Montag finds her, has her stomach pumped by the local stomach pumping service (it's a growth industry), and puts her back to bed. When she wakes in the morning, she cheerfully slips into her same happy routine, watching TV all day on giant screens, disappearing into her earbuds, shutting out her husband and the rest of the world, opting for her flat-screen "reality." Yes, they are happy. Really, they are.

But that is modern life. Maintaining the façade until you just can't anymore. For Montag, whose façade has actually been crumbling unnoticed—even by himself—for some time, the inflection point comes when he meets Clarisse, a lonely, eccentric 17-year-old neighbor who is, perhaps, the first legitimately happy person that he has ever met. She and her family do not have giant TVs. They do not drive a fast car or fill their days and nights with mindless entertainment. They sit together and *talk*. They walk in silence. They enjoy nature. Sometimes, they don't do anything but sit and think. It is the most bizarre thing Montag has ever heard of, and yet he cannot get Clarisse out of his head. At one point, he asks her why she is not in school.

> 'Oh, they don't miss me,' she said. '. . . I don't think it's social to get a bunch of people together and then not let them talk, do you? An hour of TV class, an hour of basketball or baseball or running, another hour of transcription history or painting pictures, and more sports, but do you know, we never ask questions, or at least most don't; they just run the answers at you, bing, bing, bing, and us sitting there for four more hours of film teacher. That's not social to me at all. That's a lot of funnels and a lot of water poured down the spout and out the bottom.' (Bradbury, 1953, pp. 29–30)

Clarisse's descriptions of the world work their way into his soul, and Montag's carefully constructed world begins to crumble. As he walks home from work with Clarisse each day, he realizes more and more just how disconnected and empty his life actually is, and he starts casting a critical eye on all the "normal" things around him. His wife's TV dramas, to which she devotes hours each day, are vacuous, literally without plot or meaning. He is surrounded by advertisements, constantly bombarded with visual and aural commands to *buy*. The pace of life is frenetic, and yet they never get anywhere. Perpetual stimuli but no action. He is exhausted, with nothing to show for it.

Still, he might have been able to keep up the pretense of happiness if it hadn't been for the old woman. The firemen receive a call that a woman has a stash of books hidden in her attic. Because all books are forbidden, there is no need to determine which books they are. Montag enters the house with his colleagues, and as he chops at the door to the attic, books begin to rain down around him. In a moment of panic or bravery (or, perhaps, a bit of both), Montag grabs one of the books at random and hides it in his jacket. Then he and his fellow firemen turn on their hoses, dousing the books and the entire house in kerosene. Beatty, Montag's boss, confronts the owner of the house, but the old woman is unmoved, and rather than surrender, she does not wait for the firemen to set her books alight. Instead, to Montag's horror, she pulls a matchbook out of her pocket, and, "with contempt to them all," strikes the match herself (Bradbury, 1953, p. 40).

It is at this point that Montag begins to disassociate. When he arrives home from the call, he finds his wife asleep in bed, earbuds blaring away so that even her sleep is filled with noise. He cannot shake the feeling that "he was in someone else's house, like those other jokes people told of the gentleman, drunk, coming home late at night, unlocking the wrong door, entering a wrong room, and bedding with a stranger . . ."(p. 42). When he wakes in the morning, he feels even worse, and, for the first time ever, he calls in sick to work. Or, rather, he doesn't actually call in. He simply does not go. Millie, his wife, pleads with him to get out of bed, to do what he is supposed to. He tries to explain about the old woman and how her devotion to her books has completely unsettled him, but Millie won't hear it. They argue and talk past each other until they are interrupted by a knock at the door: Montag's boss, Beatty.

Beatty saw Montag hide the book in his jacket, and his visit, though ostensibly to check on his sick employee, is little more than a veiled threat. He spends most of his time monologuing about the history of book burning (and his monologue is worth quoting at length):

> Picture it. Nineteenth century man with his horses, dogs, carts, slow motion. Then, in the twentieth century, speed up your camera. Books cut shorter. Condensations. Digests. Tabloids . . . Classics cut to fit fifteen-minute radio shows, then cut again to fill a two-minute book column . . . *now at last you can read all the classics, keep up with your neighbors*. . . . Now let's take up the minorities in our civilization, shall we? . . . Don't step on the toes of the dog lovers, the cat lovers, doctors, lawyers, merchants, chiefs, Mormons, Baptists, Unitarians, second-generation Chinese, Swedes, Italians, Germans, Texans, Brooklynites, Irishmen, people from Oregon or Mexico. . . . Authors full of evil thought, lock up your typewriters. They *did*. Magazines became a nice blend of vanilla tapioca. There you have it, Montag. It didn't come from the Government down. There was no dictum, no declaration, no censorship to start with, no! Technology, mass exploitation, and minority pressure carried the trick. . . . With school turning out more runners, jumpers, racers, tinkerers, grabbers, snatchers, fliers, and swimmers instead of examiners, critics, knowers, and imaginative creators, the word 'intellectual,' of course, became the swear word it deserved to be. . . . We must all be alike. Not everyone born free and equal, as the Constitution says, but everyone *made* equal. Each man the image of every other; then all are happy, for there are no mountains to make them cower. . . . So! A book is a loaded gun in the house next door. Burn it. . . . Serenity, Montag. . . . Give the people contests they win by remembering the words to more popular songs or the names of state capitals or how much corn Iowa grew last year. Cram them full of noncombustible data, chock them

> so damned full of 'facts' that they feel stuffed, but absolutely 'brilliant' with information. (Bradbury, 1953, pp. 54–62)

But Montag does not hold steady. He cannot. Though Beatty gives him 24 hours to turn the book in for burning, Montag decides instead to keep the book.

This is Montag's point of no return, and things begin to move quickly (for the sake of time and space, and with full awareness of the irony, given the nature of the monologue quoted above, I am greatly condensing the action). He returns to work after calling out "sick," but he's only been there for a few minutes when they get a call. Montag, who seems to live in a perpetual daze at this point, doesn't even realize where they have been called until the firetruck pulls up in front of his house. In this moment, it all clicks. His wife has discovered his hidden book and has turned him in. Montag dutifully lights his own house on fire, disassociating, "far away . . . running with his mind . . . gone, leaving this dead soot-covered body to sway in front of another raving fool" (Bradbury, 1953, p. 118).

Beatty tries to arrest Montag. In response, Montag turns off the safety on his flame thrower and points it at his boss. Again, he is disassociating, and he "glance[s] to his hands to see what new thing they had done" (p. 119). Beatty sees this and laughs.

"Well, that's one way to get an audience. Hold a gun on a man and force him to listen to your speech. Speech away. What'll it be this time? Why don't you belch Shakespeare at me, you fumbling snob" (p. 119)?

But Montag doesn't quote Shakespeare or anyone else. He just pulls the trigger.

And now Montag is on the run. He is a wanted murderer, a dangerous criminal, and the entirety of the law is after him. Helicopters shine spotlights from the sky, bathing dark alleyways in artificial light. His name and face are plastered on every screen in every home, and citizens go to the windows and step onto their porches, hoping to catch a glimpse of Montag the fugitive as he hides in the shadows. To throw his pursuers off his scent, he hides in a gas station bathroom, puts on some old clothes, and makes his way to the river. He climbs in and lets the river carry him downstream, certain that he will be caught at any moment.

But that moment never arrives. After drifting downriver for what feels like an eternity, Montag climbs onto the bank, cold and wet. He breaks through the undergrowth and stumbles quite literally onto an old, disused railroad track. He follows it away from town until he sees the glow of a fire ahead of him. It took him some time to recognize it, however, because it was different from the fires he was used to. This fire "was not burning. It was *warming*. . . . He hadn't known fire could look this way. He had never thought in his life that it could give as well as take" (Bradbury, 1953, p. 145–146). Huddled around the fire is an odd assortment of men. They welcome him by name and offer him a cup of coffee. One of the men gestures to a small, portable television. They've been watching the pursuit, and they're all amused by the fact that Montag is standing among them while, on the screen, the hunt continues in the city, far from where they are. One man, Granger, explains why: "They're faking. You threw them off at the river. They can't admit it . . . so they're sniffing for a scapegoat to end things with a bang. Watch. They'll catch Montag in the next five minutes" (p. 148). Montag and the other men watch in horror as the spotlights capture a man walking alone on the street. The man, whose face is blurred in the camera, looks up, surprised, and suddenly the police are upon him. The man screams, the camera cuts to black, and the voiced-over announcer proclaims that Montag is dead. The city is safe once more.

The real Montag, who is very much alive, trembles.

His new companions introduce themselves. They are all former professors, scholars, authors, thinkers. What's more, they are rememberers. Each man has memorized chapters of books, if not entire books. They, and the thousands like them scattered across the countryside, are the keepers of the sacred flame, the flame that gives light and heat and warmth. They are a living library:

> All we want to do is keep the knowledge we think we will need intact and safe . . . for if we are destroyed, the knowledge is dead, perhaps for good. . . . We'll pass the books on to our children, by word of mouth, and let our children wait, in turn, on the other people. A lot will be lost that way, of course. . . . And when the war's over, someday, some year, the books can be written again, the people will be called in, one by one, to recite what they know and we'll set it up in type until another Dark Age. (Bradbury, 1953, pp. 152–153)

As it turns out, they don't have to wait long for the Dark Age to arrive. Their conversation is interrupted by the sounds of bombers and jets roaring overhead, and they watch in horror as the city on the horizon, the city from which they have all fled, erupts in flames, enveloped and consumed in a nuclear inferno.

The book ends with Montag and his compatriots moving back toward the ruined city, back toward the survivors, to begin the long, painful, and hope-filled process of rebuilding. They would help the city rise like a Phoenix from the ashes, and they would help the people rise from the nightmare of isolation and disconnection. As one of the professors says, "We're going to meet a lot of lonely people in the next week and the next month and the next year. And when they ask us what we're doing, you can say, We're remembering. That's where we'll win out in the long run" (pp. 156–157).

And so they head back to the city to help the people remember.

The Critical Analysis

To talk about books and remembering from a critical perspective, we need to take a fresh look at the word *remember*. Consider it in light of its constituent parts: *re* and *member*. *Re* is a prefix meaning *again*, but *member* is a bit more complex. As a noun, *member* has two general meanings that relate to our analysis: the sense of being related to a physical body (Member, *N.*, Sense I.1.b, 2024), and the sense of being related to a social body (Member, *N.*, Sense III.9.a, 2024). Consequently, when someone loses a limb in an accident, we say they have been *dismembered*. Likewise, if a person is kicked out of a social club, we say they have lost their *membership*. In both cases, *member* refers to being a part of a larger body, be it physical or social.

So what does it mean to re-member? By metaphorical extension, remembering must involve, at least in part, the act of reconnecting the individual part to the larger body. To reattach a severed limb would be to re-member the body, just as reuniting a lost child with his parents would be to re-member the family. Of course, this is admittedly not how we generally use the term. And yet, this is precisely how the term is used both in *Fahrenheit 451* and in literature on the relationship between books and culture.

In the mid-20th century, Mortimer Adler and Robert Hutchins, both from the University of Chicago, started a foundation dedicated to collecting and preserving the greatest books from the Western Canon. They called their collection the *Great Books of the Western World* (Hutchins & Adler, 1952). It was originally published encyclopedia style, with each of the 54 volumes containing the texts from a handful of authors ranging from the ancient Greeks up through Hemingway. Along with publishing the original texts (or translated versions of the originals), the Great Books series included some training materials or "how to read this series" material.

The most important of these supplementary materials was a short book called *The Great Conversation* (Hutchins, 1952), which was intended to be an introduction to the aims, values, and methods of the Great Books series. *The Great Conversation* made the bold claim that what distinguished Western literature from all other literature was its dialogic nature. That is, the Western Canon bounces ideas back and forth, trying ideas on for size. All parties are welcome to the conversation, they said. If they contribute something meaningful, they can stay, and the Great Books series (Hutchins & Adler, 1952) is a testament to the conversations that have lasted over time.

This dialogue of ideas, Hutchins (1952) claimed, was central to the continuance and preservation of Western culture and civilization. If we were to suddenly lose these books, we would be individually, socially, and culturally lost. In Hutchins' (1952) own words,

> These books are the means of understanding our society and ourselves. They contain the great ideas that dominate us without our knowing it. There is no comparable repository of our tradition. To put an end to the spirit of inquiry that has characterized the West it is not necessary to burn the books. All we have to do is to leave them unread for a few generations. (p. 2)

A great many people took Hutchins' claim seriously, and an entire industry grew out of the belief that the books that Hutchins, Adler, and their colleagues had identified were necessary for the continuation of Western civilization. Not long after its inception, the Great Books series (Hutchins & Adler, 1952) began making its way into both K–12 and college curricula. The Great Books Foundation (which still exists today) created the Junior Great Books series (Great Books Foundation, 1993) to introduce the Great Books to a K–8 audience under the belief that "literacy and critical thinking help form reflective, knowledgeable citizens equipped to participate constructively in a democratic society" (*Who We Are*, 2024). Some schools went to the extreme, basing their entire curriculum around the notion of the Great Books. St. John's College, for example, currently identifies itself as a

Great Books school, meaning that all of its courses are based on "classics" of the Western Canon. To be clear, their list of books is slightly more flexible than the list created by Hutchins and Adler, but the general relationship between books, literacy, and cultural preservation remains the same. Thus, at St. John's, "while the list of books has evolved over the last century, the tradition of all students reading foundational texts of Western civilization remains" (Reading List, 2024).

Although the current iterations of both the official Great Books series (Hutchins & Adler, 1952) and the generalized Great Books curricula include a wider range of authors, genres, and modalities than they once did, the original collection was an almost perfect example of the "Dead, White Male" meme. Of the 129 authors represented in the original Great Books series from 1952, only four of them were women. Meanwhile, while it is impossible to know the skin tone of some of the ancient Greek authors (e.g., Homer), all the authors hail from either Europe or the United States. The great Western tradition, it would seem, did not include anyone from Mexico, Central America, or South America, and though a handful of the Roman authors may have been born in regions of North Africa, they were first and foremost citizens of the Roman empire. Not a single Native American or otherwise Indigenous author was included.

So how did it come to be that a collection that was supposed to embrace the best of the West ended up being so patently *un*representative of the people who lived (and live) in the West? Certainly, the Great Books series (Hutchins & Adler, 1952) was rooted in a tradition that placed Christian, White, Male experiences front-and-center and then called them "universal themes." Even if we assume that Hutchins and Adler were not explicitly and intentionally racist in their construction, it does not change the fact that the Great Books series (Hutchins & Adler, 1952) was assembled according to the same "literary rules" that privileged White men's words over everyone else's. And again, Hutchins' and Adler's intentions in this regard are almost beside the point. Regardless of whatever personal and private biases they may or may not have had, and regardless of whether or not they were explicitly racist, their collection was, in part, a product of our collective *implicit* racism. This *implicit racism*—which is the racism born not of consciously biased decisions but rather the racism that hides in assumptions we don't realize we're acting upon—affects the way we interpret the notions of *literature* and *literacy*. For the purposes of this chapter, we'll be looking at the ways that implicit racism in educational settings has 1) created the illusion of such a thing as "The Western Canon;" 2) led to the so-called "canon wars;" and 3) promoted a one-sided literary "conversation" in which some voices are over-represented while other voices are left out entirely.

The Myth of the Western Canon

The term *canon* has its roots in the ancient Greek *kanon*, which referred to a standardized unit of measurement. If something was canonical, it quite literally measured up, meaning that it was heavy enough or large enough for trading purposes. This literal understanding of *canon* came to be applied metaphorically. In the first few centuries CE (common era), the early Christian Church was still trying to settle on a fixed set of texts to act as their scripture. They had books of poetry and historical accounts they had inherited from Judaism, and letters, dream sequences, and a host of other types of literature that were all being used authoritatively in various Christian churches, but they did not have a single, unified set of documents. I will skip the history of how the Christian Bible came into its current form, other than to say this: by the mid-4th century, the Church had established 66 books (what we now refer to as the Bible) and *only* those 66 books as canonical. In other words, the Church established a *canon*, a set of texts that were both fixed and authoritative. Individual churches could neither add nor take away from the canon, and the canon was the standard by which the Church and its members would be judged.[1]

This metaphorical application of the canon as a "standard" by which to measure the worthiness of a text was reserved for spiritual texts for 1500 years. It was not until the mid 18th century that the term *canon* was used to refer to a collection of non-sacred texts. Interestingly enough, the first recorded secular usage of *canon* was applied to educational texts. Dutch scholar David Ruhnken (1768) was describing how ancient Greek oratory teachers used to create their syllabi. Keep in mind that oratory was a big deal in ancient Greece, and learning the skills and techniques of public speaking and persuasion was a large part of a proper education. Consequently, oratory teachers had a number of textbooks to choose from. And this is what Ruhnken was studying. Out of all the texts they had to choose from, these teachers, Ruhnken reported, picked no more than ten texts and used them *as if they were the canon* (translation mine). Such a little sentence, such a big can of worms.

The trouble with applying *canon* to a collection of literary texts is that the literary canon is not authoritative or fixed in the same way that a sacred canon can be. Unfortunately, English uses the same word for both sacred and literary canons, and most people do not distinguish between the two when talking about the canon. This confusion of terms raises some important questions:

- If we say that Christians *ought* to read the Bible or that Muslims *ought* to read the Quran, does it mean the same thing when we say that ninth graders *ought* to read *Romeo and Juliet* (Shakespeare, 1597)?
- If the canon is fixed and authoritative, which texts should be in the Western literary canon? Who decides? Who "locks it in place?" What are the penalties for "unlocking" the canon? Excommunication? Hell-fire and brimstone?
- Is there a master list of the fixed and authoritative Western Canon locked in a vault somewhere? Who made it? Is the Great Books series (Hutchins & Adler, 1952) an attempt to create such a master list?

I wish I could say that these were silly questions, but they are not. Quite the opposite, in fact. When used in reference to sacred texts, *canon* is prescriptive. It tells us which books we *should* read if we want to be a member of the community. This *should* is a moral imperative. To be a good Christian, you *should* read the Bible. To fail to do so is to fail morally, to sin, to fall from grace.

But literary canons are not prescriptive, or at least not in the moral sense. True, a teacher or curricula may require that you read this or that text. There might be a pragmatic imperative in that reading *Romeo and Juliet* (Shakespeare, 1597) will benefit you in terms of getting a grade or providing you and others a common reference point (we'll talk about cultural literacy later in this chapter). However, while failing to read *Romeo and Juliet* might have practical consequences, it does not have moral consequences. *Romeo and Juliet* is not authoritative. It does not dictate the laws and policies of Western society. People are not shunned or excommunicated because they don't like or haven't read Shakespeare. Nothing about the Western Canon carries anything near the moral weight that the Bible, the Quran, the Torah, and other sacred texts carry within their respective religious communities. In that sense, the Western Canon is not, and has never been, prescriptive, and the popular notion that there is a master list of "good" books is patently false.

And yet, myths of such a master list abound. The term *the classics* is often used as a synonym for the Western Canon, and yet there is little agreement about what make a classic a *classic*. Although some have sought to define the classics by their aesthetics and beauty of language (e.g., Bloom, 1994) their ability to teach moral truths and lead us to moral action (e.g., Adler, 1940), or their ability provide common references and allusions for members of a wide-spread community (e.g., Hirsch, 1988), the term *classics* today functions primarily as a marketing device (Barry, 2003). Consider the relationship between *the classics* and the simultaneous release of specially bound editions of those books:

> Thus we have a two-pronged approach to the word "classic" as a marketing and design tool, used by so many products that the term is rendered almost meaningless, and "classics" as the texts within the literary canon, which is used by reprint publishers in the manufacturing of new classics. . . . Many book historians have already studied the significance of the material form of the book and its psychological impact on the reader, the collector, and the culture at large . . . series packaging (often numbered as well) aids in a kind of transference of values from one book to the next, so that a lesser-known work will perhaps be uplifted (in the minds of readers) by its company on the shelf . . . [and] packaging a book in that format is an act of certification, a seal of approval that readers will consciously or unconsciously comprehend. Moreover, a display of series literature—a whole shelf of similarly packaged classics is the goal of many reader-collectors—creates a visually commanding image of authority as the *complete* and *definitive* set of classics. (Barry, 2003, p. 254)

A quick Google search of the phrase "which books are the classics?" yielded first-page results of the official websites of Penguin Books, Pan Macmillan Publishers, Barnes & Noble, Juniper Books, Half Price Books, Great Illustrated Classics, Reader's Digest, Canterbury Classics, Scholastic, Penguin Random House, Abe Books, and Easton Press. Each website contains not only its own unique list of "the classics" but also links to order and purchase your very own copies of the books.

To recap: There is no such thing as a fixed and prescriptive Western Canon, and "the classics" are a loosely defined, completely unregulated, disagreed upon collection of books that have more to do with marketing than with any coherent or shared qualities. If all this is true, why can't we shake the feeling that the canon and the classics really do exist? How do all of Montag's professor friends know which books are worth memorizing and passing down? How is it there is no canon when there clearly *is* a canon?

The Pedagogical Canon

The answer to the question above lies in the books that we *teach*. Regardless of the fact that there is no fixed canon, and despite the fact that there is no national American curriculum governing which books are taught in high school language arts classes,[2] the books that get taught in high school English classes are more or less the same. We refer to these commonly taught books as *the pedagogical canon*, and, for better or worse, the pedagogical canon of today is nearly identical to the pedagogical canon of nearly 40 years ago. In fact, a quick dig through historical records reveals that roughly half of the most frequently taught books in high schools from the 1960s are still among the most frequently taught today (Anderson, 1964). In short, although there is no fixed Western Canon, our high school English classrooms often act as if there is.

The Canon Wars of Yesterday—Positive Essentialism

It should come as no surprise that the pedagogical canon has been the subject of much debate, acrimony, and resistance. At the risk of oversimplifying a fantastically complex phenomenon, the arguments over the pedagogical canon boil down to two sides: the essentialists and what I will call the multiculturalists.

Essentialism

Essentialism is the belief that the purpose of education is to instill in students the facts, skills, and knowledge that are essential for the preservation and maintenance of society. When Hutchins (1952) said that failing to read the Great Books would lead to the collapse of Western traditions, he was making an essentialist argument. Knowledge of and familiarity with *these* books, he claimed, are essential to the continuation of the West. This essentialist argument stems, in part, from a belief in the value of cultural literacy. To be culturally literate is to be fluent in the language, references, allusions, stories, histories, and traditions of the culture. E.D. Hirsch Jr., perhaps the most prominent advocate for *cultural literacy* of the last 40 years, claims that one of the key roles of the school is to promote the common understandings that are necessary for cultural literacy and, therefore, social cohesion:

> From the start of our national life, the school curriculum has been an especially important formative element of our national culture. In the schools, we not only tried to harmonize the various traditions of parent cultures, we also wanted to strike out on our own within the dominant British heritage. . . . In this self-conscious job of culture making, schools played a necessary role. That was especially true in the teaching of history and English, the two subjects central to culture making. . . . The dominant symbol for the role of the school was the symbol of the melting pot. (Hirsch, 1983, p. 160)

In order to facilitate this "culture making" via a "melting pot" education, Hirsch advocates that certain fundamental concepts, vocabulary, and historical facts be taught at every school across the country. To be fair to Hirsch, he does not advocate memorizing vocabulary lists for the sake of memorizing vocabulary. Instead, he focuses on the ideas, common understandings, and tradition maintenance that such shared vocabulary entails. If we teach students the phrase *First Amendment*, he claims, and if we teach them about how the phrase relates to concepts of positive and negative rights, the history of the American Constitution, and the political processes necessary to revise and amend the Constitution, the phrase and the deeper understanding will always be linked. Consequently, *First Amendment* becomes "a lexical item that can hardly be used without bringing in a lot of associated information" (Hirsch, 1983, p. 168).

If we fail to teach these "uniform lists" (p. 160) of common knowledge, we run the risk of cultural fragmentation. When we lose common readings, we lose the glue that binds us together, because

> no culture exists that is ignorant of its own tradition. In a literate society, culture and cultural literacy are nearly synonymous terms. American culture, always large and heterogeneous, and increasingly lacking a common

> acculturate curriculum, is perhaps getting fragmented enough to lose its coherence as a culture. (p. 167)

I am quoting Hirsch at length, because his ideas became increasingly popular in the 1990s, forming the backbone of the modern essentialist movement. Hirsch's most influential book—*Cultural Literacy: What Every American Needs to Know*—was released in 1988 and immediately spawned an entire cottage industry of essentialist books, curricula, and educational materials. In general, the target audiences for these materials were not schools and education professionals but rather parents and the general public.

Most of the books in the extended Hirsch universe have sought to balance theory and practice. For example, in *Cultural Literacy*, Hirsch devotes the first 100 or so pages to outlining his philosophy of education and the essential nature of cultural literacy. In the second half of the book, however, Hirsch provides an alphabetized list of the names, dates, concepts, and facts that form the "oxygen of social intercourse" (Hirsch, 1988, p. 19). He expands on this list in subsequent editions of the book and others. The following example is drawn from the "Literature in English" section of *The New Dictionary of Cultural Literacy* (2002, p. 115), beginning with the letter A:

- Achebe, Chinua
- "Age cannot wither her, nor custom stale/Her infinite variety"
- Agee, James
- Ahab, Captain
- "Alas, poor Yorick"
- Alcott, Louisa May
- Alger, Horatio Jr.
- *Alice's Adventures in Wonderland*
- "All animals are equal, but some animals are more equal than others"
- "All the World's a stage"
- Angelou, Maya

Hirsch includes a brief description of each entry (not quoted here), describing the importance of the author or the quote. This dictionary, which is aimed at adults, is similar to the Core Knowledge series that Hirsch edited. Armed with provocative titles like *What Your Third Grader Needs to Know*, the Core Knowledge series framed essentialist knowledge in competitive and existential terms. For example, the back cover of the 2015 revised edition of the third grade claims that the information contained within "gives today's generation of third graders the advantage they need to make progress in school and to establish an approach to learning that will last a lifetime."

The Core Knowledge series was aimed at parents, and was part of the larger "canon wars" that began in earnest in the late 1980s and continue to this day. The premise was simple: in their efforts to respond to the demands of a pluralistic society, American schools have stopped teaching the fundamentals. Unless we correct course by reintroducing essentialist knowledge, our nation will fall apart. The titles of Hirsch's subsequent books highlight the essentialist beliefs that shared knowledge can bind people together and that the current state of American education is actually driving us apart:

- *The Schools We Need and Why We Don't Have Them* (1996)
- *The Knowledge Deficit: Closing the Shocking Education Gap for American Children* (2006)
- *The Making of Americans: Democracy and Our Schools* (2009)
- *Why Knowledge Matters: Rescuing our Children from Failed Educational Theories* (2016)
- *How to Educate a Citizen: The Power of Shared Knowledge to Unify a Nation* (2020)

At the end of *Fahrenheit 451*, Montag and his motley band of ex-professors return to the ruined city as essentialist missionaries. The knowledge they carry with them is necessary for the rebuilding of society, which is why they will pass it from person to person, helping each lonely, isolated individual to "remember." Becoming culturally literate is an act of *re-membering*, of becoming reattached to the larger body. Although it seems that the book burning in *Fahrenheit 451* was both the *cause* and the *result* of social fracture, the solution Bradbury presents is the same, either way: only by remembering our shared knowledge (through books) can we hope to be re-membered.

Multiculturalism

Before discussing the resistance to essentialist movements, it is important to note that Hirsch makes it exceedingly clear that the list of essential knowledge can and *should* change over time. Furthermore, Hirsch repeatedly claims that essentialism is the quickest and surest path toward what we, today, would call social justice. He openly advocates for the inclusion of underrepresented authors and texts into the pedagogical canon, and he consistently and, I think, effectively argues for an essentialism that does not ignore the past while striving for a better future. His advocacy for a "melting pot" education is based on the belief that the stories of the many become the story of the one. Hirsch's brand of essentialism is philosophically honest and, at least on paper, just.

The problem with essentialism, however, lies in the practice. In the late 1980s and early 1990s, just as Hirsch's books and ideas were gathering mainstream attention, American education institutions became embroiled in what were known as the "canon wars." These were heated ideological battles over which books should be included in the pedagogical canons of K–12 and higher education institutions. The essentialists argued for "the classics" and highlighted their role in perpetuating a national identity and a common culture. Multiculturalists, on the other hand, highlighted the simple fact that the great American melting pot does not, and has never, melted all things equally. In an educational system based on essentialist notions of great and enduring literature that forms our common heritage, some students will have to de-form themselves more than others in order to claim that heritage as their own. Proponents of multiculturalism claimed at the time that the push for a common culture was a veiled attempt at compulsory *assimilation*, in which students from non-dominant groups were forced to sacrifice key elements of their own identities in order to be members of the common culture (Ryan, 1997). A common U.S. culture, they claimed, was nothing more than a myth used to ensure the dominance of European traditions and the subjugation of all others (Asante, 1991), and an essentialist approach to the pedagogical canon would accomplish little more than to reinforce European histories and norms under the noble guise of maintaining a common culture.

Indeed, there is a great irony in the essentialist claim that the canon of the Western tradition plays an essential role in helping the student become a "free and responsible person" (Lawall, 1994, p. 7) when it was men who had been educated in that same tradition that both allowed for and profited from the enslavement, murder, rape, and torture of millions. The reality of American society is and always has been far removed from the common culture myth espoused by essentialists. Instead, multiculturalism highlights the ways in which the United States is made up of multiple cultures operating in parallel, sometimes harmoniously, sometimes not:

> In contrast to the idea of the melting pot, which promised to erase ethnic and group differences, children now learn that variety is the spice of life. They learn that America has provided a haven for many different groups and has allowed them to maintain their cultural heritage or to assimilate, or—as is often the case—to do both; but the choice is theirs, not the state's. They learn that cultural pluralism is one of the norms of a free society; that differences among groups are a national resource rather than a problem to be solved. (Ravitch, 1990, p. 339)[3]

A multicultural approach to education would not diminish or erase the histories and literatures of non-dominant groups but would instead celebrate them all. At least that was the promise. In practical terms, multiculturalism provided an opportunity to "rethink both the boundaries and the functions" of the pedagogical canon (Chicago Cultural Studies Group, 1992, p. 531). Of course, the idea of a multicultural canon faced fierce opposition from conservative thinkers like Harold Bloom (1994), who fought for essentialism in higher education much as Hirsch was doing in K–12 education.

The challenges facing the development of a multicultural canon were not just ideological, however; they were also practical. In the early to mid 1990s, it was often difficult to find copies of books by non-Western authors, particularly in the numbers necessary for adoption in classrooms (Godina, 1996). This was before the Internet, and book orders were completed almost exclusively though publisher-provided catalogs. If the publishers did not offer those books in the catalog, it was next to impossible to order them, assuming, of course, that you even knew the books existed. It was additionally sometimes difficult to convince school administrators to fund the purchase of new books when the school already had perfectly good books in hand. My own doctoral research, years and years ago, highlighted just how many decisions about the pedagogical canon are based not on sound pedagogy but rather on logistical practicality. It is much easier to teach the book that you already have copies of, even if you have a very good reason for teaching something else, instead.

The other primary practical difficulty facing the development of a multicultural canon was the difficulty of implementation. Early attempts to diversify the canon led to a sort of literary *tokenism*, in which teachers would select a single book by a Black, Hispanic, or other non-white author and add it to the regular curriculum. They could then pat themselves on the back for having been inclusive before returning to the "normal" essentialist programming without making any substantive changes.

Banks (1989) referred to this type of surface-level multicultural canon development as "the Ethnic Additive Approach" (p. 17), in which "content, concepts, themes, and perspectives are added to the curriculum without changing its structure" (p. 19). This approach was level 2 on a spectrum of canon integration models (1989). In level 1, the Contributions Approach, schools focus on celebrating "ethnic holidays" or perhaps making a display for Black History Month highlighting famous Black "firsts" like Jackie Robinson or Barack Obama. These are surface-level decorations that do not affect the overall white, European homogeneity of the curriculum.

In level 2, books by under-represented and historically excluded authors are added to the curriculum. Again, though, this is a surface level addition. Although the books are read and discussed, they are very obviously a departure from the regular curriculum, and they constitute a one-off event or encounter.

Level 3, the "Transformation Approach," involves a level of integration in which both the structure and aims of the curriculum are changed, "enable[ing] students to view concepts, issues, events, and themes from the perspective of diverse ethnic and cultural groups" (Banks, 1989, p. 19). This, then, can lead to level 4, the "Social Action Approach," in which students are equipped and prepared to use their newfound perspectives and knowledge to identify and solve issues and problems of social justice.

As pedagogical canons began to diversify, Banks' four levels became the go-to model for assessing the quality and depth of multicultural integration, and this model was applied in educational settings far and wide (e.g., Bagnardi et al., 2009). Unfortunately, too many classrooms adopted the "Ethnic Additive Approach" (Banks, 1989, p. 19). A Black or Hispanic author or two would be added to an otherwise all-white curriculum and prominently featured during a unit on "ethnic literature" or something similar. The net effect of this additive model, of course, is to reinforce the *otherness* of non-white authors. These authors, it was implied, are not "normal." They are "special," and their specialness must be highlighted, codified in course and unit titles, and read during "special" occasions such as Black History Month. This tokenism highlighted the otherness of the non-white experience. Instead of incorporating Black and other non-white authors as a normal and regular part of the pedagogical canon, the additive model served to highlight just how "abnormal" they actually were. The fact that schools and teachers have had to intentionally add non-white authors to a pedagogical canon that supposedly represented a common American experience should indicate just how biased, one-sided, and non-representative the mythical common culture of the West actually is.

To its credit, *Fahrenheit 451* explicitly resists the additive model; to its shame, however, its reasons for doing so are rooted in tacit whiteness. When Beatty is monologuing about the history of book burning and how society came to be so intolerant, he rails sarcastically against minority groups' desires to see themselves and their interests represented in the canon: "You must understand that our civilization is so vast that we can't have our minorities upset and stirred. . . . Colored people don't like *Little Black Sambo*. Burn it. White people don't feel good about *Uncle Tom's Cabin*. Burn it" (Bradbury, 1953, p. 58).

Although Beatty's rant against a canon that concerns itself with representation seems at first to be aimed at *everyone*, it represents a mindset that has an outsized practical effect on non-white readership. By default, the American pedagogical canon caters to the interests, traditions, norms, and practices of white America. To make the claim that the canon should not be subject to the whims of either white or Black is to tacitly argue for a white canon, despite whatever intent one may have. The staying power and cultural inertia of a white pedagogical canon—as illustrated by the Great Books series (Hutchins & Adler, 1952)—must be met with an equal and opposing force if it is to be changed. Beatty's charge that *both* white and Black readers are to blame for the demise of the canon and subsequent social fragmentation ignores a very simple reality: *Uncle Tom's Cabin* is a fictionalized account of the historical reality that white people enslaved Black people, whereas *Little Black Sambo* is a caricature of Black people as subhuman and infantile that was used to justify centuries of Black enslavement at the hands of white people. The individual offense and cultural damage caused by the two texts are not the same. One is more egregious than the other. If both books remain in the canon unchecked, and if a counter-example is offered for neither, then the canonical power dynamic between white and Black racial inequality is allowed to continue. And while it is certain that both texts should remain in the historical record, it is far less certain that both should remain in the canon. In other words, if the books we read create our culture, as both Beatty and Hirsch suggest, then although we should remain aware of *Little Black Sambo*, perhaps we should, in fact, stop reading it.

Unfortunately, the multicultural movement of the 1990s ultimately failed to radically alter the pedagogical canon in any long term or substantive way, although it did provide us with the language for discussing, diagnosing, and evaluating efforts at canonical inclusion.

The Canon Wars of Today—Negative Essentialism

The Florida Example

As I write this chapter, books are once again at the center of our national educational debates. In 2022, the Florida State Legislature passed House Bill 1467 which stipulated that "each district school board must establish a process by which the parent of a public school student or a resident of the county may contest the district school board's adoption of a specific instructional material" (H.B. 1467, 2022). The new law allowed for *any* resident of a Florida county to challenge a school's pedagogical canon, regardless of whether they had children attending Florida schools. The law, which was ostensibly aimed at keeping explicit materials out of schools, quickly became a flashpoint of controversy. Supporters of the law claimed that school libraries had become havens for pornography and LGBTQ+ propaganda. Florida Governor Ron DeSantis, who signed the bill into law, framed it in essentialist terms:

> You have some groups that want to take away classic books like 'To Kill a Mockingbird,' but they want things like, 'Gender Queer: A Memoir,' which is a cartoon-style book with graphic images of children performing

> sexual acts. That is wrong. . . . They want to eliminate 'Of Mice and Men,' but 'Lawn Boy,' a book containing explicit passages of pedophilia is somehow accepted. (Farrington, quoting DeSantis, 2022)

DeSantis's appeal to the virtues of the "classics" should be familiar. He does not mention that *To Kill a Mockingbird* contains explicit descriptions of rape, domestic abuse, and murder, or that *Of Mice and Men* contains a brutal description of an attempted lynching and subsequent mercy killing. The classics are necessary for maintaining the "proper" American way of life. It is these new books that represent danger.

While schools must, indeed, ensure that they are not making sexually explicit materials available to students, particularly younger students, the term *pornographic* is often applied to materials that are not necessarily sexually explicit but that foreground non-heterosexual relationships or non-traditional gender expression. In the 2020–2021 school year, 41% of the 1648 titles banned in American schools either explicitly addressed LGBTQ+ themes or featured LGBTQ+ main or secondary characters, and yet only 22% of the books banned contained sexual content (Friedman & Johnson, 2022, n.p.).

By the 2022–2023 school year, state book bans had increased to 3362 titles, led by Florida, which banned 1406 different books (Meehan et al., 2024). Because Florida law allowed anyone in the county to challenge a book, and because there was little to no guidance on what, precisely, constituted reasonable grounds for a challenge, Floridians were able issue challenges to any book that they deemed offensive for any reason. The result was a book-banning frenzy. The Escambia County school district, for example, was compelled to ban the dictionary due to a complaint that it contained depictions of sexual conduct (Thornton, 2024).

In 2023, anti-book-banning activists attempted to have the Bible removed from all Florida schools by claiming that it was obscene and not age-appropriate given its frequent references to murder, incest, rape, sexual immorality, masturbation, and even infanticide (Schwarz, 2023). Despite the fact that the Bible *does* contain explicit references to all these topics, Governor DeSantis criticized attempts to ban the Bible as "performative" and "fraudulent" attempts to minimize parents' actual concerns about book content (Parnell, 2024). In order to combat attempts to ban the Bible and other "classic" literature, DeSantis signed an updated law in 2024, requiring book challengers to have children who were students in Florida schools. This update was necessary, he claimed, because some people were "trying to weaponize [the book challenge process] for political purposes" (Houghtaling, 2024).

The example of Florida's attempts to control the pedagogical canon highlights a contemporary version of essentialism that draws on opposed and othering binaries between "us" and "them." When *I* fight for the "traditional" Western Canon, it's in the name of parents' rights, but when *you* attempt to challenge that same canon, it's "performative" and weaponized. When *our* books contain graphic depictions of violence and sexual activity, it's ignored or justified, but when *your* books do it, it's pornographic. When *my* people are represented in classroom literature, it's unquestioned, but when *your* people are represented, it's the result of an "agenda." *My* group's behavior is "normal," but that same behavior in *your* group is "deviant." The grotesque purpose of the contemporary essentialist pedagogical canon is not to be a melting pot that joins you and me together into a new, stronger whole. Instead, the pedagogical canon is meant to act as a crucible, burning off all the impurities and leaving behind only what is ostensibly true, good, and valuable.

Diversity, Equity, and Inclusion

The contemporary battle between essentialists and multiculturalists extends far beyond the pedagogical canon. Positive attempts at multicultural representation (that is, attempts to represent through *addition*) have been met with fierce resistance not only regarding educational curriculum but also in educational structures. With a growing awareness that racism is a matter of systemic structural inequity just as much as it is individual bias and prejudice (Tatum, 2007), educational institutions across the country have created structures and policies designed to promote *diversity, equity, and inclusion (DEI)*. DEI can be thought of both as a set of values/aspirations and as a set of policies and procedures intended to enact those values. Though there is no single agreed-upon definition for DEI (Arsel et al., 2022), visible DEI efforts have become commonplace in both K–12 and higher education settings. These efforts range from the verbal, such as position statements, mission statements, and websites—to the pedagogical, such as courses, committees, workshops, and curricula—to the structural, such as administrative positions, revised policies, and financial restructuring. Some of these efforts are performative, the equivalent to levels 1 or 2 on Bank's model of multicultural inclusion. Others are transformative (Gibbs et al., 2023). The impact of these combined efforts on student learning is still being studied, though early data shows that DEI efforts may have a positive impact on the recruiting, admission, and retention of a more ethnically and racially diverse student population (e.g., Conway et al., 2021), although the results are less encouraging when it comes to the retention of a more diverse faculty (Banks, 2022).

But our focus here is not so much on DEI efforts themselves as it is on the *resistance* to DEI. Much like a more representative pedagogical canon, DEI efforts are under social and political attack (Lange & Lee, 2024). The attacks on DEI efforts come in many forms. Some are efforts to ban *critical race theory (CRT)* in K–12 curriculum. For the record, critical race theory emerged in the 1970s as a specialized theory about racism and legal studies (Delgado & Stefancic, 2023). It is usually taught in graduate school, and it is not part of K–12 curricula. However, CRT became a proxy term used to attack and discredit *any* race-related curricular or instructional materials. For example, the 1619 Project, a multimedia history curriculum that details the long-term impact of slavery on American history and culture, was decried by President Trump (2020) as "toxic propaganda" and "ideological poison" that will "dissolve the civic bonds that tie us together. It will destroy our country." Trump frames his attack on the 1619 Project in essentialist terms, albeit in an inverse fashion. Whereas Hutchins, Hirsch, and other essentialists have claimed that we must read books X, Y, and Z to maintain our social cohesion, Trump claims that we must *not* read or participate in the 1619 Project due to its threat to our "civic bonds." This is a sort of negative essentialism that focuses not on what we must *do* to preserve our union but rather on what we must *avoid*.

Attacks on CRT have led some states to pass laws forbidding K–12 schools from teaching about historical and on-going structural racism in the United States. For example, in Tennessee, teachers are forbidden to teach the following concepts:

- An individual, by virtue of the individual's race or sex, is inherently privileged, racist, sexist, or oppressive, whether consciously or subconsciously;

- An individual, by virtue of the individual's race or sex, bears responsibility for actions committed in the past by other members of the same race or sex;
- An individual should feel discomfort, guilt, anguish, or another form of psychological distress solely because of the individual's race or sex;
- A meritocracy is inherently racist or sexist, or designed by a particular race or sex to oppress members of another race or sex;
- This state or the United States is fundamentally or irredeemably racist or sexist;
- Promoting division between, or resentment of, a race, sex, religion, creed, nonviolent political affiliation, social class, or class of people;
- Ascribing character traits, values, moral or ethical codes, privileges, or beliefs to a race or sex, or to an individual because of the individual's race or sex. (SBO 623, 2021)

The law is pushing back against a misrepresentation of CRT—namely, that it promotes *racial essentialism* (which is not to be confused with the educational essentialism we have been discussing in this chapter). Racial essentialism is the ascribing of moral, character, or behavioral traits to an individual or group of individuals simply by virtue of their race. Of course, CRT does not promote racial essentialism. On the contrary, the actual CRT explicitly states that Black people are *not* a monolith. However, the Tennessee law is a response to a bogeyman, a mythical curriculum that teaches white students that they are oppressive simply because they are white. Again, neither CRT nor the 1619 Project makes such claims. However, both CRT and the 1619 Project *do* highlight the structural nature of racism, showing that although individual white people may not be oppressive, the legal, political, and social systems of the United States have oppressed Black people, and white people have benefitted from that oppression. Acknowledging that such a system exists and that such a system has benefitted some more than others is not the same as promoting racial essentialism. But, if social cohesion and cultural unity depend on ensuring that certain stories are *not* told, then the negative essentialism of today's canon wars makes a perverted sort of sense. The problem of the pedagogical canon has been solved; once we've identified all the books we *shouldn't* read, we'll just read whatever's left.

Conclusion

Negative essentialism is part of what led to the social collapse in *Fahrenheit 451*, at least according to Beatty's account. When canons are created based not on what we should read but rather on what we *shouldn't*, we end up with something very much like what is happening in America today—social cohesion based on exclusion and rabid orthodoxy. To be clear, this is not merely a phenomenon of the political right. Though the negative essentialism examples from this chapter focus on conservative legislation and policies, the unwritten social policies of so-called "cancel culture" that have flourished in progressive spaces are no less negatively essentialist. In both extremes, canonicity boils down to which texts you're *not* allowed to read, which opinions you're *not* allowed to express, and which words you're *not* allowed to say.

Positive essentialism suffers from a different set of ills, primarily in implementation. The school day is time-bound, and even with the most well-intentioned teachers and systems, it is not possible to include all the material necessary for a true melting-pot experience. Someone's story will always be left out, if for no other reason that there are simply not enough hours in the day. This leads to important and uncomfortable questions of power and authority: who decides what gets read and what doesn't? How often do we update the pedagogical canon? How do we account for local interests in the name of *local* social cohesion, not just national? Given a seemingly endless list of cultural texts from which to choose, how do we even begin to sort through them without inadvertently reverting to a white-dominated status quo?

The great promise of essentialism as presented in *Fahrenheit 451* is its ability to help us re-member, to attach ourselves to one another, to become part of a larger social body. The great danger of essentialism, however, is its ability to exclude, to gatekeep, to detach us from one another. *Fahrenheit 451* highlights the double-edged nature of the essentialist sword, a sword that can just as easily cleave us apart as it can cleave us together.

Questions for Reflection

1. Is multicultural essentialism possible? What would it take to create and maintain a pedagogical canon that creates cohesion among *multiple* cultures?

2. How do we keep an essentialist pedagogical canon from turning into a weapon for maintaining the status quo?

3. If you had to create a canon to promote social cohesion, which texts would you choose? Are there any texts that you would intentionally leave out? What would your "required reading" list be if you were in charge of American culture?

4. What kinds of processes can you put in place in your educational context to make sure that your pedagogical canon is open to change? What are the systems and structures that make change difficult?

5. How can we balance local or student interest with the essentialist need for promoting common knowledge? When does local literacy become more important than cultural literacy? How do we include the voices of smaller groups without losing what is necessary for the group as a whole?

6. Pretend that you had to create a dictionary of cultural literacy, much like Hirsch did. How would you go about it? Who would you include in the process? How would you know when you were done?

Endnotes

1. This is a wildly over-simplified account of how the Biblical Canon came to be formed. There are, of course, sects and branches of Christianity that *do*, in fact, take away from and add to the canon, each insisting that it and it alone has the "true" version. Wars have been fought over which translation of the Biblical Canon is the "real" word of God. Furthermore, there is wild disagreement over how the canon should be interpreted, especially as it comes to guiding the life of the Church and of individual Christians. Nevertheless, the Bible has been a marvelously stable text over time, all things considered.

2. Although the Common Core State Standards (CCSS) do outline the skill and knowledge outcomes that should result from high school language arts courses, they do not dictate which texts should be taught, leaving those decisions to states, local districts, and individual teachers. Furthermore, the CCSS are *not* national. They do not come from the federal government. They were created by a private organization, and although many states have voluntarily chosen to align with CCSS, there is no federal legislation mandating such alignment. As I write this, only 40 states are using the CCSS.

3. Ravitch, who went on to become the Assistant Secretary of Education under President George W. Bush, was actually an early critic of multiculturalism and a chief architect of the high-stakes testing movement that blossomed under No Child Left Behind. However, later in her career, she came to reverse her positions on, well, almost everything, becoming a staunch *opponent* of standardized testing and great advocate for educational justice.

References

Adler, M. (1940). *How to read a book: The art of getting a liberal education.* New York, NY: Simon & Schuster.

Anderson, S.B. (1964). *Between the Grimms and "The Group": Literature in American high schools.* Princeton, NJ: Educational Testing Service.

Arsel, Z., Crockett, D., & Scott, M. L. (2022). Diversity, equity, and inclusion (DEI) in the Journal of Consumer Research: A curation and research agenda. *Journal of Consumer Research,* 48(5), 920–933. https://doi.org/10.1093/jcr/ucab057

Asante, M. (1991, Spring). Multiculturalism: An exchange. *The American Scholar, 60*, pp. 267–272.

Bagnardi, M., Bryant, L., & Colin, J. (2009). Banks multicultural model: A framework for integrating multiculturalism into nursing curricula. *Journal of Professional Nursing,* 25(4), 234–239. https://doi.org/10.1016/j.profnurs.2009.01.010

Banks, J. A. (1989). Approaches to multicultural curriculum reform. *Trotter Review, 3*(3), pp. 17–19. https://scholarworks.umb.edu/trotter_review/vol3/iss3/5

Banks, T. M. (2022). Black talent: Practical retention strategies. In Allen & Stewart (Eds.), *We're not OK: Black faculty experiences and higher education strategies,* 183–197. Cambridge, United Kingdom: Cambridge University Press.

Barry, R.R. (2003). The Neo-Classics: (Re)Publishing the "Great Books" in the United States in the 1990s. *Book History 6*, 251–275. https://doi.org/10.1353/bh.2004.0002.

Beach, R., & O'Brien, D. (2005). Playing texts against each other in the multimodal English classroom. *English in Education,* 39(2), 44–59. https://doi.org/10.1111/j.1754-8845.2005.tb00616.x

Bloom, H. (1994). *The Western Canon: The books and school of the ages.* New York, NY: Harcourt Brace.

Bradbury, R. (1953). *Fahrenheit 451.* New York, NY: Ballantine Books.

Brownstein, B. (2020, Sept. 29). Fahrenheit 451 predicted people would demand tyranny. *American Institution for Economic Research.* https://www.aier.org/article/fahrenheit-451-predicted-people-would-demand-tyranny/

Chicago Cultural Studies Group. (1992). Critical multiculturalism. *Critical Inquiry, 18*(3), 530–555. https://doi.org/10.1086/448644

Conway, D. M., Saidman-Krauss, Bekah, & Schreiber, Rebecca. (2021). Inclusivity in admissions and retention of diverse students: leadership determines dei success. *Rutgers Race & the Law Review,* 23(1), 1–38.

Delgado, R., & Stefancic, J. (2023). *Critical race theory: An introduction* (Vol. 87). New York, NY: NYU press.

Ebbers, F. A. (1991). Resources and reviews: A unit on Fahrenheit 451 that uses cooperative learning. *English Journal,* 80(6), 100–101. https://doi.org/10.2307/820642

Emmons, S. (2014). We're not in Kansas anymore. In E. Dial-Driver, J. Ford, & S. Emmons (Eds.), *Fantasy Media in the classroom: Essays on teaching with film, television, literature, graphic novels and video games,* 74.

Farrington, B. (2022, March 25). *DeSantis signs bill targeting explicit books in schools.* AP News. https://apnews.com/article/entertainment-florida-ron-desantis-school-boards-libraries-da50c9c4091868e121484425d290385b

Friedman, J., & Johnson, N. F. (2022). *Banned in the USA: The growing movement to censor books in schools.* Pen America. https://pen.org/report/banned-usa-growing-movement-to-censor-books-in-schools/

Gibbs, C., Achebe, N., Johnson, B., Nwaiche, C., & Ortiz, D. V. (2023). Constructing college-level diversity, equity, and inclusion (DEI) minors—Moving from performative to transformative DEI. *The Radical Teacher,* (127), 41–50. https://www.jstor.org/stable/48756582

Godina, H. (1996). The canonical debate: Implementing multicultural literature and perspectives. *Journal of Adolescent & Adult Literacy, 39*(7), 544–549.

Great Books Foundation. (1993). *Junior Great Books.* Great Books Foundation.

Hajiyeva, M. (2024). Chronotopic contrasts: Unraveling temporal dynamics in utopian and dystopian narratives. *Path of Science, 10*(3), 4001–4006. https://doi.org/10.22178/pos.102-14

Hamblin, C.F. (1968). Bradbury's "Fahrenheit 451" in the classroom. *The English Journal, 57*(6), pp. 818–819, 824. https://doi.org/10.2307/812029

H.B. 1467. (2022). https://www.flsenate.gov/Session/Bill/2022/1467

Hirsch, Jr., E. D. (1983). Cultural literacy. *The American Scholar,* 159–169. https://www.jstor.org/stable/41211231

Hirsch, Jr., E. D. (1988). *Cultural Literacy: What every American needs to know.* New York, NY: Random House.

Hirsch, Jr., E. D. (1996). *The schools we need and why we don't have them.* New York, NY: Random House.

Hirsch, Jr., E. D. (2002). *The new dictionary of cultural literacy.* New York, NY: Houghton Mifflin.

Hirsch, Jr., E. D. (2006). *The knowledge deficit: Closing the shocking education gap for American children.* New York, NY: Houghton Mifflin

Hirsch, Jr., E. D. (2009). *The making of Americans: Democracy and our schools.* New Haven, CT: Yale University Press.

Hirsch, Jr., E. D. (Ed.), (2015). *What your third grader needs to know.* New York, NY: Bantam Books.

Hirsch, Jr., E. D. (2016). *Why knowledge matters: Rescuing our children from failed educational theories.* Cambridge, MA: Harvard Educational Press.

Hirsch, Jr., E. D. (2020). *How to educate a citizen: The power of shared knowledge to unify a nation.* New York, NY: Harper Collins.

Houghtaling, E. Q. (2024, April 17). *Ron DeSantis suddenly pretends he hates the thing he loves the most.* The New Republic. https://newrepublic.com/post/180774/ron-desantis-pretends-hates-book-ban

Hutchins, R.M. (1952). *The great conversation: The substance of a liberal education.* Chicago, IL: Encyclopedia Brittanica.

Hutchins, R. & Adler, M. (1952). *The Great Books of the Western World*. Encyclopedia Brittanica.

Kelley, E. (2024). Coloring in the lines. In D. Cook & N. Bryan (Eds.), *Critical race theory and classroom practice*. New York, NY: Routledge. https://doi.org/10.4324/9781003172253

Lange, A. C., & Lee, J. A. (2024). Centering our humanity: Responding to anti-DEI efforts across higher education. *Journal of College Student Development, 65*(1), 113–116. https://doi.org/10.1353/csd.2024.a919356

Lawall, S. (1994). Introduction: Reading world literature. In S. Lawall (Ed.), *Reading world literature: Theory, history, practice*. Austin, TX: University of Texas Press.

Meehan, K., Friedman, J., Baêta, S., & Magnusson, T. (2024). *Banned in the USA: Mounting pressure to censor*. Pen America. https://pen.org/report/book-bans-pressure-to-censor/

Member, N., Sense I.1.b. (2024). *Oxford English dictionary*. Oxford, United Kingdom: Oxford UP. https://doi.org/10.1093/OED/8871405382.

Member, N., Sense III.9.a.(2024) *Oxford English dictionary*. Oxford, United Kingdom: Oxford UP. https://doi.org/10.1093/OED/5154243289.

Owsianik, J. (n.d.). *Best futurists ever: How Ray Bradbury's Fahrenheit 451 foretold the social tensions and technology of today*. https://rossdawson.com/futurist/best-futurists-ever/ray-bradbury-fahrenheit-451/

Parnell, M. (2024, Feb. 22). *Bible ban? Florida lawmakers respond to calls to have Bible removed from schools*. https://www.wtsp.com/article/news/education/education-bills-bible-schools-books/67-734c2875-9b21-4a10-a0c4-13c19923b2b5

Ravitch, D. (1990). Multiculturalism: E pluribus plures. *The American Scholar, 59*(3), 337–354. https://www.jstor.org/stable/41211801

Reading List. (2024). *Great-Books-reading-list*. Saint John's College. https://www.sjc.edu/academic-programs/undergraduate/great-books-reading-list

Ruhnken, D. (1768). *Historia critica oratorum graecorum*.

Rundle, M. (2012, June 6). *Ray Bradbury dead: Five tech predictions the sci-fi author got right*. https://www.huffingtonpost.co.uk/2012/06/06/ray-bradbury-dead-how-accurate-predictions-fahrenheit-451_n_1574126.html

Ryan, M. B. (1997). The American canon wars: A view from Mexico. *Journal of American Culture, 20*(2), 171–176. https://doi.org/10.1111/j.1542-734X.1997.2002_171.x

SBO 623. (2021). Tennessee General Assembly. https://wapp.capitol.tn.gov/apps/Billinfo/default.aspx?BillNumber=HB0580&ga=112

Schwarz, R. (2023, June 7). *How the Bible became conservative book bans' unintended target*. The Week. https://theweek.com/book-ban/1024016/how-the-bible-became-conservative-book-bans-unintended-target

Shakespeare, W. (1597). *The tragedy of Romeo and Juliet*.

Sisario, P. (1970). A study of the allusions in Bradbury's "Fahrenheit 451." *The English Journal, 59*(2), pp. 201–201+212. https://doi.org/10.2307/811827

Stotsky, S., Traffas, J., & Woodworth, J. (2010, May). Literary study in grades 9, 10, and 11: A national survey. In *Forum: A Publication of the ALSCW* (Vol. 4, pp. 1–75).

Tatum, B. (2007). Defining racism. In P. Rothenberg (Ed.), *Race, class, and gender in the United States*, 123–130. New York, NY: Worth Publishers.

Thornton, C. (2024, Jan. 12). *Wait, did Florida ban the dictionary? Why one county is pulling Merriam-Webster from shelves.* USA Today. https://www.usatoday.com/story/news/nation/2024/01/12/escambia-county-florida-dictionary-ban/72202686007/

Trump, D. J. (2020, Sept. 17). Remarks by President Trump at White House conference on American History. *National Archives Museum.* Retrieved September 12, 2021, from https://trumpwhitehouse.archives.gov/briefings-statements/remarks-president-trump-white-house-conference-american-history/

Wagner, B. A., & Novak, B. (1981). Morality reasoning among high school students. *The Clearing House, 55*(2), 73–79. https://doi.org/10.1080/00098655.1981.9958215

Who we are. (2024). *Who We Are.* www.greatbooks.org

CHAPTER THREE

Calculating the Future: Algorithms, Agency, and Oppression in Asimov's *Foundation* Trilogy

The Text: *Foundation* (Asimov, 1951); *Foundation and Empire* (Asimov, 1952); *Second Foundation* (Asimov, 1953). Books.

Introduction

THE SO-CALLED "GOLDEN AGE" of science fiction began in the 1940s and extended through the 1950s. This was a time before big blockbuster science fiction films. Full-length science fiction novels were relatively rare, and television was still in its infancy. If you wanted to find good science fiction, you had to look to the magazines.

One of the premier sci-fi magazines of the day was *Astounding Science Fiction*. Like most trade magazines of the time, *Astounding Science Fiction* used inexpensive paper to keep publication costs down. The cheap paper was generally made from the pulpy leftovers at the paper mill, meaning that some of the pulp residue ended up in the pages of the magazines. This is where the term *pulp fiction* comes from, and, in the 1940s, *Astounding* was the premier publisher of pulp science fiction in the country.

Though the paper may have been low quality, the stories *Astounding* published were not. In May 1942, *Astounding* published a short story by a young and relatively unknown Russian immigrant named Isaac Asimov.

Asimov, who was 22 at the time and a graduate student in Chemistry, was a history buff. He had read historical accounts of the fall of the Roman Empire and the role of European monasteries in preserving knowledge throughout the so-called Dark Ages, and it led him to ask a simple question: If there were a galactic empire, and if it were to collapse, how could a galaxy-wide dark age be prevented? Asimov's 1942 short story, *Foundation*, was his first attempt at answering that question.

Over the next eight years, *Astounding* published seven more of Asimov's stories about the fall and eventual rise of a galactic empire. In 1951, the first four stories were collected into a single novel and given the title *Foundation*, which is the text we know today. The remaining four stories were collected into two additional novels and published soon after. The books were an immediate critical and commercial success, and Asimov, who by this time had finished graduate school and was a professor of biochemistry at Columbia College, never looked back. He would go on to write and edit more than 500 books in his lifetime.

Although Asimov's other stories were highly successful, and although his three laws of robotics, first introduced in *I, Robot* (1950), may have had the greatest impact on a specific scientific discipline[1], his original *Foundation Trilogy* may have had the greatest impact on the social sciences in general, informing the development of such disparate disciplines as organization theory (Phillips & Zyglidopoulos, 1999), law (Williams, 2022), diplomacy (Jazbec, 2018), sociology (Seligman, 1998), economics (Krugman, 2012), and energy policy (Mišík & Kujundžić, 2021).

The *Foundation Trilogy* also had an enormous impact on pop culture, winning the Hugo Award for "Best All-Time Series" in 1966 and going on to directly influence generations of authors, writers, and creators. In 2021, the Apple+ streaming service released the first season of a *Foundation* TV show, with a second season following in 2023.

So what is it, exactly, that has made *Foundation* so popular with both scientific and popular audiences, and what does it have to do with critical pedagogy? The answer lies with the character Hari Seldon, who dies early in the first book but whose shadow looms over everything in the entire *Foundation* universe. As we will discuss below, Seldon was a mathematician who, while the galactic empire was seemingly at its height, developed a new algorithm for studying and predicting the behavior of the entire human race. He called his algorithm *psychohistory*, and it allowed him not only to predict the impending fall of the galactic empire but also to name the conditions necessary for the rise of a new empire in the not-too-distant future.

Algorithms, of course, are front and center in our contemporary discussions of educational equity. Google search results, ChatGPT, the spellcheck function in your Word processor, and the sudden boom in artificial intelligence that seems to be accelerating every day are all examples of algorithmic processes. We will get into the details later in this chapter, but suffice it for now to say that algorithms in educational spaces are increasingly being used not just to predict student performance but rather to dictate it. This leads to a host of uncomfortable questions, of which the two most important are:

- how much control do we have over our own educational futures?
- how much of our decision-making ability have we handed over to machines?

As *Foundation* demonstrates, the line between an algorithm that predicts what you will do and a society that allows the algorithm to determine what you *must* do is very, very thin indeed.

The Story

A quick note: Although the bulk of our analysis will be based on the third book in the trilogy, Second Foundation *(Asimov, 1953), we need to set the stage with an overview of what happens in the first two books. With this in mind, the summary of the first two books will be brief and woefully truncated. I cannot encourage you highly enough to read the entire trilogy for yourself.*

Prophets are never appreciated in their own time. That's especially true for Hari Seldon, mathematician and, at this very moment, thorn in the emperor's side. It's not as if Seldon *wants* the Galactic Empire to collapse. It's just that his calculations show that imperial collapse that will happen 500 years in the future is virtually a statistical certainty, and, well, his calculations are never wrong.

Seldon tries explaining this to the head of the Grand Commission, who has called him to a tribunal to face charges of treason. The courts (Judicial and Imperial) are concerned with a new branch of statistics that Seldon has developed. He calls it *psychohistory*, and he claims that it can use be used to accurately predict the actions of humanity. It cannot predict the actions of an individual human, mind you. Individuals operate more or less randomly, and it is impossible to create a mathematical and statistical model for predicting what any one person may do. But add all those people together into the thousands of trillions of human beings who populate the 25,000,000 planets of the Galactic Empire, and you have a data set large enough to make predictions with astonishing accuracy. A man may not be predictable, but mankind is.

It is precisely the size and scope of the Galactic Empire that makes its collapse inevitable. As Seldon explains to the Grand Commissioner,

> the psychohistoric trend of a planet-full of people contains a huge inertia. To be changed it must be met with something possessing a similar inertia. Either as many people must be concerned, or if the number of people be relatively small, enormous time for change must be allowed. (Asimov, 1951, p. 27)

When the Grand Commissioner points out that Seldon has roughly 100,000 followers, all scientists who could, if they tried, stop the imperial collapse from happening, Seldon shakes his head sadly:

> Consider that Trantor [the Imperial capital where the trial is taking place] has a population of over forty billion. Consider further that the trend leading to ruin does not belong to Trantor alone but to the Empire as a whole and the Empire contains nearly a quintillion human beings. (p. 27)

The statistical mass of the impending collapse is too great to be countered by so few people in such a short time, Seldon continues. In 500 years, the Empire will finally die, and the human beings spread across the galaxy will enter into a galactic Dark Age. Vast quantities of human knowledge will be lost. Interstellar travel and trade will grind to a halt. Civilizations and cultures will decay. Wars will be endless. And this new galactic dark age of humanity, which psychohistory tells us is a statistical inevitability, will last for 30,000 years.

Unless . . .

There is one option, Seldon tells the Grand Commissioner. Although Seldon and his 100,000 followers may not be able to keep the Empire from collapsing, they *can* reduce the Dark Age of suffering to a short 1,000 years. How? By collecting, archiving, preserving, and protecting the entirety of human knowledge. Seldon proposes that he and his followers be allowed to set up two foundations. The first foundation will be devoted to creating the Encyclopedia Galactica, which will be the official record of human knowledge that will see humanity through the dark times ahead. He doesn't say much about the second foundation.

Although Seldon proposes that he be allowed to set up his foundation on the Imperial capital of Trantor, the Grand Commissioner has other ideas. He grants Seldon his charter but exiles him and his followers to an unknown planet at the far end of the galaxy—Terminus. And although the Grand Commissioner feels that he "won" the encounter—exile is, after all, a harsh punishment—Seldon feels pretty good about it. After all, this turn of events is precisely what he, and psychohistory, had predicted.

And so, the Foundation, now firmly settled on Terminus, falls into a pattern of growth and crisis, growth and crisis. A mere 50 years after being established, for example, the Foundation faces its first existential threat. As the Empire's power has waned, the planets nearest to Terminus have declared independence, each ruled by a self-styled monarch/warlord. More importantly, the planets of the periphery have lost or forgotten how to maintain critical technology. Terminus, being a colony of scientists, is the only planet in the area to still have atomic power, for example. The rest have gone back to coal. Still, they are strong, and Terminus is without defense. Though it is *officially* protected by the Empire, it is *practically* on its own.

In addition to the external threat of warmongering neighbors, Terminus is fighting an internal battle, as well. Though there is a nominal civilian leader—the mayor—the colony's charter holds that it is to be officially governed by the "board of trustees"—that is, by the leaders of the encyclopedia project. The academic leadership insists that the sole purpose of the colony is the creation of the encyclopedia. The mayor insists that Terminus has, at this point, a population of well over 1,000,000, most of whom were born there and have nothing to do with the encyclopedia whatsoever. Internal and external tensions rise to the point that there is only one way forward. The planet Anacron *will* attack, and the board of trustees *will* remove the mayor from his position. The time for weighing options has passed, and it is precisely at this moment that the Time Vault, a special room constructed when the colonists first arrived, opens, and a hologram of Hari Seldon appears.

It would seem that events are unfolding precisely as Seldon has predicted. Seldon, who was too old and infirm to join the colonists when they left Terminus some 50 years before, has programmed the Time Vault to open at key moments in the Foundation's "history." Each of these key moments is called a "Seldon Crisis," and each represents a specific moment in time when the cultural, economic, political, and social tension both within and around the Foundation will come to a head, converging until there is only one way forward, shutting down all alternative paths of action and leaving only the path predicted by Seldon's psychohistorical model. In this moment, the hologram tells the board of trustees and the mayor, who all happen to be in the vault, the first crisis has arrived. They are learning the truth: The nominal reason for establishing the Foundation—that is, the creation of the Encyclopedia Galactica—was all a ruse. The *real* reason for the creation of the Foundation is to plant the seeds of a new Galactic Empire. The Foundation will grow, spread, and, eventually fill the vacuum left by the collapse of the current Empire. If all goes according to plan—and there's a 98.5% chance that it will—this will take only 1000 years.

Faced with Seldon's revelation, the board of trustees admits defeat. That doesn't really matter though, because while they were all in the vault, the Mayor's men had staged a quiet coup on his behalf, and soon after, he wards off the threat of invasion by pitting the neighboring planets against one another. It was the only way keep the Foundation safe. As Seldon's hologram said, forces had converged until there was only one way forward.

And so the growth/crisis pattern continues for the next 200 years. To pacify its neighbors, the Foundation offers to help them rebuild their atomic power infrastructure and to train their people to work and maintain it. But they don't teach them the science; instead, the Foundation creates a religious cult in which the mysteries of atomic power are the miracles of the Great Spirit. The priests who run the reactors are all Foundation-trained, and when the neighboring planets once again threaten to attack, the High Priest—himself a Foundation nuclear scientist who knows exactly what he's doing—calls on his priests to shut down all the power across the periphery. After all, an attack on the Foundation is an attack on the Great Spirit. Thus, the Foundation weathers another attack *and* consolidates power in the local systems. The Time Vault opens. The hologram emerges. The second crisis has passed, and the plan is intact.

As time passes, the crises grow more complicated, but the general pattern remains the same. As the Federation expands its territory, other planets, having heard about the "priesthood," refuse to use nuclear power. The Federation "conquers" them through trade and economic cunning. Once the populace grows used to luxuries like Foundation-made kitchen appliances that cook meals in 1/10th of the time, they don't want to give them up. Planets that would not fall to religious manipulation succumb to the might of the market. The Time Vault opens. The crisis has passed. The plan remains intact.

The Empire, though dying and more or less vanished in the periphery, remains strong in the galactic core. A cunning and strikingly competent general hears of the Foundation and, accurately recognizing the danger it poses, gathers the remnants of the great Imperial Navy to crush these upstarts. He is winning and has almost managed to capture Terminus when he and his ships are suddenly recalled to Trantor and put on trial for treason against the emperor. The Time Vault opens. Even though the Foundation's efforts did not bring about the victory, Seldon's hologram announces that the general's defeat was a statistical inevitability. When the Empire and the emperor are weak, a strong general must be perceived as an *internal* threat and dealt with as a political rival. The political, cultural, and social forces of the Imperial aristocracy and bureaucracy guaranteed that the emperor would not allow a strong general to flourish. The Foundation's success, hologram Seldon reminds them, is not a matter of individual heroics or choices. The economic and sociological forces measured by psychohistory and represented by its statistical models make the Foundation's success a mathematical certainty. One person could no more stop it than an ant could stop a speeding train. The plan remains intact.

Or does it?

The next Seldon Crisis involves the unionization of the Federation's millions of space-tug drivers and asteroid miners. At least that's what Seldon's hologram says it's about when the Time Vault opens. But the people in the vault are confused, because although the union issue had been important a few months back, a new threat has emerged. A warlord from the planet Kalgon has been slowly and steadily taking over Federation planets, pushing through Federation defenses as if they are not even there. No one knows what this warlord looks like or just how he is achieving his victories. They only know that he is called the Mule, that he commands absolute loyalty from every one of his subjects—even those he has taken by force—and that he is about to lay siege to Terminus, the Federation home world. Unless something unforeseen takes place, the Mule will undo 500 years of Federation expansion in six short months. So the people listening to Seldon's hologram droning on about unionization and better conditions for the workers cannot help but wonder just what the heck he is talking about.

The truth is that the Mule was not predicted in Seldon's plan. He is an outlier, a random piece of data that could not be accounted for in a data set of quintillions. Quite simply, psychohistory could not predict the random genetic mutation that would take place in the Mule's DNA, rendering him just a little bit different from every other human ever born. The Mule has no super strength, no above-average intelligence, no powers of invisibility. What he does have, and what he was born with, however, is the ability to read and control others' emotions. The Mule is able to capture cities, planets, and entire systems almost without lifting a finger, because he can, quite simply, make people loyal to him. He can sense betrayal before it happens, and he can twist the tendrils of his enemies' minds so that opposing him becomes quite literally unthinkable.

The Mule *does* go on to defeat the Foundation, occupying Terminus and laying waste to the Seldon Plan. He's well on his way to creating a new galactic empire of his own. There is just one thing standing in his way, however: the Second Foundation.

If you recall, when Seldon proposed the Foundation to the emperor, he simultaneously proposed that a *second* Foundation be established on the opposite side of the galaxy, at Stars End. Whereas the First Foundation was a colony of physical scientists, the Second Foundation was . . . well, that's really the question, isn't it? No one knows. No one, perhaps, except the Mule.

The Mule is convinced that the Second Foundation is actually made up of *psychic* scientists. That is, just as the First Foundation has expanded the horizons of physical science, conquering the realms of the atom and the stars, the Second Foundation has expanded the horizons of the *mind*, conquering the mental and psychological realms. If the First Foundation is to be the beneficiary of the Seldon Plan, the Second Foundation is the guardian of the Plan. Their job is to ensure that the course of human affairs proceeds according to the dictates of psychohistory. When humanity deviates too far from Seldon's statistical modeling, the Second Foundation gives a little nudge to get things back on track. Some emotional control here, a bit of mental alteration there . . . nothing serious. Just enough to ensure that the events of human history unfold as they're supposed to. And, up to this point, they've been doing a pretty good job.

But the Mule was a variable that no one had accounted for. Convinced that the Second Foundation is the last remaining threat to complete galactic dominion, the Mule launches a galaxy-wide manhunt. He knows they're there, even though almost no one has ever even heard of them. He can *sense* them. After all, the powers that he was born with are the same powers that the Second Foundation has developed through time, study, and training. The details of the Mule's search are fascinating, but they are too detailed for this summary. Suffice it to say that although he *does* find them, they manage to "disable" his psychic powers. The threat to the Seldon Plan posed by the Mule is neutralized.

Except that it's not. For although the Mule has been dealt with, the Second Foundation had to essentially blow its cover in the process of saving the galaxy. It has announced its existence to the First Foundation. The First Foundation, in turn, is now aware that their collective fate is being controlled by a far-away group of secret mental scientists, and they resent it. Now that humanity knows it is being "watched," great masses of people begin behaving in ways that they normally wouldn't, and history strays even further from the Seldon Plan, despite the incapacitation of the Mule.

Everything that happens from this point on is *not* a part of the Seldon Plan. The Second Foundation is desperate to get things back on track, and the First Foundation is desperate to locate the Second Foundation and destroy it. These adventures are well worth reading.

As the maintainers of the Seldon Plan, the Second Foundation has a great allegiance to psychohistory and its statistical models. As the First Speaker, leader of the Second Foundation claims,

> a [Second Foundationer] must not only be aware of the mathematical intricacies of the Seldon Plan, he must have a sympathy for it and for its ends. He must *love* the Plan; to him it must be life and breath. More than that, it must even be as a living friend. (Asimov, 1953, p. 120–121, italics original)

Because loyalty to the Plan trumps all, the Second Foundation's only obligation to the mass of humanity is making sure that they adhere to the "proper" statistical models. Consequently, they view humankind as "gigantic forces amenable to statistical treatment" (Asimov, 1953, p. 117). Of course, maintaining the Plan is about more than just mathematics; instead, it is about the survival of the Plan's "philosophies and aims" (p. 125). The Second Foundation is tasked with ensuring that the "stubborn and stupid" (p. 117) mass of humanity does nothing to threaten the promised future: a new galactic empire in which the First Foundation supplies the "physical framework" while the Second Foundation supplies the "mental framework of a ready-made ruling class" (p. 127).

In the end, the Second Foundation finds it necessary to sacrifice some of their own in order to maintain the statistical integrity of the Plan. They allow 50 Second Foundationers to be caught, imprisoned, tortured, and, presumably, executed by the First Foundation. It was a horrible sacrifice to make, but it was ultimately successful. The First Foundation, believing it has defeated the Second, begins to behave "normally" again. The Plan is back on track. The keepers of the algorithm are satisfied, and everything is now as it should be. Statistically, that is.

The Analysis

It may at first seem a bit strange to examine algorithms through a lens of critical pedagogy. Even if we extrapolate from the abstract to specific iterations of algorithms, such as ChatGPT, the relationship between algorithms and the uncovering of hidden power structures in education is not immediately obvious. To be sure, there are grotesque examples, such as the algorithms that drive facial recognition software used by law-enforcement agencies being unable to recognize non-white faces, leading to rampant misidentification and disproportionate numbers of false arrests (e.g., Garvie & Frankle, 2016; Lohr, 2022; Taylor et al., 2023). But these are extreme examples. Day-to-day use of algorithms, such as Google searches and Amazon purchase recommendations, do not appear to merit critical attention because it is not immediately apparent how they might be covering up, hiding, or otherwise obscuring hidden educational power structures.

I assert, however, that algorithms are, in fact, perhaps the single most important site of educational resistance today. The central issue of the Foundation series was the tension between the extent to which human beings were able to chart their own courses through the universe and the extent to which their choices and futures had been predetermined. This is the same tension facing American learners in 21st-century classrooms. The rhetoric being tossed around higher education spaces right now is that we must teach our students how to use AI in their own educations, because they *are* going to use it, with or without our guidance. This is an example of what Pronzato (2021) calls a narrative of "dependency, powerlessness, inevitability and trajectorism" (p. 13). AI *is* coming, we're told. There is no stopping it. We should stop fighting and accept that students *will* use algorithms to finish their assignments just as teachers *will* use algorithms to grade papers. Edutopia, an educational foundation long dedicated to highlighting creative and student-focused learning strategies, features posts by educational researchers and thinkers who assure us that AI can only improve our practices: Teachers who use AI to plan their lessons are more effective and efficient (Ma, 2024); students who use AI tutors will benefit from personalized learning scenarios (Mollick, 2024); and schools that use AI to automate routine tasks will have more time for learning (Finley, 2023). Each of the posts featured on Edutopia's website includes direct hyperlinks to various AI software companies, facilitating the easy purchase of the life-changing programs that we will all inevitably be using.

It is difficult to ignore the constant barrage of advertisements, reports, and news stories touting the virtues and unstoppable nature of the algorithmic development. Consequently, it becomes difficult to imagine an education future that does not "reproduce current ideological trends or cede control and power to external, mostly corporate, stakeholders" (Markham, 2021, p. 384). The role of for-profit corporations in perpetuating this rhetoric of algorithmic inevitability cannot be ignored, and we will address it later in this chapter. For now, though, let's begin our analysis by defining our terms. Because, although we use the term freely, for many of us, a simple question remains: What exactly is an *algorithm*?

The Algorithmic Process

It is tempting to speak of algorithms as concrete *things*. In reality, though, algorithms are *processes*. When I asked the algorithms running the Google search engine for the definition of *algorithm*, it told me that an algorithm is "a process or set of rules to be followed in calculations or other problem-solving operations, especially by a computer" (Algorithm, N,

2024). Other definitions from non-algorithmically driven sources are similar. For example, an algorithm is "a procedure or set of rules used in calculation and problem-solving; (in later use *spec.*) a precisely defined set of mathematical or logical operations for the performance of a particular task" (Algorithm, N. Sense 2, 2024). Interestingly, the Oxford English Dictionary also includes a definition of *algorithm* that applies specifically to the process of diagnosing a disease (Algorithm, N. Sense 3, 2024).

This reference to diagnostic processes is worth exploring. At its most fundamental, algorithmic function depends on three things: 1) existing information/data; 2) new information/data; and 3) a set of rules for reconciling the new data with the old. For example, if a patient presents with fever and a runny nose, the doctor will enter into the diagnostic process with an existing body of knowledge. They will be aware of the variety of respiratory and viral illnesses that present with these particular symptoms. Furthermore, they will be aware of the conditions that do not present with these symptoms. They will compare the new information (the patient's specific symptoms) with the database of symptoms that the doctor either has in mind or in their computer. Based on this comparison of new information with old, the doctor will immediately be able to rule out a wide variety of conditions, such as a broken leg. They will most likely be able to conduct this step of the algorithmic process before talking to or examining the patient.

The rules of the diagnostic algorithm dictate that the doctor should then seek out more information, such as the patient's medical history. They will ask a variety of questions about other possible symptoms, recent travel, lifestyle, etc. The answers to these questions will allow the doctor to immediately rule out another set of potential conditions, because the rules of the algorithm state that the absence of certain symptoms or environments negates the possibility of certain conditions. For example, if the patient has never traveled outside of Minnesota, and if the patient has not been in contact with people who have traveled recently, the doctor can almost certainly rule out a variety of diseases that are only found only in subtropical climates.

Depending on the answers the doctor gets from the patient's history, the algorithm might guide them to conduct specific tests or examinations. The results of those examinations will allow the doctor to rule out even more conditions. If the doctor's comparison of the new data to the old results in a list of possible conditions greater than one, they will gather more information. Each new piece of information allows the doctor to run new comparisons between the new information and the old. Eventually, the comparison of new information with old will result in only one possible condition, and the doctor will be able to make a diagnosis.[2]

This is an admittedly crude example, and yet it is a fair representation of a basic algorithmic process. The initial or existing data set is the result of *algorithmic training*. Before the algorithm goes "live," programmers introduce large data sets into the computer (much like the doctor attends four years of medical school and memorizes the symptoms of hundreds of diseases). The software then looks for mathematical relationships or correlations between two or more variables. When these relationships have been established, the training is refined through the introduction of new information. Each new piece of information is called *feedback*. For example, when you purchase something from Amazon, the website's algorithms compare the new information/feedback (the item you just bought) with a vast database of old information (things you have bought in the past, things that other people who also bought this item have purchased, other items that are often bought in conjunction with this item), and they make a diagnosis. In this case, the diagnosis comes in the form of a recommendation of other things that you might like to buy. When I buy motor oil for my motorcycle online, Amazon tells me that I might also like to buy oil filters, because I have bought the two items together in the past, as have the millions and millions of other people who buy motor oil. If I do, in fact, buy an oil filter, I have given the algorithm feedback that will strengthen the mathematical correlations between "motor oil" and "oil filter," meaning that the algorithm is now more likely to make that recommendation again.

Consider a video streaming service that curates a list of "movies you might like." This list is created by comparing your viewing history (new information/feedback) with the viewing history of millions of other users (old information) by conducting a series of mathematical operations (the "rules" for comparing the two sets of data) and coming to a conclusion: *you might like these movies, too*. If you do in fact watch one of those movies, then the correlation has been strengthened, and the algorithm will keep recommending those types of movies.

On the surface, these types of algorithmic applications do not appear to be overtly problematic. I *did* need to buy an oil filter, after all. The algorithm was right. But consider what might happen if the items available for me to purchase were determined solely based on an algorithmic calculation of my past purchases. I would most likely receive a fair number of notifications about sales on oil and other motorcycle parts, but I would get no information about anything else. If I watch two British murder mysteries on Netflix, the list of movies available for me to choose from suddenly all resemble murder mysteries. Netflix begins curating my choices based on my past choices and the past choices of others who have made choices similar to mine. Suddenly, all the options presented to me resemble the options I have chosen in the past. It becomes increasingly difficult for me to watch something other than a British murder mystery, because all my choices for the future have been determined by my choices in the past. If I want to watch something else, I will have to search for it manually, but because of the way my options are curated for me, I might not even be aware that other options exist. The algorithms at Netflix have decided that I like British murder mysteries, and so that is what it gives me to watch.

Algorithms of this type are known as *recommendation algorithms*. They use "historical data on interactions between users and items [to generate] personalized recommendations for the users" (Mansoury et al., 2020, p. 2145). However, these recommender systems are prone to bias:

> Recommender systems are deployed in dynamic environments. At each time step, a recommender system makes recommendations and collects user feedback. At the next time step, the recommendation algorithm is updated based on this feedback. The process alternates between these two steps, inducing a feedback loop: the recommendation algorithm influences what user behavior data it observes; this data in turn affects the recommendation algorithm, since the algorithm is trained on this data. Over time, the issue is exacerbated: the recommender system is trained on a growing set of data points that have been biased by recommendations. (Krauth et al., 2022, pp. 1–2)

The *feedback loops* described above are a well-documented and particularly dangerous element of mechanized algorithmic decision making. This is especially problematic, given that recommendation algorithms are now commonly used to curate personalized information feeds (Bodó et al., 2019). Essentially, the training of the algorithm never ends. Consequently, when a student searches for information on the Internet, the search results they obtain are based, in part, on the search engine's recommendation algorithms. The searches a student has run in the past will influence the results they obtain in their current search, and the current results will, in turn, inform the recommendation system, which will inform the next set of results, and so on. As stated, this *recommendation bias* is a well-documented phenomenon. As curated and personalized news and information feeds become the norm, recommendation bias leads to a *homogenization* of both recommendations and user behavior (Krauth et al., 2022).

Homogenization, in this context, is the process of removing difference, meaning that recommendation bias will slowly remove diversity and difference from recommendations. If you searched for information on a presidential candidate and you clicked on one of the links, your future searches for information on that presidential candidate will be informed by the first link that you clicked. Each subsequent search will compound the feedback loop, and it eventually becomes very, very difficult for you to obtain search results or curated information that does not confirm and conform to the search results that you obtained early on. Because the information used to train the algorithm early in its development is often weighted more heavily than information that retrains it later on, early search results and early feedback play outsized roles in determining future results.

Of course, if the person searching for information on the presidential candidate is not aware of the possibility of a feedback loop, they will most likely assume that the information they have obtained is free of bias. Even though the results obtained have been heavily biased by the algorithm, they will have the appearance of neutrality.[3] In this sense, the algorithm creates a sort of trajectory: the farther you go down a certain pathway, the easier it becomes to continue down that pathway, and the more difficult it becomes to choose any other alternative, because there do not appear to be any alternatives. Although you appear to have the freedom to choose whatever you want, the algorithm has, in fact, determined which choices will be made available to you and which will not. If you become aware of this process, you will realize that what seemed like free will was in fact a type of slavery. You do not get to determine your future, because your future has been determined for you by a set of statistical calculations over which you have no control.

This awareness is precisely what the Second Foundation feared. In order to avoid rebellion and a complete breakdown of the Seldon Plan, it is vital that the First Foundation remain unaware of the algorithmic processes that are guiding, shaping, and, yes, manipulating them. The Second Foundation must remain hidden. The algorithm must remain unseen. The First Foundation must believe that it is acting on its own free will. If the people of the First Foundation were to discover that a small group of elites views them as little more than variables to be manipulated in service to the algorithm, they might refuse to play along. To keep the Plan intact, it is very, very important that the people being controlled by the algorithm remain unaware of that control.

Critical Consciousness

The invisible nature of the type of social control described in the *Foundation* trilogy (Asimov, 1951–1953) has long been of great concern to critical pedagogues. The Second Foundation does not want the First Foundation to know it is being controlled. They want the First Foundation to believe that the development of their society is natural—that there are no mechanisms at work, no agendas being played out. If there are injustices or inequities, it is not because anyone has made it that way. It's just the way things are.

Behind the scenes, of course, the Second Foundation is pulling the strings. There is nothing natural about the way things are. Whatever injustice or inequities exist in the First Foundation have been planned and engineered, designed to keep the First Foundation growing according to the ideology represented by the Seldon Plan.

For a critical pedagogue, there are two issues of concern here. The first concern is fairly straightforward: one group is controlling and manipulating the other. The second concern, however, is more insidious: the First Foundation doesn't realize that it is being controlled. In Marxist social theory terms, the hidden relationship between the two groups is the result of an *oppressive ideology*. An oppressive ideology is a constructed system of values and beliefs that masquerades as "natural." It hides its own agenda, making it seem like the condition of society is the result of natural development when, in fact, it was designed to be the way it is. Generally speaking, oppressive ideologies remain hidden because it is to the benefit of the oppressor that the oppressed remain unaware of their oppression. Remember, the Second Foundation was setting the First Foundation up to build the physical infrastructure of a new empire so that they, themselves, could provide the "mental framework of a ready-made ruling class" (Asimov, 1953, p. 127).

All this brings us back to algorithms. Predictive algorithms are engineered. They "encode the biases of their developers or the surrounding society" (Baker & Hawn, 2022, p. 2). They have been designed to weigh certain types of data more heavily than others. They use complex and complicated mathematical calculations to provide results that are neither neutral nor disinterested. Algorithmic results have been shaped by the feedback provided to the machine and the initial data with which the machine was trained. If the initial data was poor or incomplete, the algorithmic results will be poor or incomplete, as well. If biased recommendations lead to biased action and biased feedback, all future predictions will compound that bias. An algorithm is the furthest thing from "natural."

When the algorithm takes the form of a doctor making a medical diagnosis, we accept it for what it is. We expect a doctor to provide biased (that is, influenced) recommendations based on the doctor's training and experience. The algorithmic process is visible for all to see, and it is expected. When the algorithmic process masquerades as "unfiltered information," however, the algorithm becomes an agent of oppressive ideology. When algorithm-driven information feeds are believed to provide fair, balanced, undistorted, and unfiltered data, the oppressive ideology is in full swing. The algorithmic results mask the nature of their own bias.

The Second Foundation fears what will happen if the First Foundation realizes that it is being algorithmically controlled. Marx referred to the oppressor's sudden awareness of their oppressed state as *critical consciousness*. Until the First Foundation realizes that they are being manipulated, they will never be free because:

> Critical consciousness is a means of perceiving the origins of the oppressive ideology in which one is immersed is a pre-requisite for the development of autonomy, and hence of genuine democratic participation. Thus it is necessary to the process of revolution, and to its success. And the individual is more likely to be able to develop her capacities if she is able to perceive, via critical consciousness, the real nature of her situation, which ideology disguises and keeps hidden from her. (Enslin, 1987, p. 65)

A crucial goal of critical pedagogy is the development and fostering of a critical consciousness that is aware of the hidden power structures and agendas used to shape, direct, and manipulate learners, teachers, institutions, and systems of education. This goal, in turn, leads us to a critical discussion of how algorithms are being used to shape education today.

Algorithms and Educational Inequity

Recommendation algorithms are a type of *predictive algorithm.* As the name suggests, predictive algorithms are used to make predictions. Often, they are making predictions about human behavior, such as predicting which purchases a customer will make or predicting which news articles a user is likely to click on. In educational settings, predictive algorithms can be used to predict student performance, such as predicting which students are likely to drop out of school (e.g., Christie et al., 2019). In this sense, predictive algorithms are often touted as a sort of "early warning system" (Liz-Dominguez et al., 2019), and there is emerging data that these algorithms may, in fact, be able to accurately predict students' future performance based on early indicators. For example:

- Ornelas & Ordonez (2017) developed an algorithm to predict which community college students would earn a C or higher based on their LMS login data;
- Thompson et al. (2018) used algorithms to accurately predict which college students would pass an introductory Biology class based on their earlier performance on tests *that had nothing to do with the course content*;
- The algorithms developed by Trussel & Burke-Smalley (2018) accurately predicted which students would graduate from college "on time" based on their household income, gender, and ethnicity; and
- Amirkhan & Kofman's (2018) algorithm used data about students' stress levels to accurately predict the long-term GPA of more than 500 college students.

Early warning algorithms such as these can be used to mathematically classify students as being at low, medium, or high risk of failure (e.g., Arnold & Pistilli, 2012), giving teachers and school administrators the opportunity to intervene and remediate *before* the student reaches the failing point. For example, if student performance on a Week One assignment is an accurate predictor of their final course grade, then the algorithm can flag certain students in need of help very early in the course, and the teacher will be able to provide targeted support and scaffolding, helping the student "change course." Predictive algorithms as early warning systems are increasingly common in both K–12 and higher education.

But what happens when the early warning system is not used to indicate students who need additional support but instead to decide which students will not succeed? In other words, what if the algorithm no longer predicts what *might* happen and instead determines what *will* happen? *Algorithmic determinism* (not to be confused with a *deterministic algorithm*) is what happens when the algorithm's predictions are used to determine a future state of affairs. With an early warning system, if the algorithm flags a student as "at risk of failing" based on their performance during the first week of class, the teacher will intervene and provide additional support. With algorithmic determinism, however, the algorithm will flag the student as "at risk," and the teacher will decide to remove the student from the class. The algorithm predicts that the student will fail, and so the teacher makes the algorithmic prediction come true. The algorithm's prediction *must* come true. The student is penalized—removed from the course—based on the mathematical prediction of what *might* happen. The predictive model developed from the data of other students determines the reality for this individual, even though this particular student has not actually failed the course. Because other students like them have failed, they too must fail.

This type of inequitable algorithmic determinism has already taken place, and on a massive scale. In 2020, the British government used algorithmic determinism to assign A-level grades to thousands of K–12 students. Due to the COVID-19 pandemic, British high school students were unable to sit in-person for the A-level exams. Because no online or distance testing option existed, the government used a predictive algorithm to assign A-level grades based not on these students' actual performance *but rather based on the historical performance data of the students who had attended their schools*. Students' A-level scores determine where they can go to college, meaning that for thousands of British students, their future education options were suddenly being determined not by their own performance but rather by a mathematical prediction of what their performance might have been—*a prediction made based on the historical academic performance of other people.*

To make matters worse, the government applied this algorithmic process only to students who attended schools with high student/teacher ratios. Students who attended schools with small student/teacher ratios—around 15 students for every one teacher—used the teachers' predictions to assign A-level scores. Basically, if you went to a large school with around 30 people in your class, the algorithm determined your score. But, if you went to a smaller school with smaller class sizes, your *teacher* decided what your score was going to be. The developers of the algorithm claimed that this was due to sample sizes and small schools not having enough historical data to make statistical predictions. Perhaps this is true. In practice, though, this meant that students in large (primarily urban) schools were given scores based on mathematical calculation of their hypothetical performance, whereas students at smaller schools (primarily *private*) were given scores based on their teachers' knowledge of their actual abilities. Predictably (ha!), this state of affairs did not sit well with the British public, and the algorithmic results were soon overturned in favor of teachers' predictions for *all* students.

It is important to note that algorithmic determinism is not a specific type of algorithm or set of statistical calculations. Instead, it is a belief system. It is the decision, conscious or unconscious, to grant the machines the power to move beyond predicting future events to determining future events, allowing statistical predictions to become self-fulfilling prophecies. It is Amazon deciding not what you might like to buy but rather foreclosing all your options until it is, in effect, determining what you *will* buy. It is a search engine algorithmically removing any content that deviates from your historical views, allowing the sites you have visited in the past to determine the sites you are able to visit in the future. It is the gradual stripping of agency, the gradual removal of choices, the gradual and inexorable creation of a calculated future. As it has been, so it must continue to be.

Without critical consciousness, we remain unaware that our futures have been determined for us. The algorithm has curated a personalized news feed that locks us into to hearing only one perspective, and yet, as far as we know, we have been presented with the news in full. This limited, selected, and calculated news *is* the news, as far as we are concerned, blithely unaware that we are algorithmically bound. This is the state of affairs that the Second Foundation is fighting to maintain: complete control through algorithmic determinism.

This kind of determinism is grossly at odds with human agency. Primarily, algorithmic determinism contradicts the inherently flexible, dynamic, and often contradictory nature of human identity (Polonski, 2016). Instead of preparing people to forge a new and unimagined future, algorithmic determinism binds them to a well-worn past, choking off choices and pruning pathways until only one option remains. But, because people's opinions, abilities, and preferences grow and change, the options and pathways determined by the algorithm often represent a "striking gap between our real interests and their digital reflection" (Koponen, 2015). Algorithmic determinism cannot account for a future that is different from the past.

Unfortunately, algorithmic determinism is already having a detrimental effect on learners (e.g., Baker & Hawn, 2022; Hu & Rangwala, 2020; Kai et al., 2017; Ocumpaugh et al., 2014; Yu et al., 2020; Yudelson et al., 2014). Some elite universities in the United States, for example, are using algorithmically deterministic processes to decide which students will and will not be admitted. Given how labor intensive it is to conduct an admissions review, and given the increasing numbers of applicants to elite institutions, some universities have taken the admissions-decision process away from human beings and handed it to machines (Lee et al., 2024). Applicants will be admitted (or not) based on algorithmic computations, not a human review of their application materials. To determine the impact that algorithmically-determined admissions processes might have on individual applicants, Lee et al. (2024) looked at data from more than 14,000 college applicants in the 2022–2023 application cycle. They found that the predictive models used by a handful of elite universities had been trained to make decisions based on variables in two categories: 1) controllable factors, such as test scores, classes taken, and intended majors; and 2) uncontrollable factors, such as parental income, place of birth, race, and gender.[4] Their analysis yielded two interesting and disturbing conclusions:

- Due to the arbitrary nature of the initial training and modeling, the sorting algorithm often arbitrarily assigned applicants within binary categories. Placement in one binary instead of the other often had an outsized impact on the applicant's overall score, affecting admission.

- When the algorithms used race-blind admission (when race was not factored in as part of the application decision), the number of historically underrepresented students categorized into the top tier of applicants dropped by 62%.

This last point is especially disturbing. Historically underrepresented students' scores on controllable factor variables often differ from those of their white counterparts due to inequitable distribution of educational resources, systemic racism, and other structural inequities in American K–12 education. A human admissions officer can take these factors into account, even when not directly considering race. However, if the algorithm has not been trained to account for systemic inequities in its modeling, such inequities will not factor into the algorithmic outputs. Furthermore, Lee et al. (2020) are quick to note that the removal of historically underrepresented students from the top tier of applicants did *not*, in fact, increase the academic merit of the top tier pool. In short, because algorithms are trained on historical data, they are, unless very, very carefully constructed, prone to reenact historical inequities. And, because the humans at these institutions have placed admissions decisions in the "hands" of the algorithm, inequitable algorithmic predictions are likely to lead to inequitable algorithmic determinism, in which the sins of the past are necessarily replicated in the future.

This same algorithmic determinism is playing an increased role in K–12 schools, particularly in the so-called "tracking" movement. Tracking is essentially the process of sorting students into differentiated academic pathways, such as "vocational" tracks and "academic" tracks. Third graders who are identified as "gifted," for example, may be placed in accelerated math courses. They will remain in the accelerated pathway through middle and high school, eventually culminating in Advanced Placement (AP) math courses. Students who were *not* placed on the accelerated path in elementary school may not have the opportunity to take Advanced Placement courses when they reach high school, despite their actual math skills and abilities.

Tracking has a long history of inequity in the United States. For example, In the 2020–2021 school year (the most recent data available), Black students represented 15% of the overall K–12 student population. However, in that same year, only 7.7% of all AP science students and only 6% of all AP math students were Black. At the same time, white students accounted for 45% of the overall K–12 population and yet made up 51% and 53% of AP science and math students, respectively (Office for Civil Rights, 2024). Black students were underrepresented in AP classes, whereas white students were *over*represented. Although the overrepresentation of white students is much less egregious than it used to be,[5] the underrepresentation of Black students in AP classes has actually gotten slightly worse.

The causes of these disparities are long-standing and complicated—a complex interplay of social, structural, and historical inequalities that manifests in inequitable tracking processes—and providing a full account of these complexities is beyond the scope and intent of this chapter. However, the emerging use of algorithms to sort students into academic tracks is perpetuating these already existing inequalities (Rafalow & Puckett, 2022). For example, the Boston School district collaborated with researchers at MIT to develop an algorithm designed to "reengineer its school choice and assignment system, with the goal of providing parents with equitable access to good schools that are close to home" (Boston Area Research Initiative, 2018, p. 10). Home prices and segregated neighborhoods have long been identified as variables leading to inequitable tracking practices (Lofton, 2024), and perhaps the district sought to provide an algorithmic counterbalance to these factors. Regardless of the intent behind it, however, the algorithm failed to reduce the inequitable distribution of school assignment and placement. In the district's own words:

> [The plan] carried with it the potential for positive and negative impacts on school composition. On the one hand, it might increase the potential for schools to act as gathering places for individual neighborhoods, strengthening bonds within the community, at the school, and between home and school. On the other, in doing so it might limit the geographic and, in turn, racial diversity of individual schools, thereby undermining one of the basic goals of school choice. **[The plan] appears to have done little to achieve the former, desired outcome while modestly moving towards the latter, unwanted one . . .** This appears to be an unintended consequence of the system's design. . . . It largely maintained status quo, inheriting but not counteracting inequities that existed under the previous system. (pp. 69–70, emphasis mine)

The Boston case has a "happy" ending in that the district's administrators recognized and named the algorithm's failures. However, the rightful questioning and interrogation of algorithmic outputs can happen only when the users of the algorithm are 1) aware that they are, in fact, using an algorithm, and 2) aware that the algorithms they use are prone to recommendation bias. Unfortunately, these levels of algorithmic critical consciousness are uncommon, necessitating an educational push toward a new type of data justice.

Toward a New Data Justice

The so-called "digital divide" generally refers to differing levels of access and fluency with digital tools and technologies. Those who have easy access to and operational knowledge of digital technologies are at an advantage over those who do not. Historically, this divide has fallen along socio-economic demographic lines. However, a new, more important digital fault line is emerging—a divide based not on access or skill but rather on awareness. On one hand, people who have reached a level of critical consciousness—that is, people who have achieved a degree of awareness of the dangers posed by recommendation bias and algorithmic determinism—are more likely to be able to seek out alternatives not provided by the algorithm or to question the seemingly neutral results the algorithm provides. The greater the level of algorithmic awareness, the greater the level of skepticism and even distrust of algorithmic results. On the other hand, people who are not aware of the biased nature of algorithms are more likely to have favorable and positive attitudes about algorithmic processes. The less awareness they have, the less they question the results (Gran et al., 2021; Shin et al., 2022).

Unfortunately, levels of algorithmic awareness appear to fall along a demographic fault line. People from higher socio-economic backgrounds achieve algorithmic awareness at higher rates than those from lower socio-economic backgrounds (Cotter & Reisdorf, 2020). Furthermore, the people creating and designing the algorithms themselves constitute a socio-economically homogenous group (Beer, 2009; Noble, 2018). Because algorithms do not necessarily correct for the social inequalities embedded in their training data, and because algorithmic processes tend to reinforce existing inequalities, groups of socio-economically privileged people are creating biased algorithms that are, at some point down the line, being used by and, to a degree, *against*, people who are not aware of the inequitable nature of algorithms (Cotter & Reisdorf, 2020; Eubanks, 2017; Noble, 2018).

Promoting algorithmic awareness is therefore a critical step in promoting data justice. This awareness will come about only through intentional educational efforts, because simply using algorithms does not necessarily facilitate awareness of algorithmic processes (Powers, 2017; Swart, 2021). Fortunately, a growing body of evidence suggests that it is not necessary to provide people with a complete technical understanding of algorithmic processes in order to increase their algorithmic awareness and critical consciousness. Instead, providing learners with a general overview of algorithmic processes may be enough to raise their level of critical consciousness to the point that they recognize the potential algorithmic inequities, even if they cannot express those inequities in technical terms (Aprin et al., 2023).

The imperative for educators is clear: We must teach algorithmic awareness. This is different from teaching students how to create algorithms. Although there is a growing body of research that details effective instructional STEM strategies for teaching students how to *create* algorithms and other machine learning applications (Martins & Gresse von Wangenheim, 2023), it is unclear the extent to which the general student population is being taught the general principles of algorithmic function. This general knowledge must not be relegated to the STEM classroom. The impact of algorithms surpasses the boundaries of the STEM classroom, crossing all disciplines, affecting every aspect of academic and civic life (Berry, 2022). It is therefore incumbent on teachers of *all* disciplines to explicitly address the role of algorithmic processes in shaping and, if we are not careful, determining the parameters of the possible, both in formal education and beyond. This is not simply a matter of preparing students for 21st-century jobs: This is a matter of preparing them for a life of agency and active participation, because, "if algorithms play a crucial role in providing the conditions for participation in public life, lack of awareness seems to pose a democratic challenge" (Gran et al., 2021, p. 1791).

Conclusion

There is no escaping the algorithms. In the terms of agricultural activist Wendell Berry (2010), "We're all complicit in the things we may be trying to oppose" (n.p.). And, to be clear, the critical response to the explosion of algorithms in education is not resistance to algorithms, per se. Instead, the call is for the development of a critical consciousness, an awareness of the biases, limitations, and foreclosed possibilities inherent in algorithmic function. When students have an awareness of the ways that algorithms use the trends of the past to create the conditions of the future, they can imagine new ways of being that diverge from the algorithmic output. When teachers provide students with the language and experiences to understand the ways that algorithms can trap and enslave, students can make conscious choices that consider algorithmic output but are not *determined* by it. Because algorithms mask the constructed and biased nature of their outputs, it is incumbent upon educators at all levels and of all subjects to instill in their students the awareness necessary to use algorithms as helpful tools without giving up their own human agency, working toward an equitable world in which the future is not determined by the past.

Questions for Reflection

1. How are algorithms used in my specific educational setting? Which algorithms am I aware of? How can I discover the ones that I'm *not* aware of?
2. How have my personal, educational, and professional choices been limited or foreclosed by algorithmic processes? How has my past been used to determine my future?
3. How can I teach algorithmic awareness in my discipline? What do I need to learn?
4. How will my own growing awareness of algorithmic processes change my work as a learner and teacher?
5. How can I promote critical consciousness among my students, colleagues, and peers when I, myself, am still learning?

Endnotes

1. Asimov actually invented the term *robotics*, as in "the study of robots."
2. In case you're wondering, the patient had a common cold.
3. Note that *bias* and *neutrality* are not being used in reference to the *content* of the results. In this case, *bias* means something like "influenced by the algorithm and the feedback loop," whereas "neutrality" means "free from influence." The results themselves might present unbiased and neutral information about the candidate in question. Or maybe not. The algorithm is not concerned whatsoever about the accuracy of the results.
4. There were many, many more variables than the ones listed here (>30).

5. In the 2011–2012 school year, white students accounted for roughly half of the overall K–12 population and yet made up more than 61% of all AP math students (Office for Civil Rights, 2024).

References

Algorithm, N. (2024). *What is an algorithm?* Google search results.

Algorithm, N., Sense 2. (2024, June). *Oxford English dictionary*. Oxford, United Kingdom: Oxford University Press. https://doi.org/10.1093/OED/1112230738.

Algorithm, N., Sense 3. (2024, June). *Oxford English dictionary*, Oxford, United Kingdom: Oxford University Press. https://doi.org/10.1093/OED/1113254159.

Amirkhan, J.H., & Kofman, Y.B. (2018). Stress overload as a red flag for freshman failure and attrition. *Contemporary Educational Psychology*, 54, 297–308. https://doi.org/10.1016/j.cedpsych.2018.07.004.

Aprin, F., Peters, P., & Hoppe, H. U. (2023). The effectiveness of a virtual learning companion for supporting the critical judgment of social media content. *Education and Information Technologies*, 1–34. https://doi.org/10.1007/s10639-023-12275-6

Arnold, K.E., & Pistilli, M.D. (2012). Course signals at Purdue: Using learning analytics to increase student success. In *Proceedings of the 2nd International Conference on Learning Analytics and Knowledge (LAK '12)*, 267–270. https://doi.org/10.1145/2330601.2330666

Asimov, I. (1950). *I, robot*. New York, NY: Gnome Press.

Asimov, I. (1951). *Foundation*. New York, NY: Gnome Press.

Asimov, I. (1951–1953). *The foundation trilogy*. New York, NY: Gnome Press.

Asimov, I. (1952). *Foundation and empire*. New York, NY: Gnome Press.

Asimov, I. (1953). *Second foundation*. New York, NY: Gnome Press.

Baker, R. S., & Hawn, A. (2022). Algorithmic bias in education. *International Journal of Artificial Intelligence in Education*, 1–41. https://doi.org/10.1007/s40593-021-00285-9

Beer, D. (2009). Power through the algorithm? Participatory veb cultures and the technological unconscious. *New Media & Society, 11*(6), 985–1002. https://doi.org/10.1177/1461444809336551

Berry, D. (2022). *AI, ethics, and digital humanities* (Version 1). University of Sussex. https://hdl.handle.net/10779/uos.23309129.v1

Berry, W. (2010, Nov. 8). Everything worthy is under fire. In Healy (Ed.), *Counterpunch*. https://www.counterpunch.org/2010/11/08/quot-everything-worthy-is-under-fire-quot/

Bodó, B., Helberger, N., Eskens, S., & Möller, J. (2019). Interested in diversity: The role of user attitudes, algorithmic feedback loops, and policy in news personalization. *Digital journalism*, 7(2), 206–229. https://doi.org/10.1080/21670811.2018.1521292

Boston Area Research Initiative. (2018). *An evaluation of equity in the Boston Public Schools' Home-Based Assignment Policy*. https://www.bostonpublicschools.org/cms/lib/MA01906464/Centricity/Domain/162/Final%20Evaluation%20of%20Equity%20in%20BPS%20HBAP.pdf

Christie, S. T., Jarratt, D. C., Olson, L. A., & Taijala, T. T. (2019). *Machine-learned school dropout early warning at scale.* Proceedings of the 12th International Conference on Educational Data Mining (EDM 2019), 726–731.

Cotter, K., & Reisdorf, B. C. (2020). Algorithmic knowledge gaps: A new horizon of (digital) inequality. *International Journal of Communication, (14)*21.

Enslin, P. (1987). Can Marxism offer a coherent notion of education. *Journal of philosophy of education, 21*(1), 59–74. https://doi.org/10.1111/j.1467-9752.1987.tb00143.x

Eubanks, V. (2017). *Automating inequality: How high-tech tools profile, police, and punish the poor.* New York, NY: St. Martin's.

Finley, J. (2023, March 13). *6 ways to use ChatGPT to save time.* https://www.edutopia.org/article/6-ways-chatgpt-save-teachers-time

Garvie, C., & Frankle, J. (2016). Facial-recognition software might have a racial bias problem. *The Atlantic, 7*(04), 2017.

Gran, A. B., Booth, P., & Bucher, T. (2021). To be or not to be algorithm aware: A question of a new digital divide? *Information, Communication & Society,* 24(12), 1779–1796. https://doi.org/10.1080/1369118X.2020.1736124

Hu, Q., & Rangwala, H. (2020). *Towards fair educational data mining: A case study on detecting at-risk students.* Proceedings of the 13th International Conference on Educational Data Mining (EDM 2020), 431–437.

Jazbec, M. (2018). Isaac Asimov's Foundation Trilogy and its perception of diplomacy: Envoys, protocol, talks. *European Perspectives,* 9(1), 111–137

Kai, S., Andres, J. M. L., Paquette, L., Baker, R. S., Molnar, K., Watkins, H., & Moore, M. (2017). *Predicting student retention from behavior in an online orientation course.* Proceedings of the 10th International Conference on Educational Data Mining, 250–255.

Koponen, J.M. (2015, June 25). The future of algorithmic personalization. *Techcrunch.* https://techcrunch.com/2015/06/25/the-future-of-algorithmic-personalization/

Krauth, K., Wang, Y., & Jordan, M. I. (2022). Breaking feedback loops in recommender systems with causal inference. *arXiv preprint arXiv:2207.01616.* https://doi.org/10.48550/arXiv.2207.01616

Krugman, P. (2012). Asimov's Foundation novels grounded my economics. *The Guardian.* https://www.theguardian.com/books/2012/dec/04/paul-krugman-asimov-economics

Lee, J., Harvey, E., Zhou, J., Garg, N., Joachims, T., & Kizilcec, R. F. (2024). *Algorithms for college admissions decision support: Impacts of policy change and inherent variability* (No. hds5g). Center for Open Science.

Liz-Domínguez, M., Caeiro-Rodríguez, M., Llamas-Nistal, M., & Mikic-Fonte, F. A. (2019). Systematic literature review of predictive analysis tools in higher education. *Applied Sciences,* 9(24), 5569. https://doi.org/10.3390/app9245569

Lofton, R. (2024). Plessy's tracks: African American students confronting academic placement in a racially diverse school and African American community. *Race Ethnicity and Education,* 27(5), 559–578. https://doi.org/10.1080/13613324.2021.1924141

Lohr, S. (2022). Facial recognition is accurate, if you're a white guy. In K. Martin (Ed.), *Ethics of Data and Analytics* (pp. 143–147). Auerbach Publications. https://doi.org/10.1201/9781003278290

Ma, S. (2024, May 22). *How generative AI tools assist with lesson planning.* https://www.edutopia.org/article/ai-tools-lesson-planning

Mansoury, M., Abdollahpouri, H., Pechenizkiy, M., Mobasher, B., & Burke, R. (2020, October). Feedback loop and bias amplification in recommender systems. In *Proceedings of the 29th ACM international conference on information & knowledge management* (pp. 2145–2148). https://doi.org/10.1145/3340531.3412152

Markham, A. (2021). The limits of the imaginary: Challenges to intervening in future speculations of memory, data, and algorithms. *New Media & Society, 23*(2), 382–405. https://doi.org/10.1177/1461444820929322

Martins, R. M., & Gresse Von Wangenheim, C. (2023). Findings on teaching machine learning in high school: A ten-year systematic literature review. *Informatics in Education,* 22(3), 421–440. https://doi.org/10.15388/infedu.2023.18

Mišík, M., Kujundžić, N. (2021). The future is nuclear: Energy weapon in Isaac Asimov's *Foundation.* In Mišík, M., & Kujundžić, N. (Eds.), *Energy Humanities. Current State and Future Directions.* Cham, Switzerland: Springer. https://doi.org/10.1007/978-3-030-57480-2_9

Mollick, E. (2024, June 4). *Using AI tutors to flip your classroom.* https://www.edutopia.org/article/using-ai-tutors-flipped-classroom

Noble, S. U. (2018). *Algorithms of oppression: How search engines reinforce racism.* New York, NY: New York University Press.

Ocumpaugh, J., Baker, R., Gowda, S., Heffernan, N., & Heffernan, C. (2014). Population validity for educational data mining models: A case study in affect detection. *British Journal of Educational Technology,* 45(3), 487–501. https://www.learntechlib.org/p/148344

Office for Civil Rights. (2024). Summary—National data. *Civil Rights Data Collection.* https://civilrightsdata.ed.gov/profile/us?surveyYear=2020

Ornelas, F., & Ordonez, C. (2017). Predicting student success: A naïve Bayesian application to community college data. *Technol. Knowl. Learn,* 22, 299–315, https://doi.org/10.1007/s10758-017-9334-z

Phillips, N., & Zyglidopoulos, S. (1999). Learning from *Foundation*: Asimov's psychohistory and the limits of organization theory. *Organization,* 6(4), 591–608. https://doi.org/10.1177/135050849964002

Polonsky, V.W. (2016, Nov. 6). Algorithmic determinism and the limits of artificial intelligence. *Oxford Internet Institute.* https://www.oii.ox.ac.uk/news-events/algorithmic-determinism-and-the-limits-of-artificial-intelligence/

Powers, E. (2017). My news feed is filtered? Awareness of news personalization among college students. *Digital Journalism,* 5(10), 1315–1335. https://doi.org/10.1080/21670811.2017.1286943

Pronzato, R. (2021). Critical pedagogy as a practice of resistance to algorithms. *AoIR Selected Papers of Internet Research.*

Rafalow, M. H., & Puckett, C. (2022). Sorting machines: digital technology and categorical inequality in education. *Educational researcher,* 51(4), 274–278. https://doi.org/10.3102/0013189X211070812

Seligman, M. (1998). *Learned optimism.* New York, NY: Alfred A. Knopf.

Shin, D., Kee, K. F., & Shin, E. Y. (2022). Algorithm awareness: Why user awareness is critical for personal privacy in the adoption of algorithmic platforms. *International Journal of Information Management, 65*, 102494. https://doi.org/10.1016/j.ijinfomgt.2022.102494

Swart, J. (2021). Experiencing algorithms: How young people understand, feel about, and engage with algorithmic news selection on social media. *Social media + society, 7*(2), 20563051211008828. https://doi.org/10.1177/20563051211008828

Taylor, S. M., Gulson, K. N., & McDuie-Ra, D. (2023). Artificial intelligence from colonial India: Race, statistics, and facial recognition in the global south. *Science, Technology, & Human Values, 48*(3), 663–689. https://doi.org/10.1177/01622439211106083

Thompson, E.D., Bowling, B.V., & Markle, R.E. (2018). Predicting student success in a major's Introductory Biology course via logistic regression analysis of scientific reasoning ability and mathematics scores. *Res. Sci. Educ, 48*, 151–163. https://doi.org/10.1007/s11165-016-9563-5

Trussel, J.M., & Burke-Smalley, L. (2018). Demography and student success: Early warning tools to drive intervention. J. *Educ. Bus. 93*, 363–372. https://doi.org/10.1080/08832323.2018.1496893.

Williams, C. (2022). Framing the future: The Foundation series, foundation models and framing AI. *Law, Technology and Humans* 4(2):109–23. https://doi.org/10.5204/lthj.2452

Yu, R., Li, Q., Fischer, C., Doroudi, S., & Xu, D. (2020). *Towards accurate and fair prediction of college success: Evaluating different sources of student data.* Proceedings of the 13th International Conference on Educational Data Mining (EDM 2020), 292–301.

Yudelson, M. V., Fancsali, S. E., Ritter, S., Berman, S. R., Nixon, T., & Joshi, A. (2014). *Better data beat big data.* Proceedings of the 7th International Conference on Educational Data Mining, 205–208.

CHAPTER FOUR

Stepping into a Larger World: Knowledge and Community in *Star Wars*

The Text: *Star Wars* (Lucas, 1977). Film.

Introduction

YOU HAVE PROBABLY SEEN *Star Wars* (Lucas, 1977). Most people have. And even if you haven't seen it, you are probably familiar with the basic storyline and cast of characters. You've almost certainly heard of the evil Darth Vader and the heroic Luke Skywalker. You've undoubtedly heard someone say "use the Force" or seen someone wave a stick around like a lightsaber. You're surely aware of Yoda, the little green Jedi Master, and heard his irregular syntax, you probably have.

To be sure, it is almost impossible to live in the West and not have at least a passing familiarity with *Star Wars*. The film franchise, which began in 1977, now encompasses countless books, TV shows, video games, and various other types of media, and it has infiltrated nearly every aspect of American culture. It has been referenced by presidents when discussing foreign policy, and if the rumor is to be believed, its soundtrack was used by Al-Qaeda when creating anti-Western propaganda videos (King, 2015). Of all the science fiction texts discussed in this book, *Star Wars* is by far the most popular.

The original *Star Wars* movie has led to countless sequels, prequels, TV shows, cartoons, books, video games, toys, and other media. It would be impossible to analyze the entirety of the *Star Wars* corpus in 50 books, much less a single chapter. So the focus of this chapter is limited to a few scenes from the original *Star Wars* movie. Furthermore, the analysis is limited to a handful of characters: Han Solo, the rogue pilot and skeptic; Luke Skywalker, the "student;" and Obi-Wan Kenobi, the Jedi master and "teacher."

Obi-Wan Kenobi is perhaps among the most recognizable characters of any 20th-century literary genre (Martín, 2019). As a mentor to young Luke Skywalker, he fills the archetypal role of the "mystic-helper" (Campbell, 1949), the bearded and wizened hermit who provides both sage advice and tokens of magical power that the hero will need on his quest (much like Gandalf in *The Lord of the Rings* or Dumbledore in *Harry Potter*). Obi-Wan's mentoring role in the *Star Wars* (Lucas, 1977) narrative is so archetypal that his name is often used as a synonym for "mentor" or "spiritual advisor" in literature, popular culture, and even in academia. References to Obi-Wan Kenobi can be found in academic scholarship researching topics such as public health care (Geronimus et al., 2016), religious education (Rossiter, 2005), social identity (Gunnels, 2009), adult education (Darwin, 2000), the teaching of gifted students (Grassinger et al., 2010), psychopathology (Friedman, 2015), organizational administration (Nielsen, 1980), jurisprudence (Mullins, 2016), and even artificial intelligence (Eger & Martins, 2017). Obi-Wan's influence has even extended beyond the metaphorical: In one study, adolescent males suffering from migraines were taught to use the Jedi relaxation techniques modeled by Obi-Wan (Rozensky & Pasternik, 1985). The intervention worked.

The proliferation of scholarly work using "Obi-Wan" as a synonym for "mentor" indicates that Obi-Wan Kenobi is not merely an example of a mentor archetype. In many ways, he has *become* the mentor archetype, at least in Western consciousness. For the purposes of this chapter, however, we will be looking at Obi-Wan's beliefs and practices related specifically to teaching and learning. Even more specifically, we will be examining Obi-Wan to learn more about what it means to learn in community and to resist *epistemicide*, which is the destruction of other ways of knowing. As we will see, Obi-Wan's resistance extends beyond teaching Luke how to use specific weapons or how to disable and destroy military installations. He is much more subtle than that. That is, he teaches Luke a different way to think about how to know something. He is not just fighting against the Empire's weapons: He is fighting against their entire philosophy of knowledge.

In *Star Wars* (Lucas, 1977), Obi-Wan's interactions with Luke highlight two important elements of critical pedagogy:

1. Learning is a communal practice; and

2. Knowledge is relational.

But enough overview. Let's begin the story.

The Story—Part One

Luke Skywalker, the young and reluctant farm-boy hero of the original *Star Wars* trilogy, feels like his life is passing him by. He lives on the desert planet of Tatooine, a seemingly forgotten world in a part of the galaxy that no one ever visits. All his friends have left, headed off for distant stars and distant adventures, and Luke is stuck at home, helping his aunt and uncle run the family's moisture farm.

Luke hates farming, but he loves his family, and so he helps his uncle purchase some used robots, two droids named R2D2 (Artoo) and C3PO (Threepio), to do chores and odd tasks around the farm. The droids are a mess, probably having been stolen, and Luke's uncle sends him to clean them up and get them ready for the fields. Luke grudgingly obliges.

While giving Artoo some basic maintenance, Luke accidentally triggers a small snippet of message hidden within the droid's data banks. It is a hologram projection of a young woman repeating "Help me, Obi-Wan Kenobi. You're my only hope." When commanded to play the rest of the message, Artoo claims to be the property of Obi-Wan Kenobi, and he can only play the full message for his master. Luke does not know anyone named "Obi-Wan," but he is vaguely aware of a strange, old hermit named Ben Kenobi living out beyond the Dune Sea. Luke cannot think too much about it, though, because he has chores to do, and he leaves the droids alone while he gets back to work.

When Luke wakes up in the morning, he discovers that Artoo has run away, apparently to look for his old master, Obi-Wan Kenobi. Luke and Threepio set out to find Artoo and bring him home. Of course, nothing goes quite according to plan, and, as they find Artoo, they are attacked by the Sand People, the native dwellers of Tatooine. Just as all seems lost, the Sand People turn and flee, scared away by a mysterious cloaked figure. The cloaked figure is none other than Old Ben Kenobi, the strange desert-dwelling recluse. He brings Luke and the droids back to his hut to rest and recuperate.

Luke and Ben get to talking, and Ben confirms that he is, in fact, Obi-Wan Kenobi, though he has not gone by that name for many years. He tells Luke that he, Obi-Wan, was once a Jedi Knight who long ago fought alongside Luke's own father on behalf of the Old Republic before the Evil Galactic Empire came to power. At this point Ben pauses, rummages through a chest, and pulls out an old-fashioned weapon which he hands to Luke. It was, he tells Luke, [Luke's] father's lightsaber. A lightsaber, Obi-Wan explains, is the weapon of the Jedi Knight. The Jedi were the guardians of the Old Republic and masters of the Force. According to Obi-Wan, "the Force is what gives a Jedi his power. It's an energy field created by all living things. It surrounds us and penetrates us. It binds the galaxy together" (Lucas, 1977).

At this point, Artoo plays the full message. It turns out that the Rebel Alliance, a band of freedom fighters who are trying to overthrow the Empire, have hidden some stolen military blueprints inside Artoo. The message asks Obi-Wan to rejoin the fight against the Empire by escorting Artoo and the blueprints he carries to the Rebel Alliance on the planet Alderaan. Obi-Wan looks Luke in the eye and says, "You must learn the ways of the Force if you're to come with me to Alderaan" (Lucas, 1977).

And just like that, the stage is set.

The Critical Analysis

There is much to discuss when it comes to Obi-Wan Kenobi, teaching, and learning, and there are so many questions to ask: Is Obi-Wan working from a set curriculum? Is he making it up as he goes? Are there Jedi learning standards to which he and Luke must adhere? Are there "best practices" that he can draw from? All these questions are questions of community. Obi-Wan is not the first person to train Jedi.[1] He, himself, had a teacher at one point in time. Even though Luke and Obi-Wan are alone, and this is a one-on-one teacher/student scenario, none of this is happening in isolation.

Learning as a Communal Activity

In order to understand the relationship between learning and community, we must first understand the term *communities of practice*. A community of practice is bound together not by shared biology or shared geography but rather by shared action. In other words, members of a community of practice *do* things together. The term *community of practice* describes the ways that groups of people gather together to engage in a central, commonly practiced task. Plumbers might be a community of practice, for example, because they engage in a common activity: plumbing. But it doesn't stop there. They use the same jargon and the same tools. They (we hope) adhere to the same standards. They belong to the same professional organizations. Most importantly, they learn from and with one another. In fact, most plumbers still learn in something akin to an apprentice model, where the rookie follows the veteran, doing what they do.

Becoming a member of a community of practice involves both the development of domain-specific skills *and* the development of a community-based identity. Lave (1991) highlights the synchronous and inseparable development of skills and identity as part of the learning process:

> [We should] consider learning not as a process of socially shared cognition that results in the end in the internalization of knowledge by individuals, but as a process of becoming a member of a sustained community of practice. Developing an identity as a member of a community and becoming knowledgably skillful are part of the same process, with the former motivating, shaping, and giving meaning to the latter, which it subsumes. (p. 65)

When Obi-Wan invites Luke to come with him to Alderaan and learn the ways of the Force, he is, in effect, inviting Luke to join a community of practice. To Obi-Wan, learning the ways of the Force means, in part, adopting the practices of the Jedi (e.g., learning to wield a lightsaber). Consequently, when Obi-Wan gives Luke the lightsaber, he is providing him with the tools that the community uses, and skill-based fluency involves mastery of the physical and martial techniques and skills unique to the Jedi order.

Obi-Wan's teaching extends beyond equipping Luke with the technical skills to be a functional Jedi, however. On the contrary, he is also inviting Luke to become a new kind of person and to identify as a member of the Force community, as one who is connected to all things via the Force. While Luke and Obi-Wan are talking, Obi-Wan mentions Luke's uncle, with whom Luke now lives. Obi-Wan had wanted to give Luke the lightsaber at an earlier date, but Luke's uncle had forbidden it, fearing that Luke would "follow old Obi-Wan on some damn fool idealistic crusade" (Lucas, 1977).

Indeed, Luke repeatedly refers to his uncle's displeasure when refusing to accompany Obi-Wan to Alderaan, noting that he's "already late" and "in for it as it is" (Lucas, 1977) suggesting that his current self-identity is one of dutiful and obedient ward, destined to sit on the sidelines and not get involved in intergalactic conflict. He tells Obi-Wan as much: "I can't get involved. I've got work to do. It's not that I like the Empire. I hate it, but there's nothing I can do about it now" (Lucas, 1977). Obi-Wan's invitation to learn the ways of the Force is, in part, an appeal to Luke to reenvision his self in relation to the goings on of the universe. Becoming a Jedi involves learning more than lightsaber technique: It involves seeing oneself in a new way in relation to the universe. As Luke learns how to act like a Jedi, he is also learning to *be* a Jedi in the existential sense, thereby fully identifying with the Jedi/Force community.

Critical pedagogy is deeply concerned with community. On one hand, critical pedagogy calls into question the deeply individualistic nature of American capitalism. The rugged individual is bound to no one, responsible to no one, and responsible *for* no one. In its extreme, rugged individualism celebrates its lack of human connection. Recent developments in higher education demonstrate this extremism. For example, advocates for large-scale, AI-driven, online education often highlight their institutions' abilities to tailor learning to meet the specific needs, desires, and goals of the individual. While this individualization is not an issue in and of itself, these institutions also often highlight that this level of individualization frees the learner from the relational obligations of learning within a community. When everything is individualized, "there is no waiting for slower-to-learn classmates to catch up" (Bell, 2019, n.p.). The learner's responsibilities are solely to themself, and the less they are slowed down by other people, the more they will learn. Both learning and life are, it is claimed, individual pursuits, because learning and life are *zero-sum* endeavors. The term *zero-sum* has been borrowed from game theory, but it fits quite nicely with critical pedagogy. A zero-sum game is one in which there must be winners and losers. It is not possible for both players or both teams to win, nor is it possible for them to tie. One must win and one must lose. Zero-sum individualism, then, is the belief that I can be successful/fulfilled only if you are not. My learning depends on you *not* learning. A scenario in which we help each other learn is literally unthinkable, and so we create individualized tracks of education in which I am not held back by slower learners.

If this sounds like a competition, that's because it is. The language of competition has been officially written into our educational structures at all levels. The Obama-era educational laws that replaced *No Child Left Behind* (2001) were referred to as *A Race to the Top* (H.R. 1532, 2011). Of course, in a race, there are winners and losers, and the metaphorical implication is that not every student can "win." This same language of winners and losers is echoed by the U.S. Department of Education (2023), which has as part of its official mission statement the claim that the purpose of education is to "promote student achievement and preparation for global competitiveness" (n.p.). Note that we do not educate for global *cooperation*, in which all learners benefit. Instead, we educate under the assumption that there will be winners and losers, and that teaching and learning are a zero-sum game.

Critical pedagogy rejects this kind of individualism and zero-sum mentality. Instead, the critical pedagogue highlights the inherently relational nature of learning and education. Critical pedagogue and activist Paulo Freire (1970) describes true education as that which enables individuals to see that they are, in fact, members of a class and community. Although oppressive educational structures work to separate individuals from one another, a radical education exists in order to reconcile individuals with themselves, with one another, and with the world around them.

Freire's point about reconciliation is worth unpacking. Too often, he claims, our formal and official educational practices serve to separate us from the world around us, building separation into our educational structures. Learners are kept separate from other learners through both classroom infrastructure and a host of rules and policies that limit and sometimes even prohibit student interaction. Learners are separated from their teachers by classroom power structures. They are separated from their own interests by being subjected to curricula that were created and selected without any learner input. They are separated from the values of their community through the system's allegiance to standardized learning goals and processes. Learners have limited choices and even less agency, meaning that they often have to ask permission to attend to their most basic bodily needs. And, in a system that sees students as empty vessels who need to be filled with information, learners are separated from the creation and generation of knowledge. Knowledge is an object to be acquired, and the more efficiently a learner is filled with outside information, the better the learner they are.

The net effect of this separation, Freire claims, is that learners are dehumanized. They are individualized and alone, disconnected from the relationships that make us human. At his most cynical, Freire argues that this disconnection is, in fact, the purpose of an oppressive education, because a cog in a machine is a better cog when it forgets that it is actually a human being.[2]

A critical pedagogue must fight against this individualization, separation, and lack of connection. Instead, they must foster the practices, relationships, and ways of knowing that *reconcile* learners with the world around them:

> The pursuit of full humanity, however, cannot be carried out in isolation or individualism, but only in fellowship and solidarity; therefore it cannot unfold in the antagonistic relations between oppressors and oppressed. No one can be authentically human while he prevents others from being so. (Freire, 1970, p. 85)

If a critical pedagogue's job is, in part, to reconnect learners with the world around them, with their own agency and power, and with their fellow human beings, then the critical nature of Obi-Wan Kenobi's teaching becomes clear. Luke feels disconnected and powerless. In the face of galactic evil, he says there is "nothing he can do" (Lucas, 1977). He faces punishment for making his own decisions. He is engaged in work that he finds neither exciting nor liberating. His only companions are non-human. He is, in every way, individualized, isolated, and alone.

Obi-Wan's invitation to come to Alderaan and learn the ways of the Force is, in fact, an invitation to reconnect. By doing what the Jedi do, Luke will *become* a Jedi, like his father. Obi-Wan is inviting Luke to reconcile with his past and his family. He is inviting him to be a member of a group. He is inviting him to be transformed through the process of learning in and with a community of practice.

Communities of practice share more than simply common practices, however; they also share common ways of knowing. Let us return to our story.

The Story—Part Two

Even though Luke has told Obi-Wan that he cannot go with him to Alderaan, fate, it seems, has other plans. Luke returns to the farm only to discover that his aunt and uncle are dead. They have been killed, murdered by Imperial Stormtroopers. Luke and Obi-Wan quickly put two and two together: The Stormtroopers are looking for the stolen military plans that Artoo is carrying. Luke and his companions are in danger, and they need get away. Fast.

Luke, Obi-Wan, and the two droids head to Mos Eisley, the nearest spaceport. They convince a rogue pilot, Han Solo, to smuggle them off the planet in his ship, the *Millennium Falcon.* Imperial forces are checking all the outbound ships, and our heroes very nearly get caught. Somehow, they manage to evade capture, and they escape to the safety of hyperspace. Next stop, Alderaan.

Meanwhile, Imperial officials are fuming about the loss of the stolen plans. They have captured Princess Leia, a leader of the Rebel Alliance, and they threaten to use the Death Star to destroy her home planet of Alderaan if she does not reveal the location of the secret Rebel base. She refuses to talk, and Grand Moff Tarkin gives the order to fire. With one shot, Alderaan is completely destroyed, reduced to space dust. An entire planet, billions of people, animals, and other living creatures wiped off the galactic map in a split second.

Back on the *Millennium Falcon*, Obi-Wan Kenobi is overcome with a wave of dizziness, and he nearly collapses into his chair. Luke asks him if he's ok. "I felt a great disturbance in the Force," Obi-Wan replies. "As if millions of voices suddenly cried out in terror and were suddenly silenced. I fear something terrible has happened." He forces a weak smile. "You'd better get on with your exercises" (Lucas, 1977).

Luke nods, unconvinced, and returns to what he was doing. Obi-Wan has given Luke his first official lesson in lightsaber technique. A small training drone hovers in the air, and Luke is trying to block its tiny laser bursts with his lightsaber. He is failing miserably, and he is repeatedly stung by the drone's fire. Han Solo returns from the cockpit, and all eyes turn to Luke's training.

Luke avidly tracks the drone with his eyes, lightsaber raised.

Obi-Wan: "Remember, a Jedi can feel the force flowing through him."

Luke [*eyes still on the drone*]: You mean it controls your actions?

Obi-Wan: Partially, but it also obeys your commands.

The drone shoots Luke in the leg.

Han [*laughing*]: Hokey religions and ancient weapons are no match for a good blaster at your side.

Luke [*turning off the lightsaber and shifting his gaze to Han*]: You don't believe in the Force, do you?

Han: Kid, I've flown from one side of this galaxy to the other. I've seen a lot of strange stuff, but I've never seen anything to make me think there's one, all-powerful force controlling everything. No mystical energy field controls my destiny. It's all a lot of simple tricks and nonsense.

Obi-Wan [*laughing slightly at Han and rising from his chair*]: I suggest you try it again, Luke. This time, let go your conscious self, and act on instinct.

Obi-Wan places a helmet on Luke's head. The helmet has an opaque visor, fully blocking Luke's eyesight.

Luke: With the blast shield down, I can't even see. How am I supposed to fight?

Obi-Wan: Your eyes can deceive you. Don't trust them.

Luke reignites his lightsaber, which reactivates the drone. As soon as he turns toward the drone, it shoots him in the shoulder. He winces.

Obi-Wan: Stretch out with your feelings.

Luke raises his lightsaber. Though he cannot see the drone, he tracks its movement with his body. The drone fires three shots in rapid succession, and Luke successfully blocks all of them.

Obi-Wan: You see? You can do it.

Han: I call it luck.

Obi-Wan: In my experience, there's no such thing as luck.

Han leaves the room. Luke removes his helmet and approaches Obi-Wan.

Luke: You know, I did feel something. I could almost see the remote.

Obi-Wan: That's good. You've taken your first step into a larger world. (Lucas, 1977)

The Critical Analysis

The second aspect of Obi-Wan's critical pedagogy is the way that he challenges the epistemology of the Galactic Empire. *Epistemology* is a branch of philosophy devoted to the study of knowledge. When we talk about a person's or a group's epistemology, we are essentially talking about their rules for knowing. For example, most scientists embrace an epistemology based on *empiricism*, meaning that knowledge is governed by the senses. The only things we can know, the scientist might say, are the things that we can see, touch, taste, feel, or hear. If it can be sensed, it can be measured and tested. We can perform experiments, and those experiments can be replicated. Knowing, then, is a matter of obtaining information in very specific ways. If we can't sense it—if it's not empirical—we can't know it, because we can't follow all the epistemological rules that the scientific community generally agrees upon.

But not everyone agrees with an epistemology based on empiricism. A deeply religious person, for example, might claim to know something based on divine revelation. God spoke to them in a dream, and, based on that experience, they *know* a specific thing to be true. The rules for knowing are different in different communities. In fact, the same scientist who adheres to an empirical epistemology in the laboratory might rely on an entirely different epistemology in their private life.

Knowledge is Relational

The issue of epistemology becomes even more important when we consider how the dominant group in any society often assumes its way of knowing to be the "right" one. Groups who know differently are marginalized, and their epistemologies are often weaponized against them, held up as evidence of how "backwards" or "uncivilized" they are. This has certainly been true for indigenous peoples around the world. As a general rule, Western epistemologies see knowledge as an object that exists separately from the individual, the subject. This is where we get phrases such as "X is *objectively* true." We in the West treat knowledge like a *thing*. We can trade it, buy it, pass it around to our friends, and, if we want, discard it. Because knowledge is an object, it can be owned. The phrase "intellectual property" is steeped in a Western epistemology that assumes that knowledge can belong to one person. If I own an idea, you need my permission to use it. This is the basis for all the rules about citation that you learned in your high school English classes. If knowledge is objective, then it is found by studying objects. If knowledge is objective, it is stored and contained in objects. Just think of the role that books and other printed materials have played in the storage and preservation of Western knowledge. We store our objective knowledge in special places, such as libraries and museums, and when we want to know more about the world, we look beyond ourselves. When knowledge is an object, then it can be treated just as any other object. In extreme cases, it can be turned into capital and used to buy other goods. The phrase "the knowledge economy" is prototypically Western in that it acknowledges the objective nature of knowledge *and* the Western tendency to turn everything into a commodity.

Not everyone shares this objective view of knowledge, however. As Western European settlers established colonies all around the globe, they encountered indigenous communities whose epistemologies were profoundly different from their own. In many indigenous communities, the development of knowledge is a matter of relationships between subjects, not a matter of a subject collecting and acquiring objects. If knowledge is subjective, then it is relationally bound. Knowledge is not owned but shared. It is held not in objects but rather in people. If knowledge is *subjective*, then to know more about a tree is not to learn about an object that is separate from me but rather to learn about a being with whom I am in relationship. If knowledge is subjective, then it cannot be property to be hoarded. Instead, it manifests in mutual obligations. To know a thing is to respond to it, just as it responds to me. To know a tree is to understand its needs—water, pruning, etc.—and to use that information to act responsibly toward it. The tree will respond to my actions by producing fruit. Knowledge yields mutual benefit (Kimmerer, 2013). This is in profound contrast to the way objective epistemologies treat knowledge as a commodity to be bought and sold, because in subjective epistemologies, knowledge is both the basis for and the result of healthy, sustainable relationships.

It is not difficult to imagine the epistemological clashes that took place when Western colonists arrived on indigenous lands. It is not difficult to imagine how the colonists' epistemologies allowed them to see these "new" lands—and the people who were already on them—as objects to be conquered, controlled, and commodified. And it is equally easy to imagine the horror with which the indigenous peoples watched the colonists destroy the land in wanton and willful ignorance.

I have created a bit of a *straw man* argument here, and neither indigenous nor Western epistemologies can be reduced to simple labels. There is enormous complexity, variance, and nuance in both traditions, and I am using the broadest of all possible brush strokes to describe a fantastically complicated phenomenon.

Nevertheless, my general statements about Western objectivity and indigenous subjectivity do accurately represent two fundamentally different epistemologies. In the West, knowledge is an object to be acquired, allowing the knower to exert dominion over the natural world and make it serve the knower. In many indigenous communities, knowledge is a byproduct of relationship, obligating the knower to care for that which is known and to be cared for in turn.

The abuses that European colonists inflicted upon indigenous communities defy description. In North America, Australia, and New Zealand, indigenous children were stolen from their families and communities and forced to attend Western-style boarding schools. There, they were forced to abandon all vestiges of their cultures. They were not allowed to speak their own languages or wear their own clothes. They were forced to talk, act, dress, learn, and *think* like Europeans. They were often beaten. They were often murdered.[3]

The devastation that European colonists wrought upon indigenous communities was genocidal. It was also a clear example of *epistemicide*, which is the devaluing and destruction of alternative epistemologies. When European powers removed indigenous children from their communities, they were destroying a way of knowing, because, for many of these communities, the only way to know is in relationship with the members of the community. Robin Wall Kimmerer (2013) chronicles this epistemicide in her description of the forced relocation of her ancestral tribe. When her Anishinaabe people were removed from their lands, they were also removed from relationship with the land around them, particularly the trees.

> We have always known that the plants and animals have their own councils, and a common language. The trees, especially, we recognize as our teachers. . . . In the old times, our elders say, the trees talked to each other. They'd stand in their own council and craft a plan. But scientists decided long ago that plants were deaf and mute, locked in isolation without communication. The possibility of conversation was summarily dismissed. Science pretends to be purely rational, completely neutral, a system of knowledge-making in which the observation is independent of the observer. And yet the conclusion was drawn that plants cannot communicate because they lack the mechanisms that *animals* use to speak. (pp. 18–19)

Western empiricism, which has so often been used to dominate and subjugate the "other," is facing increasing scrutiny in educational and academic settings. Indigenous scholar Kathleen E. Absolon (2011), also an Anishinaabe person, notes that the word *research* "has a lot of colonial baggage attached to it" (p. 21), because it was so often assumed by Western scholars that indigenous methodologies did not exist. Western educators too often serve as "gatekeepers" of official knowledge, refusing to take other ways of knowing seriously (pp. 19–20). In an attempt to reassert the validity of indigenous ways of knowing, particularly within educational settings, Absolon uses the term *harvesting* instead of *data-collection*, because harvesting recognizes the interdependence and relationship between the knower and that which is being known.

The clash between objective and relational epistemologies can clearly be seen in Luke's attempts to learn to use a lightsaber. Learning the ways of the Force involves adopting the epistemology of the Jedi, which means reimagining the nature of reality and one's place in the natural order. The Galactic Empire's emphasis on dominance through technology provides a stark contrast to the nature of universal connectivity as outlined by Obi-Wan. The Force is the connective tissue between all living things, and to learn of the Force is to recognize one's interdependence with the natural order, in which we "recognize with sympathy our fellow members, human and nonhuman, with whom we share our place" (Berry, 2012, p. 14). Learning the ways of the Force, therefore, means learning to imagine the fullness of the place. It means acknowledging relationship with the other, a category that includes beings, animals, plants, land—indeed, *all* matter. Because of this relationship, we must also admit our obligations to both the human and the nonhuman. Without this imagination, Berry warns, we cannot live in a place without subjugation and destruction. Indeed, the Galactic Empire's solution to the problem of the Rebel Alliance is to destroy the entire planet of Alderaan, a destruction that causes "a great disturbance in the Force" (Lucas, 1977). The Empire cannot imagine anything other than itself. It cannot recognize shared space. Its only obligation is to itself, and anything outside itself is subject to control and domination. In the Imperial mind, knowledge is reduced to technological power, which allows for and enables domination. In the Jedi mind, however, knowledge is relational. It expands beyond the boundaries of the self and encompasses all that exists. The Imperial knows in order to subjugate nature; the Jedi knows in order to be in relationship with nature, and the only way to fully know is to imagine.

The scene in which Luke trains with the lightsaber is particularly important for its repeated emphasis on sight as a means of knowing. Both Han and Luke appeal to empiricism, claiming knowledge through sight (and via sensory organs). Han dismisses the idea of the Force because he has "never seen" (Lucas, 1977) any evidence of it. Similarly, Luke claims that his ability to engage with the drone depends on his ability to see. Without this ability, he cannot accurately perceive the world around him.

Obi-Wan's response both rejects Han's and Luke's appeal to empiricism and simultaneously outlines his alternative: instinct, or the *mind's eye*. Empirically derived data, Obi-Wan warns, is not to be trusted. His insistence on the eyes' ability to "deceive" underscores his epistemological orientation that knowing and learning begin not by sensing the external but rather by embracing the internal. In short, learning to become a Jedi means first seeing that which is already inside you, and only then aligning it with the outer world.

The relationship between inner and outer worlds has long been a hallmark of Romantic education. Obi-Wan's claim that the Force emanates from "all living things" and "binds the galaxy together" was predicted almost exactly 150 years earlier in the opening lines of German educator Friedrich Fröbel's (1826) foundational pedagogical text, *Die Menschenerziehung, or, The Education of Man*: "An eternal law works and reigns over all; it speaks in external nature, in the internal spirit, and in the unity of the two. . . ." (p. 1, translation mine).

Fröbel, who is perhaps best known as the creator of *kindergarten*, was, like Obi-Wan Kenobi, an epistemological radical. He insisted that the primary purpose of education was not to help learners know the world as an object but rather to know themselves *in relation to the world*. This kind of relational knowledge has two components.

First, relational knowledge requires me to acknowledge that I am not as independent as I think I am. Instead, I am bound by and responsible to beings other than myself. This responsibility runs counter to the rugged individualism that dominates Western thought and tradition. Extreme self-determination stems from a faulty imagination in that it fails to recognize the relational boundaries of our actions and desires. When we are in relationship with other beings, we do not have complete and total freedom over our own selves. The boundaries that accompany relationships *do* place limits on our individualism, and, for some people, the idea of these kinds of limits leads to fear. This is the fear behind Han Solo's insistence that "no mystical energy field controls [his] destiny" and Luke's concern that the Force "controls [his] actions" (Lucas, 1977). If you are deeply committed to protecting your complete and total independence, you will, of course, resist anyone who suggests that we are all *interdependent*. The imaginative act that acknowledges obligations and decenters the self can only be seen as radical in this context. Indeed, Obi-Wan is dismissed by those around him. Luke's uncle refers to him as a "crazy old man" (Lucas, 1977). Obi-Wan's ideas, according to Han Solo, are little more than "tricks and nonsense" (Lucas, 1977). Even Luke himself refers to Obi-Wan as "strange" (Lucas, 1977). Within the context of the Imperial and empirical empire, Obi-Wan lives in the margins, out on the edge of the Dune Sea. This marginalization highlights both his archetypal role as the hermit/wizard and, more importantly, the critical nature of his imagination.

Farmer and activist Wendel Berry (2012), too, notes the critical nature of imagination. Non-imaginative ways of knowing are reductive, he claims. They disconnect us from the world and people around us, because they replace relational knowledge with statistical knowledge: "Statistical knowledge is remote, and it isolates us in our remoteness. It is the stuff itself of unimagined life. We may, as we say, 'know' statistical sums, but we cannot imagine them" (p. 25). The connectedness of relational knowing as modeled by Obi-Wan is set in stark contrast against the isolated independence of both Han (whose surname is "Solo") and of the Empire itself, which serves only its own corporate interests. As Berry notes, "we don't . . . have to worry about governmental or corporate affection" (p. 15). If affection entails acting responsibly toward and recognizing the being-ness of both local and universal eco-systems, then it must be predicated upon a radical imagination that transgresses the boundaries of the self.

Still, this radical imagination does *not* devalue the individual. As both Fröbel and Obi-Wan contend, a true education results in the unity of the inner and outer worlds. Consequently, just as the individual may be influenced by this unity—a possibility confirmed by Obi-Wan's admission to Luke that the Force would only "partly" control his actions—the individual is also able to influence the unified world. As Obi-Wan states, the Force "also obeys your commands" (Lucas, 1977). Whereas Han Solo equates submission to the Force as relinquishing control of his destiny, Obi-Wan resists such simple binary distinctions. Learning the ways of the Force involves both control and submission, both the cultivation of the inner life and a bending of the will to a reality larger than the self. To learn the ways of the Force is to acknowledge the both/and of the inner and the outer and to reject the totalizing schemas of technological imperialism and rugged individualism.

To be clear, however, Obi-Wan's radical imagination does not reject technology or the individual, per se. On the contrary, the imagination is radical in that it reestablishes the appropriate relationships of all things. This is achieved not by denying the value of technology and the knowledge it allows for but instead by recognizing its value in relationship to the human. Berry (2012) frames this as a matter of propriety of scale:

> By the means of such [technical and statistical knowledge] a category assumes dominion over its parts and members. . . . The fact is that humans are not much to be trusted with what I am calling statistical knowledge, and the larger the statistical quantities the less we are to be trusted. . . . Propriety of scale in all human undertakings is paramount, and we ignore it. We are now betting our lives on quantities that far exceed all our powers of comprehension. (pp. 24–25)

The radical imagination highlights the disproportionate role that technology has come to play in contemporary ways of knowing. As we come to rely on technologically mediated ways of knowing, Berry warns, we assume both knowledge and power that we do not have. When knowing is reduced to the manipulation of numerical representation, decisions can be made outside of relational contexts. A disproportionate emphasis on technology as both the means and the source of knowledge distances the individual from the larger world. In Fröbel's terms, it fails to recognize the relationship between the inner and the outer. Isolation and remoteness allow for the individual and/or abstract entity (such as a corporation, a for-profit testing company, or an evil Galactic Empire) to view itself as separate from the other, free from both obligation and responsibility. The Empire's decision to destroy an entire planet should not be read as an indictment of technology but rather an indictment of an epistemology that prizes technologically mediated quantification, isolation, and abstraction over all else.

The *Star Wars* extended universe (Lucas, 1977–present) assures us that both the Jedi's lightsabers and the Empire's Death Star share the same root technology and scientific base—the Kyber Crystal. However, whereas the Jedi harvested natural crystals and designed lightsabers with each particular crystal's structure in mind, the Empire developed synthetic crystals in order to increase the power output for militaristic purposes. These artificial crystals were "highly unstable and explosive" ("Kyber Crystal," 2021, n.p.). In Berry's terms, the Empire failed to *imagine* the crystals. Although it possessed technical and statistical knowledge about the crystals, it did not "know" them. Their understanding of the world had become "less creaturely and more engineered" (Berry, 2012, p. 23). The Empire's abuse of the crystals is a symptom of an "increasing abstraction and unconsciousness of our connection to our [re]sources in the land" and of knowledge that has become "increasingly statistical" (p. 23). For Berry the farmer and for Obi-Wan the Jedi, technology is neither to be feared nor shunned; it is, however, to be used only in connection and relationship with the being and forms with whom we share the world and the universe. Therefore, Obi-Wan's primary task as a teacher, and Luke's primary task as a learner, is to cultivate an imagination that looks beyond both the Imperial and empirical boundaries between self and other, and, by taking this radical perspective, unifies the two.

Conclusion

What binds these two scenes together is their focus on relationship. Critical pedagogy highlights the relational, interdependent nature of both learning *and* knowledge. The ways we learn and know are impacted by, and have an impact on, the people and environment around us. Seemingly "neutral" ways of knowing are, in fact, power laden, based on philosophical assumptions about the relationship or "position" between the knower and the thing being known. The more independent we believe ourselves to be, the less obligation we will feel to our fellow learners and to the world that we are knowing. In contrast, the more that we recognize the ways that our learning and knowledge depend on others, the more we will recognize our corresponding obligations and responsibilities to others.

We often do not recognize the ways that we have kept students separate from their own learning or the ways that we have participated in epistemicide. Even as I write this chapter, I am forced to reflect on some of the ways that I have devalued my students' ways of knowing, albeit unintentionally.

As a critical pedagogy lens helps us see, that is the way the system is designed, and unless we are actively swimming against the tide, we will default to the "neutral" position, which is, as we know, not neutral at all. Just as all education is political, our assumed ways of knowing are equally political. As you grow in critical pedagogy, you will learn to recognize and value the ways of knowing your students bring to the classroom, and you will be able to create meaningful learning experiences that allow them to connect with themselves, their knowledge, and their communities of practice.

Questions for Reflection

1. Has my own education ever left me feeling "disconnected?" What specific practices might have contributed to this sense of isolation?

2. Do my students or the learners I am responsible for feel connected to their learning? If not, what have I done that has kept them separated from their learning?

3. Am I connected to my own learning, particularly in my own professional development?

4. Have I allowed students to connect their learning to their lives in ways that I did not expect and that perhaps defy standard or "normal" practice?

5. Do the power structures in my classroom allow for students to question basic assumptions about knowledge and connection?

6. What are my own epistemological assumptions? How have those assumptions informed my own teaching and learning?

7. Have I unwittingly participated in epistemicide? In what ways might I have unintentionally devalued other ways of knowing?

8. Have I mistaken "statistical" knowledge for relational knowledge? What impact has that had on my students, their learning, and their lives?

Endnotes

1. See Chapter Six to learn more about what Obi-Wan's own education must have been like.
2. Freire's thoughts on education are unpacked in greater detail in Chapter Six.

3. See Chapter Seven for an examination of the role of language in epistemicide, particularly in relation to the education of Native American students in the so-called "Indian Boarding Schools."

References

Absolon, K. E. (Minogiizhigokwe). (2011). *Kaandossiwin: How we come to know.* Halifax, Nova Scotia: Fernwood Publishing.

Bell, J. (2019, April 22). Here's how Western Governors University Ohio is disrupting higher education. *Columbusceo.com.* https://www.columbusceo.com/story/news/education/2019/04/22/here-s-how-western-governors/5311769007/

Berry, W. (2012). *It all turns on affection.* Berkeley, CA: Counterpoint Press.

Campbell, J. (1949). *The hero with a thousand faces.* New York, NY: Pantheon Books.

Darwin, A. (2000). Critical reflections on mentoring in work settings. *Adult education quarterly,* 50(3), 197–211. https://doi.org/10.1177/07417130022087008

Eger, M., & Martens, C. (2017, September). Character beliefs in story generation. *Proceedings of the AAAI Conference on Artificial Intelligence and Interactive Digital Entertainment* 13(1) https://doi.org/10.1609/aiide.v13i2.12990

U.S. Department of Education. (2023). *Mission statement.* Retrieved from https://www.ed.gov/

Freire, P. (1970). *Pedagogy of the oppressed.* New York, NY: Continuum.

Friedman, S. H., & Hall, R. C. (2015). Teaching psychopathology in a galaxy far, far away: the light side of the force. *Academic Psychiatry, 39*(6), 719–725. https://doi.org/10.1007/s40596-015-0340-y

Fröbel, F. (1826). *Die Menschenerziehung.* Leipzig, Germany. https://www.froebelweb.de/images/pdf/ME_www.pdf

Geronimus, A. T., James, S. A., Destin, M., Graham, L. F., Hatzenbuehler, M. L., Murphy, M. C., & Thompson, J. P. (2016). Jedi public health: Co-creating an identity-safe culture to promote health equity. *SSM-population health,* 2, 105–116. https://doi.org/10.1016/j.ssmph.2016.02.008

Grassinger, R., Porath, M., & Ziegler, A. (2010). Mentoring the gifted: A conceptual analysis. *High Ability Studies, 21*(1), 27–46. https://doi.org/10.1080/13598139.2010.488087

Gunnels, J. (2009). 'A Jedi like my father before me': Social identity and the New York Comic Con. *Transformative Works and Cultures, 3*(3). https://doi.org/10.3983/twc.2009.0161.

H.R. 1532. (2011). *Race to the Top Act of 2011.* [Government]. U.S. Government Printing Office.

Kimmerer, R.W. (2013). *Braiding sweetgrass.* Minneapolis, MN: Milkweed Editions.

King, D. (2015). Why the *Star Wars* "Imperial March" is the best music cue in movie history. *Vanity Fair.* https://www.vanityfair.com/hollywood/2015/12/star-wars-imperial-march-history

"Kyber Crystal." (2021). https://starwars.fandom.com/wiki/Kyber_crystal

Lave, J. (1991). Situating learning in communities of practice. In Lauren B. Resnick, John M. Levine, & Stephanie Teasley (Eds.), *Perspectives on socially shared cognition.* Washington, DC: American Psychological Association. pp. 63–82.

Lucas, G. (Director). (1977). *Star wars episode IV: A new hope* [Film]. Lucasfilm.

Lucas, G. (1977–present). The Star Wars Universe. Lucasfilm

Martín Alegre, S. (2019). Obi-Wan Kenobi and the problem of the flawed mentor. *Foundation: The International Review of Science Fiction, 48*(1, 132), 37–53.

Mullins, A. E. (2016). Jedi or judge: How the human mind redefines judicial opinions. *Wyoming Law Review, 16*, 325.

Nielsen, J. E. (1980). Organization: move over, Obi-Wan Kenobi. *Purchasing Administration*, 4(9), 37.

No Child Left Behind Act of 2001, Pub. L. No. 107-110, § 115, Stat. 1425 (2002)

Rossiter, G. (2005). From St Ignatius to Obi-Wan Kenobi: An evaluative perspective on spirituality for school education. *Journal of Religious Education, 53*(1), 3. https://acuresearchbank.acu.edu.au/item/850xz/from-st-ignatius-to-obi-wan-kenobi-an-evaluative-perspective-on-spirituality-for-school-education

CHAPTER FIVE

The Hidden Curriculum Strikes Back: Crime, Punishment, and Privilege in *Star Trek*

The Text: *Star Trek* (Abrams, 2009); *Star Trek II: The Wrath of Khan* (Meyer, 1982). Film.

Introduction

THIS CHAPTER IS SLIGHTLY different from the others. Instead of focusing on a specific film or book, we are going to focus on a bit of science fiction lore that is featured repeatedly in multiple films, books, and TV episodes within the Star Trek canon. I am talking, of course, about the standardized test known as the *Kobayashi Maru*, the no-win battle simulation that all Star Fleet officers must face before earning their commission. The basic premise of the simulation is simple: You are the captain of a Star Fleet ship. While on routine patrol, you receive a distress signal from the *Kobayashi Maru*, a civilian ship that has become incapacitated and drifted into the neutral zone, which is a violation of several treaties. If the *Kobayashi Maru* is discovered by the Klingons, the crew will be killed, and an intergalactic war will most certainly begin. So you, the captain, have a choice. You can go behind enemy lines and attempt to rescue the crew, which carries the risk of capture, death, and war. Or you can remain in place, leaving the stranded crew members to face an almost certain death, almost certainly leading to mutiny from the bridge crew, who cannot stand by while the *Kobayashi Maru* is sacrificed. There is, of course, no way to "win" in this scenario. Any choice you make will lead to death, dishonor, and probably war. You are damned-if-you-do, damned-if-you-don't.

This "no-win" scenario is not designed to assess whether or not you can somehow find a way to beat the odds. The simulation is specifically arranged and programmed so that you *cannot* win. You, your crew, and the crew of the *Kobayashi Maru* will die, or your crew will mutiny in the face of your inaction. These outcomes are unavoidable. Instead, the simulation is designed to assess how you handle yourself in the face of certain death. The outcome is predetermined; what matters, according to those who created the assessment, is how you conduct yourself in light of that predetermined end. It is a test of character, not a test of tactics.

It is difficult to write about the assessment called the *Kobayashi Maru* while simultaneously differentiating it from the ship that features within that assessment. From this point forward, unless otherwise noted, the phrase "the Kobayashi Maru" will refer to the assessment itself, not the similarly named spaceship.

The Kobayashi Maru was first introduced into the Star Trek universe in the 1982 film, *Star Trek II: The Wrath of Khan* (Meyer). We will discuss the details of the plot below, but it is important to understand how quickly the Kobayashi Maru became infused into the Star Trek canon. By 1989, the first Kobayashi Maru novel appeared (Ecklar). It has since appeared explicitly in multiple iterations of Star Trek episodic television (e.g., the shows *Star Trek: Lower Decks, Star Trek: Discovery, Star Trek: Picard*, and *Star Trek: Prodigy*) and implicitly in others (e.g., *Star Trek: The Next Generation, Star Trek: Voyager*). In the video game *Star Trek: Star Fleet Academy*, you can game play as a Star Fleet cadet taking part in the Kobayashi Maru simulation (rendering the video game a simulation of a simulation). The Kobayashi Maru features prominently in too many Star Trek novels, short stories, and comic books to name, although a number of fan-based websites have attempted to catalog every known instance of the Kobayashi Maru test in the entire Star Trek corpus, both canonical and apocryphal (e.g., Memory Alpha, 2024). Finally, the Kobayashi Maru test plays a central role in the plot of the 2009 reboot of the Star Trek film franchise (Abrams).

Of course, the Kobayashi Maru has made its way into the "real" universe, as well. The test, whether as a metaphor for a no-win situation or as an actual assessment tactic, has been explicitly mentioned in academic literature on such varied subjects as entrepreneurship (Carriker & Mayo, 2021), experiential learning (Bruni-Bosso & Willness, 2016), student retention (Dunlap & Lowenthal, 2010), academic leadership (Ortiz et al., 2019), global warming (Manuel, 2016), curriculum development (Whitsed & Green, 2016), ethics (Stemwedel, 2015), and growth mindset (Markle, 2020).

It has shown up in some very interesting places. For example, Lee & Skog (2014) highlight the Kobayashi Maru as a potential model for using simulations to teach no-win scenarios in medical school. Hoban (2023) suggests something similar, regarding teaching physicians how to have "end of life" conversations with dying patients. The Kobayashi Maru has been referenced in case law related to unionization (Miller, 2017) and the employment of former convicts (Garcia, 2012). Finally, and perhaps most interestingly, strategists from the U.S. Cyber Command and the U.S. Military Academy have called for military trainers to "embrace the Kobayashi Maru" because of its ability to teach students to cheat (Conti & Caroland, 2011, p. 48). We'll come back to this idea later.

This point about "cheating" will serve as our transition to a plot overview, because the "cheating" plays a large role in the scenes we're about to analyze. Indeed, when the only hard-and-fast rule of the assessment is "you cannot win," cheating takes on newfound importance and leads to a host of interesting and troubling questions: What is the difference between "cheating" and creative thinking? If the deck is intentionally stacked against you, is cheating morally wrong? What are the "rules" for learning? Who decides? Is it cheating to push back against standardized elements of a standardized assessment, particularly when the "standard" is based on a narrow and strikingly nonrepresentative cross section of humanity?

From the perspective of a critical pedagogue, the Kobayashi Maru highlights the disturbing interactions among power, rules, agency, and learning that dominate so much of American educational practice. To conduct our analysis, we will not be looking solely at the scenes depicting the test itself. Instead, we will also be examining the consequences and fallout of the Kobayashi Maru within each of these stories, allowing us to dissect the roles that simulation and high-stakes testing play in *Star Trek*'s learning spaces.

Finally, it is important to note that many of these critical questions are raised *within the Star Trek universe itself*. This is perhaps not surprising, given *Star Trek*'s long history of critically interrogating and questioning

American race and gender norms. It is a strikingly political show in this regard, and, in many ways, it provides a roadmap for how we might consider the Kobayashi Maru through a critical lens.

But enough preamble. Set phasers to learn!

The Stories

Both of the texts we will analyze tell the story of how James T. Kirk became the first and only Starfleet cadet to ever "beat" the Kobayashi Maru. Although each text recounts the same event, each emphasizes a slightly different element of the story, and while these stories are overall quite similar, they do diverge on some important plot details. The implications of these divergences will be discussed later in this chapter.

Story 1: From *The Wrath of Khan* (Meyer, 1982)

Things are not looking good for the crew of the *Enterprise*. Khan, a ruthless, half-sane evil genius, has chased them through the galaxy, hell bent on getting revenge on James T. Kirk, the former captain of the *Enterprise* who left him marooned nearly 15 years before. So far, Khan's vengeance has been successful. He has crippled the *Enterprise*, and Kirk, along with a handful of his crew members, are forced to hide deep under the surface of a lifeless planetoid. The details of Khan's obsession and his cat-and-mouse game with Kirk aren't important for this chapter; suffice it to say that Kirk and crew are trapped with seemingly no escape. There is nothing to do but wait for either an unlikely rescue or for a much more likely death.

But, because they have got some time to kill, they might as well get into their backstories. Lt. Savak, a Vulcan who is still in command school training and who has already attempted and failed the Kobayashi Maru, approaches Kirk, who is now an admiral, with a question.

> **Kirk:** What's on your mind, lieutenant?
>
> **Savak:** The Kobayashi Maru, sir.
>
> **Kirk:** Are you asking me if we're playing out that scenario now?
>
> **Savak:** On the test, sir. Will you tell me what you did? I would really like to know.
>
> **Bones** [*the ship's doctor, who has been listening to their conversation*]: Lieutenant, you are looking at the only Starfleet cadet who ever beat the no-win scenario.

> **Savak:** How?
>
> **Kirk:** I reprogrammed the simulation so it was possible to rescue the ship.
>
> **Savak** [*incredulously*]**:** What?
>
> **David** [*a scientist who is trapped with the* Enterprise *crew*]**:** He cheated.
>
> **Kirk** [*defensively*]**:** I changed the conditions of the test. Got a commendation for original thinking. I don't like to lose.
>
> **Savak:** Then you never faced that situation. Faced death.
>
> **Kirk:** I don't believe in a no-win scenario. [*He pulls out his communication device*] Kirk to Spock. It's two hours. Are you ready?
>
> **Spock** [*over the communicator*]**:** Right on schedule, Admiral. Just give us your coordinates, and we'll beam you aboard.
>
> **Kirk** [*stands and grins smugly at Lt. Savak, who is quite surprised that the supposedly crippled* Enterprise *is, in fact, standing by to rescue them*]**:** I don't like to lose. (Meyer, 1982)

They are rescued from immediate danger, but the battle with Khan continues. The *Enterprise* eventually manages to defeat Khan but sustains a fatal blow in the process. Though his ship has been disabled, Khan has activated a bomb powerful enough to destroy everything within a million kilometers. The *Enterprise*'s warp engines were damaged in the battle, and it can only limp away from the coming explosion. The bomb will go off in four minutes, and the *Enterprise* will be only a few thousand kilometers away. The bomb cannot be disabled. The warp engines cannot be repaired without manually repairing the warp core, a task which means certain and almost immediate death-by-radiation for anyone who enters the warp chamber. Kirk sees no escape. He faces, for perhaps the first time in his life, a true no-win scenario.

Spock, however, sees what Kirk cannot. While Kirk is distracted, Spock rushes down to the engine room, overpowers the guards, enters the warp chamber without protective gear, and repairs the warp core. Up in the bridge, an officer tells Kirk that the engines are back online. Kirk gives the order for warp speed, and the *Enterprise* avoids obliteration by mere seconds.

While celebrating their narrow escape, Kirk calls down to the engine room.

Kirk: Engine room—well done, Scotty.

Bones [*ship's doctor, who witnessed Spock's sacrifice*]: Jim . . . I think [his voice breaks] you'd better get down here.

Kirk: Bones?

Bones: You'd . . . you'd better hurry.

Kirk looks over and sees Spock's empty chair. A horrible realization passes across his face, as he rushes from the bridge to the engine room. When he arrives, the engineers are standing almost at attention, as if trying to honor someone. Kirk literally shoves them out of the way and tries to force his way into the warp chamber. Bones and Scotty have to hold him back.

Bones: No! You'll flood the whole compartment!

Kirk [*in anguish*]: But he'll die.

Scotty: Sir, he's dead already.

Kirk looks helplessly to Bones, who nods.

Bones: It's too late, Jim.

Kirk stumbles to the transparent door dividing the warp chamber from the rest of the engine room. He presses his face against the glass and yells. The sound cannot penetrate the door. He fumbles for the intercom switch.

Kirk: Spock!

Spock, who has been crouched in the far corner of the warp chamber, stands slowly and with great difficulty, keeping a hand on the wall to steady himself. His back is to the crew. He straightens his uniform, as if trying to maintain some dignity. He turns and walks toward Kirk. The skin on his face is sloughing off, evidence of the severe radiation poisoning from which he is now suffering. He bumps into the transparent door, and we realize he is blind. Kirk stares at him in incomprehension.

Spock [*his voice weak, burnt*]: The ship. Out of danger?

Kirk: Yes.

Spock: Don't grieve, Admiral. It is logical. The needs of the many outweigh . . . [*his voice trails off. He is clearly in great pain*].

Kirk [*finishing Spock's sentence*]: . . . the needs of the few.

Spock: Or the one. [*Spock falters, nearly collapsing*] I never took the Kobayashi Maru test. Until now. What do you think of my solution?

> **Kirk** [*looking around desperately, as if waiting for someone to come save him, to save the situation*]: Spock . . . [*it is almost a sob*].
>
> *Spock's legs fail him, and he slumps to the floor*
>
> **Spock:** I have been, and always shall be, your friend. [*He places his hand on the glass, fingers spread in the Vulcan salute*] Live long, and prosper.
>
> *Kirk places his hand on the other side of the glass, his fingers "touching" Spock's. Spock lets his hand fall, turns away from Kirk, and dies.*
>
> **Kirk:** No . . . [he, too, turns, back against the glass, defeated]. (Meyer, 1982)

Story 2: From Star Trek (Abrams, 2009)

In *The Wrath of Khan* (Meyer, 1982), everything we hear about Kirk's experience with the Kobayashi Maru comes to us retrospectively. Although we get a firsthand account from Kirk himself, it comes to us years after the exam actually took place. The exam happened when Kirk was a cadet. He's an admiral now, though, and we have only his word for what happened. The accuracy of his account depends entirely on the reliability of his memory and his willingness to tell the truth.

In the 2009 *Star Trek* reboot, however, we witness Kirk's defeat of the Kobayashi Maru for ourselves.[1] Cadet Kirk, who was recruited to Star Fleet academy after a period of prolonged juvenile delinquency, has already made a name for himself as a hot-headed, womanizing, rule-breaking scofflaw who just happens to be exceptionally charismatic and phenomenally talented. The night before the test, Uhura, a fellow cadet and soon-to-be communications officer, caught him canoodling with her roommate. To Uhura, this is just one more indication of how deeply unserious he is about command. Instead of studying, he's, well . . .

It comes as no surprise, then, when Uhura doesn't take him seriously as the "captain" during the Kobayashi Maru exam the next day.

> **Uhura** [*sarcastically, acting as the communications officer in the simulation*]: We are receiving a distress signal from the *U.S.S. Kobayashi Maru*. The ship has lost power and is stranded. Starfleet Command has ordered us to rescue them.
>
> **Kirk** [*looking entirely unconcerned*]: Starfleet command has ordered us to rescue them . . . [*he waits, as if prompting her to fill in the blank, then fills it in himself*] . . . Captain.

An alarm sounds.

Bones [also serving as a bridge officer for the simulation]: Two Klingon vessels have entered the Neutral Zone and are locking weapons on us.

Kirk: That's ok.

Bones [*incredulous*]: That's ok?

Kirk: Yeah. Don't worry about it.

The Academy faculty and administrators who are monitoring the exam behind a one-way mirror are startled and confused.

Administrator 1: Did he just say, "don't worry about it?"

Administrator 2: Is he not taking the simulation seriously?

Back on the "bridge," the situation is getting worse.

Bones: Three more Klingon warbirds decloaking and targeting our ship. I don't suppose this is a problem either?

Helmsman: They're firing, Captain.

Kirk [*smugly*]: Alert medical bay to prepare to receive *all* crew members from the damaged ship.

Uhura: And how do you expect us to rescue them when we're surround by Klingons, Captain?

Kirk [*turning to face Uhura and smiling over-sweetly*]: Alert medical.

The monitors show Klingon ships firing repeatedly on the Enterprise.

Bones: Our ship is being hit. Shields at 60%.

Kirk: I understand.

Bones [*irritated*]: Well, should we, I don't know, fire back?

Kirk has produced an apple from somewhere and begins to eat it, obviously unconcerned about the beating his ship is taking.

Kirk: Nah.

Bones [*under his breath*]: Of course not.

Suddenly, all the systems on the simulated bridge power down. Lights dim; monitors go blank. The test administrators look around in confusion. This is clearly not part of the original simulation design. The systems power back on just as suddenly as they powered down.

Kirk: Hmm. Arm photons. Prepare to fire on the Klingon warbirds.

Helmsman: Yes, sir.

Bones: Jim, their shields are still up.

Kirk: Are they? [*He takes a bite of his apple.*]

Bones [*turns to the monitors and does a double-take, surprised*]: No. They're not.

Kirk: Fire on all enemy ships! One photon each should do. Let's not waste ammunition.

Helmsman: Target locked and acquired on all warbirds. Firing.

The monitors show the Enterprise *firing on and destroying all the Klingon ships. Kirk mimics shooting with a laser pistol and makes little "pew pew" noises.*

Helmsman: All ships destroyed, Captain.

Kirk [offhandedly, as if an afterthought]: Begin rescue of the stranded crew. [*He stands and begins "lecturing."*] So. We've managed to eliminate all enemy ships, no one on board was injured, and the successful rescue of the *Kobayashi Maru* crew is underway. [*He takes another bite of his apple.*]

The faculty and administrators in the observation room are stunned.

Administrator 1: How the hell did that kid beat your test?

Spock [*who, in this storyline, designed the test and does not yet know Kirk*]: I do not know. (Abrams, 2009)

In *The Wrath of Khan* (Meyer, 1982), Kirk was commended for creative thinking. In the *Star Trek* reboot, however, Kirk is accused of "violat[ing] the ethical code of conduct pursuant to Regulation 17.43 of the Starfleet code" (Abrams, 2009). The Academy President calls him to trial, where he is questioned by Commander Spock:

Spock: Cadet Kirk, you somehow managed to install and activate a subroutine in the programming code, thereby changing the conditions of the test.

Kirk: Your point being?

Academy President: In academic vernacular, you cheated.

Kirk: Let me ask you something I think we all know the answer to. The test itself is a cheat, isn't it? I mean, you programmed it to be unwinnable.

Spock: Your argument precludes the possibility of a no-win scenario.

Kirk: I don't believe in no-win scenarios.

Spock: Then not only did you violate the rules, but you failed to understand the principal lesson.

Kirk: Please. Enlighten me.

Spock: You of all people should know, Cadet Kirk, a captain cannot cheat death.

Kirk [*pauses*]: I of all people?

Spock: Your father, Lieutenant George Kirk, assumed command of his vessel before being killed in action, did he not?

Kirk: I don't think you like the fact that I beat your test.

Spock: Furthermore, you have failed to divine the purpose of the test.

Kirk: Enlighten me again.

Spock: The purpose is to experience fear, fear in the face of certain death, to accept that fear and maintain control of one's self and one's crew. This is a quality expected in every Starfleet captain. (Abrams, 2009)

Before Kirk is able to respond, the trial is interrupted. Starfleet is under attack. Over the course of the ensuing battles, Kirk, who technically remains on academic suspension and has snuck aboard a ship, somehow receives a field promotion to first officer and then captain, even though he is technically still a cadet-in-training. He, of course, saves the day, and at the end of the film, Kirk receives an official commendation and official promotion to captain of Starfleet's flagship, the *U.S.S. Enterprise*.—all this despite the charges of cheating never having been resolved *and* the fact that he has not yet actually graduated from the academy.

In both narratives, Kirk is eventually valorized and celebrated for his "out of the box" thinking. The punishments threatened in the reboot film never materialize, and, in both films, his "cheating" on the Kobayashi Maru has no long-term negative impact on his personal or professional life.

The Critical Analysis

This chapter could cover a great many topics that are of interest to critical pedagogues. For example, there are so many questions to be asked about the role of simulation in education. Can a "fake" scenario accurately predict how learners will act when faced with the real thing, particularly if they're aware that they're in a simulation? Ecklar's (1989) novelization of Kirk's Kobayashi Maru exam raises that exact question. When one cadet decides not to help the virtual ship in distress, his actual classmates hold it against him, inferring from his actions during the test that he would do the same to them in real life. He tries to remind them that it was a simulation, that he knew it was a simulation, and that one acts differently when one knows the stakes aren't real. Nevertheless, the relational damage is done.

Indeed, educators at all levels should be thinking carefully about the increasingly blurred lines between the real and the virtual. Unfortunately, like the cadets taking the Kobayashi Maru, I have had to make some difficult decisions. Consequently, as important as the topic is, and as much as critical pedagogues are rightly concerned with the role of simulation in the education of real students, we will not be exploring the topic further in this chapter.

Another potential topic for discussion is the notion of *consequential validity*. In assessment theory, consequential validity is the idea that the decisions resulting from an assessment must be in proportion to the scope of the assessment. For example, pretend that you are taking the written exam to get your driver's license. The passing score is 80%, and you earn a 79%. Assuming that the exam is an accurate predictor of safe driving practices, it would be reasonable to tell you that you cannot get your driver's license at this time, but that you should study more and come back when you are ready.

However, if we looked at your test score and then threw you in jail for life in order to "protect the innocent pedestrians of our fair city," we could say that the exam lacks consequential validity. It is being used to make decisions far beyond the scope of its intent. The test was designed to determine whether you are ready to drive a car *now*, not whether you are a permanent danger to society.

Does the Kobayashi Maru have consequential validity? For example, if a Starfleet cadet performs poorly on the exam, does that forever bar them from promotion beyond a certain rank? Do certain doors close forever based on this one test? Are some opportunities lost for all time? Can a one-time test that someone takes at 18–20 years old be fairly used to determine all their future prospects?

Given that our education systems have been caught in the grip of high-stakes testing for the last few decades, this is not an idle question. Critical pedagogy is deeply concerned with the disproportionate role of high-stakes testing in contemporary education, raising red flags over issues of equity, practicality, and, quite often, money. The companies that make and administer high-stakes tests have a vested interest in ensuring their continued use, and the spider-web of politics, lobbying, profit, and educational law is deeply disturbing. It is also, unfortunately, beyond the scope of this chapter if for no other reason than that it merits an entire book series of its own.

Instead of looking at the role of simulation or the consequential validity of high-stakes testing, we will be exploring the notion of an academic or educational "crime," and we will be looking at the ways that we punish or discipline students for breaking the "rules" of education. As with nearly every aspect of education practice, concepts of "rules" and "punishment" are deeply intertwined with issues of inequity, particularly along racial lines. We cannot discuss the breaking of academic rules, for example, without also discussing who made the rules in the first place, who benefits from the rules being maintained or violated, what constitutes breaking the rules versus bending them, and who does, or does not, get punished when the rules are broken.

Let's begin by asking a seemingly simple but actually complex question: What is cheating?

What is Cheating?

The verb *cheat*, as it relates to the idea of deceit, has been in popular use for roughly 400 years (Cheat, 2023). In educational settings, *cheating* implies a sort of academic deception or dishonesty. This deception generally takes one of three forms:

1. Falsely representing one's knowledge;
2. Breaking the "rules" of the assessment; and
3. Misattributing one's sources.

The first two, which are generally referred to by the catch-all term *cheating*, encompass a wide variety of illicit educational activities, ranging from the fairly innocuous (e.g., not putting your pencil down when the teacher says "stop writing!") to the blatantly egregious (e.g., paying someone else to take a test for you). The two forms often overlap. For example, copying answers from your neighbor's test is both a misrepresentation of your knowledge *and* a violation of the "rules" in most assessment scenarios. The same might be said for looking at notes that you have written on the palm of your hand or referencing an outside source when completing what is supposed to be a closed-book exam. In each of these examples, the essence of the deceit is that you have either 1) misrepresented what you know; or 2) broken the rules related to the demonstration of knowledge. In general, these two phenomena go hand in hand (though there are some notable exceptions that we'll talk about later in this chapter). So, regardless of their differences in methodology and scope, the thousands of people who buy fake diplomas from online "universities" and the ninth grader who sneaks a peek at their neighbor's answer to problem number three on the algebra pop quiz are exactly the same in this regard: They do not know something, but they want you to think they do, and they've broken the "rules" to give this impression.

The third category of academic cheating is generally referred to as *plagiarism*, and it is as specific as the other category is broad. Plagiarism is a specific type of cheating that involves taking words or phrases written by someone else and passing them off as your own. This might involve copying a quote word-for-word and sticking it in your own paper without acknowledging that you got it from someone else. It might mean failing to cite a source or even summarizing someone else's idea without giving them credit for having the idea in the first place. You have taken credit for someone else's work, a phenomenon sometimes referred to as *literary theft* (Plagiarism, 2023).

This "theft" can have serious consequences in academic settings. For example, former president of Harvard University, Claudine Gay, was forced to resign her position in January 2024, after allegations that she had plagiarized small portions of her 1997 dissertation arose. A subsequent inquiry found examples of verbatim wording that she had, in fact, cited but had neglected to place in quotation marks. In other words, she gave credit to the author, but she misused the accompanying punctuation (Nguyen, 2024). This and other related charges were sufficient to cost her her job.

Literary theft is an interesting concept, however, because it is based on the assumption that knowledge and ideas can "belong" to a specific person. In academic contexts, this "belonging" is not necessarily an issue of intellectual property law. Surveys indicate that most Americans do, in fact, consider plagiarism to be a type of theft, but this theft is framed in moral, not legal, terms (Mandel et al., 2015). Most people agree that a student who copies an article word-for-word and doesn't cite the source has not broken a criminal code. There is no jail in their future. They have, however, broken a *moral* code, and should be sanctioned accordingly. This distinction between legal and moral law might explain why Claudine Gay was ousted from her job but not subject to criminal proceedings. Her supposed crime was moral, not legal.[2] She took something that did not belong to her, her critics said, which is a crime most heinous and deserving of punishment. The truth of the accusations is almost beside the point. As Frye (2020) notes, "even an unsubstantiated accusation [of plagiarism] leaves an indelible stain, and a credible complaint cannot be countered" (p. 296).

What is clear about plagiarism and about academic cheating in general is that people take it incredibly seriously. Regardless of whether or not cheating or plagiarism constitutes a legal crime (the ins and outs of intellectual property or copyright law are far beyond the scope of this chapter), the consequences for cheating can be severe. Most people consider cheating to be a violation of the most sacred academic principles. It is a "blight" and "menace" (Boahen et al., 2022, p. 89), a "scourge" that is "plaguing" our education institutions (Braga, 2021, p. 1). Accordingly, many, if not most, education institutions treat cheating as a quasi-criminal activity, crafting punitive policy measures designed to sanction or even expel cheaters, thereby deterring future "criminals." These sanctions generally apply equally to both intentional and unintentional acts of plagiarism. Consider the plagiarism policy from the University of Oxford (2021), which acknowledges that "plagiarism may be intentional or reckless, or unintentional," and yet, in the next sentence, makes clear that "under the regulations for examinations, *intentional or reckless plagiarism is a disciplinary offence*" (University of Oxford, 2021, n.p., emphasis added). No exceptions are made for the accident or honest mistake. Moral law has been violated, and the violators must be punished.

But the purpose of this chapter is not to delve into the nitty gritty of definitions and policies. It is, instead, to peel away at the arguments surrounding our common conceptions of cheating and other academic "crimes," uncovering the hidden assumptions lurking at the center. To do this, let's return to Kobayashi Maru with a simple question: What, exactly, did Kirk do wrong?

The Unwritten Rules

Schools, like all other social institutions, are governed by rules, both explicit and unwritten. Yoho & Moore (2023) frame these unwritten rules as the "social and practical schema" (p. 1) that govern the interactions among teachers, students, communities, and curricula. These are the unspoken expectations, assumptions about the world that are so basic and fundamental that they have never needed articulation, at least not within a homogenous community. For example, the college freshman who comes from a long line of college graduates most likely "just knows" to refer to his professor as "doctor so and so" without having been explicitly instructed to do so. He has learned this rule passively, not realizing that his psychological structures have been shaped in such a way that referring to a college professor by their first name (unless invited to do so) is almost literally unthinkable. Of course, not every incoming college student has learned this unwritten rule (through no fault of their own), and the airwaves at the beginning of every school year are filled with college professors bemoaning the audacity of these incoming freshmen who have the nerve to call their professors by their first names. But it is not necessarily audacity: It is most likely a simple matter of not having been exposed to the traditional unwritten rules that govern most student/professor interactions.

These unwritten rules are often cultural. For example, say that a new teacher from an urban setting gets a job in a rural school without understanding the role of the Friday night football game in the school community. They do not attend the big game, unwittingly violating the unwritten rule that *everyone* goes to the game and supports the team, and they then wonder why their relationships with students and their families are suffering. No one instructed them that attendance is culturally compulsory, because no one has ever felt the need to articulate it. It is a rule that is simply understood and passively transmitted among the community members (Yoho & Moore, 2003).

A recent online conversation among some of my academic peers highlighted the link between unwritten rules and cultural assumptions. One professor was lamenting that their students never knock on their door when they come by for office hours. They just walk in and sit down. Another professor asked this colleague if they had ever made their expectations regarding knocking clear. "I shouldn't have to," they replied. "Students should just know."

This "should" is interesting, because it implies that the students have a moral obligation to be aware of and to follow a set of rules that their professor fully admits never telling them about. According to this way of thinking, the professor's frustration with their students is not the professor's fault for not making the expectations clear; it is their students' fault for not sharing the same set of unwritten rules that the professor has.

In education contexts, it is quite often the students who suffer under the burden of unwritten rules. For example, teachers' inconsistent application of explicit school rules can often be explained by the mitigating presence of unwritten or implicit rules. This inconsistency hurts students, though, who "cannot predict what will be appropriate behaviour in particular situations, and how teachers will react to their behaviour" (Thornberg, 2007, p. 1).

In this context, a simple rule such as "raise your hand when you want to speak" becomes extraordinarily complex. Sometimes, students will get in trouble for speaking without raising their hands. Other times, they will not be censured. Still other times, they might be praised. To the outsider, the seemingly inconsistent application of the hand-raising rule would be inexplicable and, as noted above, would result in a loss of predictive ability. The outsider would not be able to predict when they would, and when they would not, get in trouble for not raising their hand.

In many cases, however, these seeming inconsistencies are not actual inconstancies. Instead, they are "refinements" of the explicit rules, governed by unwritten codes that are understood by everyone *except* the outsider or newcomer (Jackson et al., 1993, p. 13). Most insiders would be hard-pressed to explain why a particular violation of the hand-raising rule is, in fact, not an *actual* violation. They just know that this is the case. They know the specific contexts in which the rules can be bent or even broken, although they might not be able to explain those contexts to someone else.

The phenomenon of teaching and learning these unwritten educational rules, which don't appear in any rule book or on any syllabus, is often referred to as grappling with *the hidden curriculum* (Jackson, 1968). The hidden curriculum, which operates both in conjunction with and separate from formal instruction and official curriculum (Cubukcu, 2012; Giroux & Penna, 1979) is the transmission of "unstated norms, values, and beliefs transmitted to students through the underlying structure of schooling, as opposed to the formally recognized and sanctioned dimensions of the schooling experience" (Giroux, 1978, p. 148). The hidden curriculum, which is often made manifest and transmitted at the classroom level through teacher/student interactions (Apple, 2023), often contradicts official curriculum. It's not difficult to imagine a situation in which a school's official policies encourage students to think for themselves, but the classroom teacher's actions teach students that anything other than blind adherence and unquestioning obedience will not be tolerated.

As critical pedagogy has grown from a niche and specialized field of study located solely within K–12 education to a broadly applied, diverse field of inquiry that transcends traditional academic boundaries, interest in the hidden curriculum has grown in a broad range of education contexts, including higher education (e.g., Rossouw & Frick, 2023), pharmacology (e.g., Park et al., 2023), medicine (e.g., Howick et al., 2024), engineering (e.g., Alarcón et al., 2023), and business management (e.g., Schwabenland & Kofinas, 2023). Indeed, exposing the hidden curriculum and making it explicit might be considered a central goal of critical pedagogy (Portelli, 1993) because the hidden curriculum is where the *real* educational values can be found.

Again, it doesn't require a stretch of the imagination to think of a school whose official curriculum promotes "creativity" but whose classroom interactions and implicit values promote rigidity and rule-following. As I write this chapter, protests are erupting at college campuses across the country, and many critical pedagogues are highlighting the disparities between the universities' stated values—e.g., The University of Southern California's mission to "confront the status quo" (Values, 2024)—and the unspoken values communicated through action—e.g., the university's decision to have student protestors arrested (Hernandez et al., 2024). Of course, student protests, the limits of free speech, and the proper role of education institutions in maintaining social order are admittedly complex topics. Nevertheless, the hidden curriculum has been on display, the explicit liberalism of academia standing in stark contrast to the implicit conservatism of the hidden curriculum. The explicit charge to "confront the status quo" is undercut by the implicit charge not to rock the boat too hard.

This is the dilemma facing Kirk. On one hand, Starfleet's charter urges him to seek out "strange new worlds" and to go "where no one has gone before" (Roddenberry, 1966–present). And yet, when he actually does what no one has done before, when he embraces the truly novel, he is reprimanded, at least initially. Starfleet's hidden curriculum belies its official curriculum, which brings us back to the question we asked earlier: What did Kirk do wrong?

Officially, Kirk was accused of violating Regulation 17.43 of the Starfleet code. Of course, such code exists only in the fictional *Star Trek* universe, so I am unable to cite an official regulation or policy. However, it stands to reason that Kirk had been accused of some form of "cheating." But which form? He did not misrepresent what he knew, and he did not take credit for the work of others. His "crime," then, must be that of violating the "rules." But why break the rules? What advantage would it give him? After all, the Kobayashi Maru was not a norm-referenced exam, designed to sort and rank students on a specific performance scale. As Spock noted, the purpose of the exam was to elicit a particular emotional response from the cadets, not to measure their tactical ability. Consequently, it's difficult to imagine the competitive advantage that Kirk would gain by cheating.

If cheating gave Kirk no advantage over other cadets, and if he did not misrepresent his knowledge or take credit for other people's work, then why the reprimand? According to Spock, Kirk failed to understand the purpose of the test. This may be true. However, a failure to understand the exam content generally leads to a low score or some other sort of pedagogical response. It does not generally result in a tribunal. A teacher might decide to reteach the content, or the student might be required to retake an exam. In extreme cases, a profound failure to understand course or exam content could lead to probation or dismissal. Such cases are not generally "criminalized," however. In Kirk's case, however, he is "accused" at a "tribunal." Starfleet is invoking the language of the criminal justice system, implying that the appropriate response to Kirk's actions are penal, not pedagogical. However, it remains difficult to understand just what Kirk has done to merit such a response.

Perhaps the reason it is difficult to pin down the true nature of Kirk's "crime" is that he has not, in fact, broken any official rules. As he argues, he is in fact operating within the parameters of Starfleet's officially stated values. If it is true that Kirk has acted within the spirit, if not the letter, of the official rules, then his true violation is much more egregious: He has violated the *unwritten* rules.

Despite official statements about the value of seeking out the strange and exploring the new, Starfleet's pedagogical practices reinforce a very different set of values. For example, classroom interactions between teachers and students reinforce rigid hierarchies, as evidenced by the academy officials referring to Kirk as "that kid" (Abrams, 2009). Though Starfleet is ostensibly an organization rooted in discovering the new, its practices seem intent on clinging to the old. The uniforms, ship naming conventions, and ranks are all quasi-militaristic, evoking not the derring-do of renegade explorers but rather the standardized hegemonic might of Imperial navies. Learning is portrayed as a power struggle between teachers and students, each of whom is trying to "beat" the other. The Kobayashi Maru is theoretically a no-win exam, meaning that it is not designed in the spirit of competition. But Kirk certainly views it competitively, stating that he does not like to lose. He is not the only one who sees the classroom as a battlefield. When the academy official asks Spock how Kirk "beat your test," the implication is that Kirk has, by extension, defeated Spock himself. Kirk says as much during his tribunal, suggesting that Spock's anger derives not from any moral wrongdoing by Kirk but rather from the simple fact that Kirk won.

Starfleet's real issue with Kirk's cheating is simple: He questioned an assumed reality that he was not supposed to question. Starfleet sets the rules, and students follow them. Starfleet defines the parameters, and students remain within them. Learning is a top-down enterprise (ha!) that reinforces long-existing power dynamics and maintains the status quo. None of this is ever said out loud, of course, because it doesn't need to be. But woe unto the student who questions the unspoken.

The eagle-eyed among you have noted by now that the two accounts of Kirk's "cheating" presented in this chapter have very different endings. In *The Wrath of Khan* (Meyer, 1982), Kirk is commended for his creative thinking. In *Star Trek* (Abrams, 2009), however, he is called before a tribunal and accused of academic malfeasance. Why the difference? While it's impossible to establish any sort of causal relationship, it's worth noting the years that the films were released. *The Wrath of Khan*, which came out in 1982, just preceded *A Nation at Risk* (National Commission on Excellence in Education, 1983), the highly influential report that paved the way for the high-stakes education accountability and reform movements of the last 40 years. The report, which referred to the diminished state of American education as an act of self-inflicted war, defined education reform in terms of winning and losing, particularly in relation to other countries. This gave rise to competitive, zero-sum oriented models of school reform that focused on "winning." Policies such as the No Child Left Behind Act (2002) and Race to the Top (H.R. 1532, 2011) encoded zero-sum competition into education law. Winning and/or losing was determined solely on the basis of student test scores, and standardized testing became ends in and of themselves. The goal of education slowly transitioned from increasing student learning (which, by extension, would increase test scores) to increasing the test scores for the sake of increasing the test scores (Martin, 2012; Shelton & Brooks, 2019). The test, itself, became king, and the number of hours, days, and weeks devoted to either preparing for or participating in standardized testing grew alarmingly (Jones, 2007; Moon et al., 2007; Polesel et al., 2014).

Although standardized tests existed and were used prior to *A Nation at Risk* (National Commission on Excellence in Education, 1983), they were not framed in terms of teacher/school accountability, and they were seen primarily as measures of student learning, not tools for school reform and comparative evaluation. In the wake of *A Nation at Risk*, however, high-stakes standardized testing took on an outsized role in American education (and, indeed, in the education systems of most industrialized nations). Even though educators at all levels protested the move toward accountability testing, highlighting the ways that high-stakes testing negatively impacted other measures of student learning and well-being, the trend persisted. It wasn't until 2015 that the United States government began to ease the high-stakes testing burden on students and teachers alike.

The *Star Trek* (Abrams, 2009) reboot was written and produced at the height of the high-stakes testing movement, and I wonder to what extent the "criminal" interpretation of Kirk's actions was a reflection of a cultural moment in which "testing" was, at least theoretically, synonymous with "excellence." I'm speculating, of course, and this is not a position that I am prepared to defend vigorously. However, the changing roles of high-stakes testing in American education are roughly mirrored in the films' depictions of Kirk's actions.

Punishment and Privilege

Despite the films' initial differences in consequence, the end result is the same in both: Kirk suffers no long-lasting impact to either person or career, and he is, in fact, celebrated for his quick thinking and roguish nature. From this perspective, both films are the same, and this similarity raises an interesting question: If Kirk broke the unwritten rules, why wasn't he *actually* punished? The answer to this question, I fear, may reside in Kirk's privilege.

Although the *Star Trek* (Roddenberry, 1966–present) universe is nominally unbiased and equally representative of all species, The United Federation of Planets is headquartered on Earth, in San Francisco. Kirk is a native speaker of English—the de-facto language of interstellar governance and commerce, and the language of native 23rd-century San Franciscans. Kirk is from Iowa, which is, from a contemporary perspective, part of the same political unit as San Francisco. Kirk is blond haired and blue eyed, and although such things are not supposed to matter in the *Star Trek* universe, we cannot ignore that the hero of our narrative is a member of the privileged class along virtually every demographic marker. This privilege must give us pause, and we must ask how Starfleet might have responded to a cheating cadet if that cadet weren't so perfectly and ideally human?

The real-world, critical analog to this question is this: Does the way we respond to students' violations of the rules depend, at least in part, on whether or not the students are members of the privileged class? Unfortunately, the answer is an unequivocal "yes."

Years of data and hundreds of studies tell a chilling story. In American schools, Black students are penalized more frequently and more severely than their white counterparts for the same behavior (e.g., Addington, 2023; Amemiya et al., 2020; Cruz et al., 2021; Davison et al., 2002; Fadus et al., 2021; Gregory et al., 2010; Petras et al., 2011; Wiley, 2021).

The historical statistics are sobering:

- Students of color are more likely to be differentially selected for discipline based on a "violation of implicit interactional codes," e.g., the breaking of unwritten rules (Vavrus & Cole, 2002, p. 108).
- Black students comprise 17% of the student population but account for 34% of school suspensions (Office for Civil Rights, 2002).
- Black students are up to 3.78 times more likely to face disciplinary action than white students (Skiba et al., 2011).

Though most studies are careful not to draw causal conclusions (e.g., Black students are disciplined more often *because* they're Black), the correlational and descriptive data are strikingly clear. Black students are disciplined at far higher rates than are their white counterparts. These disproportionate rates of discipline have long-term consequences for student learning, not to mention the fact that suspension nearly triples the likelihood that a student will enter into the juvenile justice system (Fabelo et al., 2011).

The logical question now is why? *Why* are Black students disproportionately disciplined? It's not because they behave differently than their white counterparts. Decades of students have come to the same conclusion: Despite the differentiated disciplinary rates, there are no objective differences in Black and white student behavior (e.g., Skiba et al., 2011). Instead, Black students are more likely to be disciplined based on *subjective* differences (Smolkowski et al., 2016). For example, although Black students are *less* likely than white students to be subject to mandatory discipline (e.g., school policy *requires* that behavior X receive a disciplinary referral), they are *more* likely than white students to be subject to discretionary discipline (e.g., the teachers determine for themselves whether the behavior is a violation) (Fabelo et al., 2011).

Again, why? One possible answer may lie in the disproportionately high numbers of white teachers—in particular, white women—in the American teaching workforce. For example, during the 2020–2021 school year (National Center for Education Statistics, 2023):

- Less than half (46%) of public school students were white

  BUT

- 77% of public school (K–12) teachers were women;
- 89% of public elementary school teachers were women;
- 80% of public school teachers were white; and
- 77% of K–12 public school principals were white.

There is a great disparity between the racial, ethnic, and cultural backgrounds of American students and the people charged with teaching them. But, because the unwritten rules that govern classroom behavior are so often culturally specific, it is possible that the disparity between teachers' and students' backgrounds means that teachers and students are not sharing the same tacit understanding of just when and how the official rules can be broken. It is possible that the disproportionately high rate of discretionary discipline applied to Black students might be due, in part, to unwritten rules that favor those students who share a culture with the teacher. And, because the great majority of teachers are white, white students who share the teachers' backgrounds may be able to break the rules with greater discretionary impunity, simply because they break the rules in tacitly acceptable ways.

Of course, this explanation is overly simplistic. Race, ethnicity, culture, and background are four separate constructs, and it is entirely possible for people of different races or ethnicities to share cultures or backgrounds (say, socio-economically or linguistically). Furthermore, a number of scholars attribute racial disparities in school discipline to *implicit bias* (e.g., Kupchik & Ellis, 2008; Skiba et al., 2016). Unlike explicit bias, in which a person is aware of their biases and consciously acts upon them, implicit bias is an unconscious process in which the individual is unaware of how their biases are affecting their actions:

> Unconscious processes, like implicit racial bias, are a spontaneous mental association between a race and evaluative or stereotypic thoughts. . . . Even though many Americans do not consciously believe that individuals who are Black should be treated differently, they unconsciously associate Black individuals with negative thoughts as a result of endemic antiblackness within American society. These unconscious associations often perpetuate injustices within society. (Marcucci, 2020, pp. 49–50)

School systems in which teachers have unconscious or implicit biases against Black students are more likely to interpret Black students' behavior as "problematic" and to discipline them accordingly, leading to some uncomfortable and yet necessary questions: How much is the naming of behavior as "good" or "bad" determined not on the basis of an evaluation of the behavior per se but rather based on an evaluation of the person engaged in the behavior? Is bad behavior bad because a "bad" person is doing it? What makes someone a member of the category "bad student?" Unfortunately, that categorical membership is often due to little more than projected racial identification. For example, the white student who questions the teacher might be labeled "opinionated," whereas the Black student who questions the teacher in the exact same way might be, due to his tacit and unconsciously assumed membership in the category "bad student," labeled "defiant." One student is curious. The other is a trouble-maker. Disciplinary systems focused on punishment might remove the trouble-maker from the general student population (through suspension or expulsion), enforcing a hidden curriculum that tacitly prepares disciplined students for removal from society as a whole, i.e., prison (e.g., Giroux, 2003; Hirschfeld, 2008); (Garcia & De Lissovoy, 2013). Not only are Black students more likely to be disciplined, but their behavior is also more likely to be criminalized.

Conclusion

And this brings us back to Kirk and the Kobayashi Maru. As Kirk himself argues, his actions did not really constitute "cheating," in that he wasn't trying to gain an edge or misrepresent his knowledge. But I think the text raises a more important question—one that, to my knowledge, is not addressed anywhere in the *Star Trek* (Roddenberry, 1966–present) canon: If anyone other than the blond haired, blue-eyed, handsome farm boy from Earth had done what Kirk did, would we be having a debate over whether or not his actions count as "cheating?" If a Klingon or other non-Earthling had reprogrammed the test, would they be given the benefit of the doubt? Despite Star Trek's legitimate reputation as a progressive franchise, and despite Starfleet's ostensible representation of all peace-minded species in the galaxy, the hidden curriculum of the Kobayashi Maru teaches a very clear lesson: if you're a good-looking white kid with an easy smile and a twinkle in your eye, you can get away with anything. In this respect, Star Trek (Roddenberry, 1966–present) asks us to boldly go where we've already been for far too long.

Questions for Reflection

1. Pick a relatively routine activity, such as having a classroom discussion. Which of your discussion rules are firm, and which are flexible? Do students know the difference? Are *you* fully aware, or do you "just know" when it has gone too far?

2. How do we communicate unwritten rules to students? How do we help them understand the nuance of when it's ok to break the rules?

3. In your context, which school or classroom policies are most subject to inequitable enforcement? Which groups are most subject to inequitable discipline?

4. How can you, an individual, work against a system of inequitable discipline? In what ways are you complicit in that system? How can you push back against it?

Endnotes

1. I am choosing *not* to discuss the divergent timeline/alternate universe aspect of the reboot films. Though fascinating from a science fiction perspective, they are irrelevant to our critical analysis. As much as it pains me to do so, we must leave the timeline aspect unexplored.
2. I am not making that claim that Claudine Gay did, in fact, plagiarize. I am merely summarizing the charges levied against her. In fact, there are compelling reasons to believe that the outcry against her was driven more by racism than by a sudden concern for academic integrity. These arguments are, however, beyond the scope and focus of this book.

References

Abrams, J. (Director). (2009). *Star Trek* [Film]. Paramount Pictures.

Addington, L. A. (2023). Keeping black girls in school: A systematic review of opportunities to address exclusionary discipline disparity. *Race and Justice, 13*(3), 386–402. https://doi.org/10.1177/2153368720988894

Alarcón, I. V., Sellers, V., Paul, R., & Smith, B. (2023). Transforming engineering education through social capital in response to hidden curriculum. In A. Johri's (Ed.), *International Handbook of Engineering Education Research* (pp. 380–401). New York, NY: Routledge. https://doi.org/10.4324/9781003287483

Amemiya, J., Mortenson, E., & Wang, M.-T. (2020). Minor infractions are not minor: School infractions for minor misconduct may increase adolescents' defiant behavior and contribute to racial disparities in school discipline. *American Psychologist, 75*(1), 23–36. https://doi.org/10.1037/amp0000475

Apple, M. (2023). The hidden curriculum and the nature of conflict. In A. Darder, K. Hernandez, K. Lam, & M. Baltodano's (Eds.), *The Critical Pedagogy Reader* (pp. 434–452). New York, NY: Routledge. https://doi.org/10.4234/9781003286080

Boahen, E. A., Glover, R., Boateng, K. A., & Nimo Nunoo, I. E. O. (2022). Plagiarism in higher academic institutions, a blight on intellectual integrity: an interventionist approach. *Asian Journal of Education and Social Studies*, 26(2), 88–100. http://doi.org/10.9734/AJESS/2022/v26i230626

Braga, I. (2021). Dealing with plagiarism in undergraduate education to achieve intellectual property rights. In *Proceedings of ICERI2021 Conference* (pp. 7538–7545). IATED. http://hdl.handle.net/10400.22/23731

Bruni-Bossio, V., & Willness, C. (2016). The "Kobayashi Maru" meeting: High-fidelity experiential learning. *Journal of Management Education*, 40(5), 619–647. https://doi.org/10.1177/1052562916644 2

Carriker, J. H., & Mayo, D. H. (2021). A framework for developing nascent entrepreneurs: Entrepreneurship education's Kobayashi Maru. *International Journal for Business Education, 161*(1), 4. https://doi.org/10.30707/IJBE161.1.1648090824.248879

Cheat, V., Sense 3.a. (2023). *Oxford English dictionary*, Oxford UP. https://doi.org/10.1093/OED/1084747490.

Conti, G., & Caroland, J. (2011). Embracing the Kobayashi Maru: Why you should teach your students to cheat. *IEEE Security & Privacy*, 9(4), 48–51. http://doi.org/10.1109/MSP.2011.80

Cruz, R. A., Firestone, A. R., & Rodl, J. E. (2021). Disproportionality reduction in exclusionary school discipline: A best-evidence synthesis. *Review of Educational Research, 91*(3), 397–431. https://doi.org/10.3102/0034654321995255

Cubukcu, Z. (2012). The effect of hidden curriculum on character education process of primary school students. *Educational Sciences: Theory and Practice, 12*(2), 1526–1534.

Davison, M., Penner, A. M., Penner, E. K., Pharris-Ciurej, N., Porter, S. R., Rose, E. K., Shem-Tov, Y., & Yoo, P. (2022). School discipline and racial disparities in early adulthood. *Educational Researcher, 51*(3), 231–234. https://doi.org/10.3102/0013189X211061732

Dunlap, J. C., & Lowenthal, P. R. (2010). Defeating the Kobayashi Maru: Supporting student retention by balancing the needs of the many and the one. *Educause Quarterly, 33*(4), 72.

Ecklar, J. (1989). *The Kobayashi Maru*. Pocket Books.

Fabelo T., Thompson M. D., Plotkin M., Carmichael D., Marchbanks M. P., Booth E. A. (2011). *Breaking schools' rules: A statewide study of how school discipline relates to students' success and juvenile justice involvement.* New York, NY: Council of State Governments Justice Center. Retrieved from http://knowledgecenter.csg.org/kc/content/breaking-schools-rules-statewide-study

Fadus, M. C., Valadez, E. A., Bryant, B. E., Garcia, A. M., Neelon, B., Tomko, R. L., & Squeglia, L. M. (2021). Racial disparities in elementary school disciplinary actions: findings from the ABCD study. *Journal of the American Academy of Child & Adolescent Psychiatry, 60*(8), 998–1009. https://doi.org/10.1016/j.jaac.2020.11.017

Memory Alpha. (2024). *Kobayashi Maru Scenario*. https://memory-alpha.fandom.com/wiki/Kobayashi_Maru_scenario

Frye, B. L. (2020). Plagiarize this paper. *IDEA, 60*, 294.

Garcia, A. (2012). The Kobayashi Maru of ex-offender employment: Rewriting the rules and thinking outside current ban the box legislation. *Temp. L. Rev., 85*, 921.

Garcia, J., & De Lissovoy, N. (2013). Doing school time: The hidden curriculum goes to prison. *Journal of Critical Education Policy Studies, 11*(4), 49–69.

Giroux, H. A. (1978). Developing educational programs: Overcoming the hidden curriculum. *The Clearing House, 52*(4), 148–151.

Giroux, H. A. (2003). Racial injustice and disposable youth in the age of zero tolerance. *International Journal of Qualitative Studies in Education, 16*(4), 553–565. https://doi.org/10.1080/00098655.1978.10113565

Giroux, H. A., & Penna, A. N. (1979). Social education in the classroom: The dynamics of the hidden curriculum. *Theory & Research in Social Education, 7*(1), 21–42. https://doi.org/10.1080/00933104.1979.10506048

Gregory, A., Skiba, R. J., & Noguera, P. A. (2010). The achievement gap and the discipline gap: Two sides of the same coin? *Educational Researcher, 39*, 59–68. https://doi.org/10.3102/0013189X09357621

Hernandez, A.O., Kaleem, J., & Gomez, M. (2024). LAPD arrests 93 people at USC amid Israel-Hamas war protests. *The Los Angeles Times.* https://www.latimes.com/california/story/2024-04-24/usc-pro-palestinian-encampment

Hirschfeld, P. J. (2008). Preparing for prison? The criminalization of school discipline in the USA. *Theoretical Criminology, 12*(1), 79–101. https://doi.org/10.1177/1362480607085795

Hoban, B. (2023). Kobayashi Maru. *British Journal of General Practice, 73*(736), 507. https://doi.org/10.3399/bjgp23X735405

Howick, J., Slavin, D., Carr, S., Miall, F., Ohri, C., Ennion, S., & Gay, S. (2024). Towards an empathic hidden curriculum in medical school: A roadmap. *Journal of Evaluation in Clinical Practice.* https://doi.org/10.1177/1362480607085795

H.R. 1532. (2011). *Race to the Top Act of 2011.* [Government]. U.S. Government Printing Office.

Jackson, P.W. (1968) *Life in classrooms.* London, U.K.: Holt, Rinehart and Winston, Inc.

Jackson, P. W., Boostrom, R. E., & Hansen, D. T. (1993) *The moral life of schools.* San Francisco, CA: Jossey-Bass Publishers.

Jones, B. D. (2007). The unintended outcomes of high-stakes testing. *Journal of applied school psychology, 23*(2), 65–86. https://doi.org/10.1300/J370v23n02_05

Kupchik, A., & Ellis, N. (2008). School discipline and security: Fair for all students? *Youth & Society, 39*(4), 549–574. https://doi.org/10.1177/0044118X07301956

Lee, S., & Skog, A. P. (2014). Kobayashi Maru in medical simulation: The educational utility of the no win patient scenario. *Annals of Emergency Medicine, 64*(4), S8–S9. https://doi.org/10.1016/j.annemergmed.2014.07.045

Mandel, G. N., Fast, A. A., & Olson, K. R. (2015). Intellectual property law's plagiarism fallacy. *BYU L. Rev.*, 915.

Manuel, F. (2016). The politics of global warming: Sciemocracy and the rescue of the Kobayashi Maru. *Journal of Globalization Studies, 7*(1), 3–29.

Marcucci, O. (2020). Implicit bias in the era of social desirability: Understanding antiblackness in rehabilitative and punitive school discipline. *The Urban Review, 52*(1), 47–74. https://doi.org/10.1007/s11256-019-00512-7

Markle. R. (2020). Assessment, growth mindset, and Star Trek: The Kobayashi Maru. *The College Knowledge Blog.* DIA Higher Education Collaborators. https://www.diahighered.com/post/assessment-growth-mindset-and-star-trek-the-kobayashi-maru

Martin, P. C. (2012). Misuse of high-stakes test scores for evaluative purposes: Neglecting the reality of schools and students. *Current Issues in Education, 15*(3). Retrieved from https://cie.asu.edu/ojs/index.php/cieatasu/article/view/1061

Meyer, N. (Director). (1982). *Star Trek II: The Wrath of Khan* [Film]. Paramount Pictures.

Miller, R. T. (2017). Smith v. Van Gorkom and the Kobayashi Maru: The place of the trans union case in the development of Delaware corporate law. *Wm. & Mary Bus. L. Rev.*, 9, 65.

Moon, T. R., Brighton, C. M., Jarvis, J. M., & Hall, C. J. (2007). State standardized testing programs: Their effects on teachers and students. *National Research Center on the Gifted and Talented.*

National Center for Education Statistics. (2023). Characteristics of public school teachers. *Condition of Education.* U.S. Department of Education, Institute of Education Sciences. Retrieved June 15, 2024, from https://nces.ed.gov/programs/coe/indicator/clr.

National Commission on Excellence in Education. (1983). A nation at risk: The imperative for educational reform. *The Elementary School Journal*, 84(2), 113–130.

Nguyen, S. (2024). The plagiarism allegations against ex-Harvard president Claudine Gay, explained. *The Washington Post.* https://www.washingtonpost.com/books/2024/01/04/claudine-gay-plagiarism-examples-harvard/

No Child Left Behind Act of 2001, Pub. L. No. 107-110, § 115, Stat. 1425 (2002).

Office for Civil Rights, U.S. Department of Education (2002). *Elementary and secondary school civil rights compliance reports.* Retrieved from http://www.ed.gov/offices/OCR/data.html/

Ortiz, Alisha, Ray, Julie A., Wilburn, Victor R., Odegard-Koester, Melissa, and Ball, Jeremy (2019). "Interim leadership positions: The Kobayashi Maru of academia?," *Academic Chairpersons Conference Proceedings.* https://newprairiepress.org/accp/2019/working/7

Park, S. K., Chen, A. M., Daugherty, K. K., Frankart, L. M., & Koenig, R. A. (2023). A scoping review of the hidden curriculum in pharmacy education. *American Journal of Pharmaceutical Education*, 87(3). https://doi.org/10.5688/ajpe8999

Petras, H., Masyn, K. E., Buckley, J. A., Ialongo, N. S., & Kellam, S. (2011). Who is most at risk for school removal? A multilevel discrete-time survival analysis of individual- and context-level influences. *Journal of Educational Psychology, 103*(1), 223–237. https://doi.org/10.1037/a0021545

Plagiarism, N., Sense 1. (2023). *Oxford English dictionary*, Oxford UP. https://doi.org/10.1093/OED/2684628460.

Polesel, J., Rice, S., & Dulfer, N. (2014). The impact of high-stakes testing on curriculum and pedagogy: A teacher perspective from Australia. *Journal of Education Policy*, 29(5), 640–657. https://doi-org.stmartin.idm.oclc.org/10.1080/02680939.2013.865082

Portelli, J. P. (1993). Exposing the hidden curriculum. *Journal of curriculum studies, 25*(4), 343–358. https://doi.org/10.1080/0022027930250404

Roddenberry, G. (1966–present). *Star Trek.* Paramount Global.

Rossouw, N., & Frick, L. (2023). A conceptual framework for uncovering the hidden curriculum in private higher education. *Cogent Education, 10*(1), 2191409. https://doi.org/10.1080/2331186X.2023.2191409

Schwabenland, C., & Kofinas, A. (2023). Ducks, elephants and sharks: Using LEGO® Serious Play® to surface the 'hidden curriculum' of equality, diversity and inclusion. *Management Learning, 54*(3), 318–337. https://doi.org/10.1177/13505076231166850

Shelton, S. A., & Brooks, T. (2019). "We need to get these scores up": A narrative examination of the challenges of teaching Literature in the age of standardized testing. *Journal of Language and Literacy Education, 15*(2), n2.

Skiba, R. J., Mediratta, K., & Karega Rausch, M. (Eds.), (2016). *Inequality in school discipline: Research and practice to reduce disparities.* New York, NY: Palgrave Macmillan. https://doi.org/10.1057/978-1-137-51257-4

Skiba, R. J., Horner, R. H., Chung, C. G., Rausch, M. K., May, S. L., & Tobin, T. (2011). Race is not neutral: A national investigation of African American and Latino disproportionality in school discipline. *School psychology review,* 40(1), 85–107. https://doi.org/10.1080/02796015.2011.12087730

Smolkowski K., Girvan E. J., McIntosh K., Nese R., Horner, R. H. (2016). Vulnerable decision points for disproportionate office discipline referrals: Comparisons of discipline for African American and white elementary school students. *Behavioral Disorders, 41*(4), 178–195. https://doi.org/10.17988/bedi-41-04-178-195.1

Stemwedel, J. (2015). The philosophy of Star Trek: The Kobayashi Maru, no-win scenarios, and ethical leadership. *Forbes.com.* https://www.forbes.com/sites/janetstemwedel/2015/08/23/the-philosophy-of-star-trek-the-kobayashi-maru-no-win-scenarios-and-ethical-leadership/?sh=1e1d03585f48

Thornberg, R. (2007). Inconsistencies in everyday patterns of school rules. *Ethnography and education,* 2(3), 401–416. http://dx.doi.org/10.1080/17457820701547609.

University of Oxford. (2021). *Plagiarism.* https://www.ox.ac.uk/students/academic/guidance/skills/plagiarism

Vavrus F., Cole K. M. (2002). "I didn't do nothin'": The discursive construction of school suspension. *Urban Review,* 34, 87–111. https://doi.org/10.1023/A:1015375215801

Values. USC. (2024, April 10). https://www.usc.edu/we-are-usc/the-university/values/

Whitsed, C., & Green, W. (2016). Lessons from Star Trek: Engaging academic staff in the internationalisation of the curriculum. *International Journal for Academic Development, 21*(4), 286–298. https://doi.org/10.1080/1360144X.2016.1170019

Wiley, K. E. (2021). A tale of two logics: School discipline and racial disparities in a "mostly white" middle school. *American Journal of Education,* 127(2), 163–192.

Yoho, L. M., & Moore, J. D. (2023). "There's an unspoken set of rules": Rural education in the Northern Plains. The Rural Educator, 44(4), 1–14. https://doi.org/10.55533/2643-9662.1366

CHAPTER SIX

There is No Try: Deficit Models and The Banking Concept in *The Empire Strikes Back*

The Text: *Star Wars—Episode V—The Empire Strikes Back* (Kirshner, 1980). Film.

Introduction

I WAS THE PRESIDENT of my high school's *Star Wars* fan club. I tell you this not to impress you (though it is undoubtedly having that effect) but rather to highlight that I have spent *a lot* of time thinking about Yoda.

I am not the only one who has thought a lot about Yoda, though. Even today, more than 40 years after his first appearance in the *Star Wars* franchise, Yoda's name is still synonymous with "the master of" or "the best at." A quick Google and admittedly un-scientific search of the phrase "the Yoda of" yields some interesting results, including:

- A *New York Times* article about a computer programmer known as "The Yoda of Silicon Valley" (Roberts, 2018);
- A link to a YouTube Video of freestyle rapper Harry Mack in which he calls himself the "Yoda of the Dark Streets" (Mack, 2022);
- The YODA Project, which refers to Yale University's efforts to create a

forum for sharing clinical research data and promoting so-called "open science" (Yale University, n.d.);

- A business consulting firm that trains corporations in using "The Yoda Process" to run meetings more efficiently (Tip of the Spear, 2017);
- A video series about the U.S. Constitution hosted by professor Akhil Reed Amar, whom National Public Radio dubbed "The Yoda of constitutional law" (Constitutional Accountability Center, 2013);
- An X (formerly Twitter) thread by @samuel_colvin in which he refers to his friend @davidhewittdev as "the Yoda of using Rust with Python" (Colvin, 2024); and
- The Yoda, a "smooth all green juice that will have you feeling extra revitalized by its alkaline nature" (Juice Ranch, 2022, n.p.).

Just in case you are one of the few unfortunate souls who does *not* know who Yoda is, here is some important context. *The Empire Strikes Back* (Kirshner, 1980) was released just three years after the enormously popular original *Star Wars* (Lucas, 1977). The sequel, which, when adjusted for inflation, is the 6th highest grossing film of all time, introduced the world to Yoda, the tiny, green Jedi master who is tasked with overseeing the education and training of Luke Skywalker. Although Luke's training begins in *Star Wars* (Lucas, 1977),[1] it is in *The Empire Strikes Back* (Kirshner, 1980) that we first see extended and well-developed scenes of focused and formal educational activity in the *Star Wars* (Lucas, 1977–present) universe.

Yoda, whose backwards syntax and gravelly voice are as distinctive as his long ears and diminutive stature, quickly entered (and remains in) the public consciousness as a master of both the Force *and* of teaching. For example, a 2015 article in the mainstream magazine *Wired* made the bold claim that in order to improve student learning, "we should be teaching our students the way that Yoda taught Luke" (Phillips, 2015, n.p.). The article claims that Yoda's teaching style and philosophy emerge from the Platonic tradition of ancient Greece. The Platonic tradition (the article claims) was highly individualistic, personalized, and flexible. The author cites a number of contemporary studies to support claims that personalized learning is more effective than the alternative, and the author encourages readers to support learning systems that go "faster and further" (Phillips, 2015, n.p.) to reach more students. The way of Yoda, they claim, is the way of success.

I don't think this is true, and the article mentioned just now manages somehow to misinterpret both Yoda *and* Plato. In fact, a critical analysis of Yoda's teaching methods and the philosophies on which they are based reveals a highly troubling dynamic among teacher, student, and society. Yoda's pedagogy is fundamentally *de*-humanizing. It serves the system, not the individual, despite what the article in *Wired* might claim, and despite our cultural (mis)conceptions about Yoda's pedagogical prowess. A critical analysis of Yoda in *The Empire Strikes Back* (Kirshner, 1980) reveals how oppressive pedagogical practices often masquerade as caring and humanistic, claiming to set students free while actually tightening the chains that bind them.

The Story

Dagobah is a bad place to try to land your spaceship. The planet, which is in the galactic middle-of-nowhere, is one giant swamp. There's almost no dry land, and to make matters worse, the thick cloud layer really messes with your sensors. Even if there were a good spot to land, you probably couldn't see it. So it is no surprise that Luke Skywalker, the farm-boy-turned-Rebel-soldier, ends up landing smack dab in the middle of the swamp. He and his droid companion, R2-D2, manage to swim to safety after they crash, and now they are sitting on the muddy shore along with the few supplies they managed to salvage, sopping wet, watching as Luke's X-Wing, which is their only way of ever getting off this planet, sinks beneath the algae-covered waters.

To make matters worse, Luke doesn't really understand why they are here in the first place. During one of his many near-death experiences, Luke had a vision of his first teacher, Obi-Wan Kenobi, telling him to go to Dagobah and find Yoda, the Jedi-Master who was, in fact, Obi-Wan's first teacher. Obi-Wan had begun training Luke in the ways of the Force a few years back but had managed to get himself killed not long after the first lesson, leaving Luke with no one to help him level up.

So when ghost-Obi-Wan tells Luke to find Yoda in order to continue his training, Luke is initially excited. The excitement quickly wears off, however. Crash landing in a swamp often has that effect.

As Luke and R2-D2 try to set up some sort of camp, a small, green alien appears and offers to help them find what they are looking for. Luke is immediately annoyed. The alien's "help" is more of a hindrance. He is rooting through Luke's tools, nibbling on Luke's food, and generally making a mess. Luke is about to lose his cool, and he urges the "little fella" (Kirshner, 1980) to leave them alone, because they're there to meet a Jedi-Master.

"Ooooh," the little fella responds. "Yoda. You seek Yoda" (Kirshner, 1980)! He offers to take Luke and R2-D2 to Yoda's home, and the three of them set off together.

But they don't go to see Yoda. They take a detour and end up at the alien's hut to escape the rain. Luke warms himself by the fire while the alien cooks dinner, and the two settle into an uncomfortable conversation:

Luke: How far away is Yoda? Will it take us long to get there?

Alien: Not far. Yoda not far. Patience. Soon you will be with him.

The alien moves to the fire to stir the soup.

Alien: Why wish you become Jedi?

Luke [*picking at his soup*]: Mostly because of my father, I guess.

Alien: Oh. Father. Powerful Jedi was he. Mmmm. Powerful Jedi.

Luke [*interrupting*]: Oh, come on. How could you know my father? You don't even know who I am. [*Luke grows angry.*] And I don't even know what I'm doing here. We're wasting our time! [*Luke throws his bowl down in frustration.*]

The alien is silent for a moment. He sighs, and begins talking to someone off screen.

Alien: I cannot teach him. The boy has no patience.

The voice of Obi-Wan Kenobi, Luke's very dead former teacher, fills the air.

Obi-Wan: He will learn patience.

Luke starts and looks around the room, searching for the source of the voice. The alien, meanwhile, turns from the fire and looks straight at Luke.

Alien: Much anger in him. Like his father.

Obi-Wan: Was I any different when you taught me?

Alien: Mmm. [*He once again faces Luke, appraising him, judging him.*] He is not ready.

Luke [*realizing the truth*]: Yoda?

The alien nods.

Luke: I *am* ready. I . . . Ben . . . I can be a Jedi. Ben, tell him I'm . . . [*In his excitement, Luke tries to stand and hits his head on the low ceiling.*]

Yoda: Ready, are you? What know you of ready? For 800 years have I trained Jedi. My own council will I keep on who is to be trained. Jedi must have the deepest commitment. The most serious mind. [*He turns, as if talking directly to Obi-Wan Kenobi.*] This one, a long time have I watched. All his life has he looked away to the future, to the horizon. Never his mind on where he was! [*He turns back to Luke and pokes him hard with his cane.*] Hmm? What he was doing. Hmm! Adventure? Ha! Excitement? Ha! A Jedi craves not these things. [*He turns directly to Luke, looking him in the eye.*] You are reckless . . . [and] too old to begin the training.

Luke: But I've learned so much.

Yoda sighs. He pauses, and then turns his head, as if talking to Obi-Wan.

Yoda: Will he finish what he begins?

Luke: I won't fail you. I'm not afraid.

Yoda immediately turns back to Luke. He draws closer, eyes narrowed. Luke draws back.

Yoda: Oh? You will be. You will be. (Kirshner, 1980)

And so Luke's training begins. The first step in his new curriculum is to tame his body, and so he begins a grueling exercise regimen, running and climbing his way through the swamp while Yoda, who is strapped to Luke's back like a toddler going for a hike with his dad, lectures him about the nature of the Force.

"Run!" (Kirshner, 1980)Yoda yells.

Luke, who is already running, picks up the pace.

"Yes," Yoda continues. "A Jedi's strength flows from the Force. But beware of the dark side. Anger, fear, aggression—the dark side of the Force are they. Easily they flow, quick to join you in a fight. Once you start down the dark path, forever will it dominate your destiny. Consume you it will."

Luke pauses to catch his breath. "Is the dark side stronger?"

"No," Yoda assures him. "Quicker. Easier. More seductive."

"But how am I to know the good side from the bad?" Luke asks, clearly confused.

Yoda shakes his head, frustrated by Luke's question. "You will know when you are calm, at peace, passive." He pauses before continuing. "A Jedi uses the Force for knowledge and defense. Never for attack" (Kirshner, 1980).

This answer doesn't satisfy Luke. "But tell me why I can't . . ."

"No!" Yoda interrupts. "No! There is no why!" He sighs in frustration. "Nothing more will I teach you today. Clear your mind of questions" (Kirshner, 1980).

Despite Luke's insistence on asking questions that Yoda doesn't want to answer, his training seems to be working. Things are going well until his X-Wing, which had been partially submerged up to this point, disappears completely beneath the water. R2-D2 bleep-bloops in alarm, distracting Luke and causing him to lose his concentration and drop the rocks he had been lifting with the Force. He runs to the water's edge and cries out in despair. "Oh no! We'll never get it out now."

Yoda scowls. "So certain are you?" He sighs. "Always with you it cannot be done."

Luke shrugs. "Alright. I'll give it a try."

"No!" Yoda counters. "Try not. Do, or do not. There is no try."

So Luke tries to lift the X-Wing from the swamp using the Force. But he can't do it, and he collapses on the sand. "I can't," he gasps. "It's too big."

Yoda is unimpressed. "Size matters not. Judge me by my size, do you? Hmm?"

Luke shakes his head.

Yoda grunts. "Hmm. And well you should not. For my ally is the Force, and a powerful ally it is. Life creates it, makes it grow. Its energy surrounds us and binds us. Luminous beings are we. Not this crude matter." He pinches Luke's shoulder by way of demonstration. "You must feel the Force around you. Here, between you, me, the tree, the rock, everywhere." He pauses in response to Luke's unasked question. "Yes, even between the land and the ship" (Kirshner, 1980).

Luke stands and brushes himself off. "You want the impossible," he says before storming off.

Yoda sighs, shakes his head, and promptly uses the Force to lift the ship out of the water and fly it over to dry land. Luke comes running and stares, mouth hanging open, as Yoda sets the ship down, safe and sound. "I don't believe it," Luke gasps.

Yoda nods, as if his deepest suspicions have been confirmed. "*That*, is why you fail."

The incident with the X-Wing seems to have been a turning point for Luke, and his training goes into high gear. Soon, Yoda has him standing on his hands and lifting various objects with his mind all while settling into some sort of Zen-like state.

"Good," Yoda whispers as Luke's eyes close in calm concentration. "Through the Force, things you will see, other places. The future, the past. Old friends, long gone."

Luke's eyes fly open, and he tumbles to the ground, dropping all the objects he has been levitating.

Yoda, who seems to be perpetually sighing, sighs again. "Control. Control! You must learn control!"

Luke struggles to his feet. He is in a daze and greatly troubled. "I saw . . . I saw a city in the clouds."

Yoda nods. "Friends you have there."

Luke blinks. He turns to Yoda in desperation. "They were in pain!"

Yoda is quiet for a moment. "It is the future you see," (Kirshner, 1980) he says gently.

Luke recoils. "The future." He turns, as if to walk away, then turns back. "Will they die" (Kirshner, 1980)?

Yoda closes his eyes, looking. "Difficult to say," he says finally. "Always in motion is the future."

Luke turns again, this time resolutely. "I've got to go to them."

Yoda lets him walk a few steps before calling out. "Decide you must, how to serve them best. If you leave now, help them you could, but . . ." He lets the silence draw out. "You would destroy all for which they have fought and suffered."

Luke nods, but he is unconvinced. When we see him next, he is packing up the X-Wing and getting ready to take off. Yoda watches forlornly from below.

"Luke," he says almost desperately, "you must complete the training."

Luke grunts as if in pain. "I can't keep the vision out of my head. They're my friends. I have to help them."

Yoda shakes his head. "You must not go!"

"But Han and Leia will die if I don't," Luke retorts.

Before Yoda can respond, the voice of Obi-Wan Kenobi breaks in. "You don't know that." A shimmering image of Obi-Wan appears. "Even Yoda cannot see their fate."

Luke steps toward his teachers. "But I can help them! I feel the Force."

"But you cannot control it," Obi-Wan counters. "This is a dangerous time for you, when you will be tempted by the dark side of the Force."

"Yes, yes!" Yoda chimes in. "To Obi-Wan you listen." He then reminds Luke of all his failures, citing specific examples of all the times that Luke has fallen short of the Jedi standard.

Luke turns back to preparing the X-Wing. "But I've learned so much since then. Master Yoda, I promise to return and finish what I've begun. You have my word" (Kirshner, 1980).

Yoda won't let it go. "Only a fully trained Jedi knight, with the Force as his ally, can conquer Vader and his emperor. If you end your training now, if you take the quick and easy path . . . you will become an agent of evil."

Obi-Wan agrees. "Patience."

Luke has had enough. He whirls around. "And sacrifice Han and Leia" he spits out, furious that his teachers are asking this of him.

Yoda doubles down. "If you honor what they fight for . . . yes."

Luke quiets and nods. "I understand" (Kirshner, 1980). He pauses, and Yoda dares to hope that maybe he's gotten through to his wayward student. But the moment passes. Luke tells R2-D2 to fire up the engines, and the X-Wing lifts off, soaring through the atmosphere toward the cloud city of Luke's visions where his friends are waiting to be rescued.

The Critical Analysis

An examination of Yoda's teaching is remarkable not because of how good or effective he is but rather because of just how pedagogically unsound his methods are. This "unsoundness" is not an issue of style or outdated practices. The pedagogical canon is neither fixed nor static; practices come in and out of favor much like planets whose elliptical and eccentric orbits bring them close to the sun for a time before hurtling them off into the dark, distant reaches of space (Harris, 1991). Instructional techniques that are popular today may be considered anachronistic or old-fashioned tomorrow. And, in many cases, these same techniques will circle back around to once again enjoy their time in the sun.

But the elliptical canonicity of specific pedagogical practices is not the heart of the issue. The fundamental flaw in Yoda's pedagogy is not a matter of technique; it is, instead, a matter of philosophy. Yoda's methods are unsound not so much because of *how* he interacts with his student (although the *how* is indeed problematic) but rather because of what the *how* reveals about the *why*. In other terms, Yoda's instructional practices lay bare his underlying assumptions about the nature of the teacher/student relationship and the primary purposes of teaching and learning.

To understand more about Yoda's flawed and disturbing philosophical assumptions, we turn to 20th-century educator and activist, Paulo Freire.

Paulo Freire and "Pedagogy of the Oppressed."

Paulo Freire's contribution to critical pedagogy cannot be overstated. His book, *Pedagogy of the Oppressed* (Freire, 1970), is perhaps the most well-known critical pedagogy text of the 20th century, and it is based on Freire's work educating impoverished peoples in his native Brazil. It is a staple of both undergraduate- and graduate-level teacher preparation programs, and Freire's thoughts on the relationships among power, education, and oppression continue to shape and form our contemporary understandings of critical pedagogy.

The Banking Concept of Education

Freire describes the power dynamics of oppressive education systems by using a system of binary lenses. These lenses divide the classroom in two, drawing clear lines between opposing parties. On one side of the room we have the teacher, who, acting as an agent of the system, operates with a stamp of official authority. As an agent of the state or, at the very least, a representative of the dominant power structure, the teacher is responsible for maintaining the processes, protocols, and principles that keep the system working. Consequently, the power differentials in the classroom can and should be viewed as a microcosm of the power differentials in society at large. When the teacher maintains order/power in the classroom, she is, in effect, teaching students how to function properly in their pre-existing societal roles.

And how are students to function? What are these roles? Because the teacher and the student are binary and opposing forces, the student can be read as the inverse or negation of the teacher. Whatever the teacher is expected to do, the "good" student is expected to do the opposite. For example, if a teacher is expected to provide a set of rules that clearly define acceptable and unacceptable behavior, the student is expected to *follow* those rules without question.

These binary and oppositional roles extend to nearly every facet of classroom life, from instructional practices and curricular sequencing to classroom management and student participation. Consider the following questions about the typical school classroom:

- Who is allowed to speak at will, and who must ask permission to speak?
- Who has freedom of movement, and who is confined to a desk?
- Who makes decisions about classroom protocols, and who must adhere to those protocols?
- Who determines what will be learned, and who learns what they are told to learn?
- Who decides the appropriate way to demonstrate understanding, and who must provide predetermined evidence of understanding whenever asked?
- Who controls when others may eat, stand, go outside, or use the restroom, and whose body is being controlled?
- Who possesses official knowledge, and who must be filled with that knowledge?
- Whose fitness for their classroom role is determined by their action, and whose fitness is determined by their passivity?
- Who acts, and who is acted upon?

As I hope you can see, these are not idle questions. For Freire (and, sadly, for many of those reading this book), these questions highlight the gross classroom power differentials that are too often the ostensible hallmark of a "good" and "effective" learning space. The good students are the well-behaved students, the students who quietly do their work, obey the rules, and do not assert their own agency. The good students are those who memorize what they're told to memorize and then repeat it for the test, regardless of whether they will remember any of it after the test or whether it is relevant to their lives in any appreciable way. The good student participates eagerly in the system that rewards their compliance with a favorable credit rating (such as a 4.0), regardless of how much they have actually *learned*. In fact, the good student does not question the fact that their entire K–12 education can be reduced to a number. A good student receives what they are told to receive, end of story.

Freire (1970) referred to this as the *banking concept* (p. 76) of education. Just as a person might make a deposit into a bank account, the teacher deposits knowledge into the willing and passive student. The student does not determine the value of the knowledge; that determination has already been made. Freire's (1970) own words say it best:

> [In the banking concept of education], the teacher's task is to organize a process which already occurs spontaneously, to "fill" the students by making deposits of information which he or she considers to constitute true knowledge. And since people "receive" the world as passive entities, education should make them more passive still, and adapt them to the world. The educated individual is the adapted person, because she or he is better "fit" for the world. Translated into practice, this concept is well suited to the purposes of the oppressors, whose tranquility rests on how well people fit the world the oppressors have created, and how little they question it. (p. 76)

This banking concept, Freire argues, is rooted in dehumanization. It strips the learner of their humanity and agency, rendering them little more than empty vessels, waiting to be filled and emptied according to the needs and whims of those charged with filling them.

Yoda and The Banking Concept

Unfortunately for poor Luke Skywalker, Yoda seems to have stolen a page right out of the oppressors' pedagogical playbook. In one of their very first encounters, Luke presumes to assert his own readiness to learn the ways of the Force. Yoda's response—"What know you of ready?" (Kirshner, 1980)—is telling. He questions Luke's ability to make his own learning decisions. Luke's opinions about his own education do not matter. He knows nothing, or at least nothing of importance. Only Yoda, with his 800 years of Jedi-training experience, is to be trusted.

Tabula Rasa

In philosophical terms, Yoda views Luke as *tabula rasa*—a blank slate. Contrary to Romantic philosophies that urge learners to look within themselves to discover the knowledge hidden deep inside (see Chapter Four), enlightenment philosophies of learning begin with the assumption that the learner is born with no innate knowledge. Although people are born with the mental and physical structures that will enable them to learn, they come into the world with absolutely no knowledge in their minds. Learning, then, is not a matter of looking inward, because there's nothing there to see. On the contrary, learning requires looking outward. It is an empirical endeavor. The learner uses their senses to take in the world around them. When they have absorbed enough information, they are able to begin thinking about what they have seen. Eventually, they are able to learn through reasoning. Before they can reason, however, they have to put some words on the empty page of their minds. Consider the words of enlightenment philosopher John Locke (1690):

> The senses at first let in PARTICULAR ideas, and furnish the yet empty cabinet, and the mind by degrees growing familiar with some of them, they are lodged in the memory, and names got to them. Afterwards, the mind proceeding further, abstracts them, and by degrees learns the use of general names. In this manner the mind comes to be furnished with ideas and language, the MATERIALS about which to exercise its discursive faculty. And the use of reason becomes daily more visible, as these materials that give it employment increase. (Chapter II, section 15)

Although the precise details of Locke's argument are beyond the scope of this chapter, his general belief that the mind of the learner is an "empty cabinet" that needs to be "furnished" is the basis of Yoda's attempts to reject Luke as his student. When Yoda asks Luke "what know you of ready?," he is working from the assumption that Luke has come to him as an empty vessel. His question—*what do you know?*—is rhetorical. He doesn't expect Luke to answer, because he already knows the answer: Luke doesn't know anything. He is *tabula rasa*. There's nothing written on the Word document of his mind.

The reason that Luke's mind is empty is because he has never really looked at the world around him. He has been looking inward, using his imagination, instead of focusing his attention outward, using his senses to gather empirical information that he can then use to start reasoning. Consider Yoda's description of Luke: "All his life has he looked away to the future. Never his mind on where he was! What he was doing!" (Kirshner, 1980). Luke's failure to approach the world empirically means that he has not yet gathered the necessary raw materials for reasoning. He is incapable of reaching informed decisions, incapable of guiding his own learning, incapable of shaping the process of his own education, even to the slightest degree. According to Yoda, Luke is behind before he has even begun.

The Deficit Model

In Yoda's estimation, Luke is a problem in need of a solution. He has arrived in the learning space underprepared and incapable. Yoda lists his flaws: he is too old; he is not ready; he is reckless; he lacks focus; he has no patience. According to Yoda, the reason Luke cannot learn is not because the learning environment isn't conducive to learning or because his teacher is not up to the task. Instead, Luke cannot learn for the simple reason that he, himself, is broken. His failures are not due to external factors; instead, his failures are due to his own internal qualities (or, rather, lack of qualities).

In contemporary educational speak, this mindset is referred to as the *deficit model* or *deficit thinking*. In American education history, the deficit model rose to prominence in the late 1980s and continued through the 2010s (and, in many ways, continues to this day). The "achievement gap" between Black and white K–12 students provides a good example. On one hand, there is the documented fact that Black students graduate from high school and enter college at lower rates than their white counterparts. Simply acknowledging the reality of the achievement gap is not, in and of itself, an example of deficit thinking. However, when researchers, politicians, and educators in the late 1980s tried to identify the *cause* of the achievement gap, they did so by highlighting the so-called "deficiencies" in the Black community. Black students, it was claimed, performed poorly in schools due to inherent deficiencies in their cultural, communal, and familial institutions. A common rhetoric began to emerge: Black parents don't care; Black children are not exposed to meaningful experiences outside school; Black children begin school "not ready" to learn; Black families don't value education; Black learners come from a "culture of poverty" (Ladson-Billings, 2007). These deficiencies, it was said, explained and accounted for the differences in performance between Black and white students. If these explanations were accurate, then the first step in closing the achievement gap would be to "fix" what is broken in Black students' bodies and lives.

Of course, this simplistic and casually racist attribution of *deficit* as a way of explaining differences in performance between Black and white students is utterly absurd, and yet this language of deficit thinking nevertheless remains disturbingly common, especially in teacher preparation programs. I recently interviewed a pre-service teacher who said that she wanted to work specifically with students of color. When I asked her why, she said that "so many students of color are missing an important figure . . . [and] a teacher can fill the void" (Delamarter, 2023, p. 189). Her stereotyped and demonstrably incorrect assumptions about the nature of Black families and the ability of the teacher to "fix" what is broken were deeply unsettling, but they are prime examples of deficit thinking.

Far too often, deficit thinking morphs from being an explanation of difference and becomes, instead, a defining factor of the "other." When one group—usually the dominant group—views itself as "normal," any deviation from that self-ascribed normality is viewed as abnormal. As the prefix "ab" suggests, any behavior or trait that deviates from the norm is defined by its deviance. Consider the oft taken-for-granted phrase *disabled students*. The prefix "dis" tells us all we need to know. The behaviors, traits, and skills of the dominant group are the norm. Consequently, there is no need for a qualifier or adjective before "students." Learners in this group are almost never called "abled students." They are simply "students." No prefix is necessary, because they are the "normal" ones.

But learners whose behaviors, traits, and skills deviate from the so-called norm *are*, in fact, given a qualifier. They are defined by their deviance from the norm. The "*dis*abled" student is the one who learns differently and, by extension, deficiently. "Abled" is the assumed norm. It is so assumed that it doesn't even need to be said when referring to mainstream students. The qualifier is only used when referring to the "other." The deficit thinking of the dominant group is encoded into the adjective "*dis*abled."

And this is where critical pedagogues raise a crucial point: Difference does not necessarily equate to deficiency. In fact, deficit thinking is so dangerous because it ignores the *strengths* associated with difference (e.g., Davidson & Orsini, 2013; Prizant & Field-Meyers, 2015; Silberman, 2015). For example, deficit thinking related to neurodivergence, such as autism, has led educators and researchers to focus almost exclusively on autistic learners' "weakness" and to ignore almost completely their cognitive strengths, such as attention to detail (Dinishak, 2022). This hyper focus on perceived "weakness" is exactly what Yoda has done with Luke. Difference has been equated with deficiency, and Yoda seems almost eager to highlight all of Luke's faults, gleefully citing his differences from the "normal" student (e.g., "he is too old") as justifications for refusing to teach him. Luke has been reduced to his perceived flaws. He has been defined by his so-called deficiencies, and his entire learning experience is rooted in the unquestioned assumption that any learning that takes place will happen *in spite of*, not because of, his fundamental (and unalterable) traits.

Funds of Knowledge

What would Luke's learning experience have been like if Yoda had begun their teacher/student relationship not by giving a litany of Luke's supposed weaknesses but instead by listing all the assets that an older learner might bring to the learning space? It is not difficult to imagine how age and experience might be an asset when learning the ways of the Force, and yet Yoda apparently never even considers this possibility. The idea that a learner might be defined not by their deficiencies but rather by their assets is often referred to as an *assets-based* approach to learning. Fundamental to an assets-based approach is the assumption that each learner enters the learning space with their own *funds of knowledge*. The teacher's job is not to fill students with the proper currency but rather to tap into and grow the funds they already have. As noted, this assumption stands in direct and stark contradiction to the deficit thinking that Freire laments when describing the banking concept of education.

Research into funds of knowledge as an integral part of equitable education first began in the 1980s (Ramos & Kiyama, 2021). Interestingly, learners' funds of knowledge are often not academic, per se, or at least not initially. For example, researchers have highlighted the ways that households, families, and communities have accumulated specific knowledge related to specific occupational tasks, household responsibilities, and even basic survival (e.g., Moll et al., 1992; Velez-Ibanez, 1988). While the relevance of these specific funds of knowledge may not be immediately apparent in an academic setting, these funds may be converted into assets as part of the educational process (Rios-Aguilar et al., 2011). Think of this as a sort of currency exchange, in which the "foreign money" that a learner has brought from home can be turned into legal tender that can be used in the classroom and other academic settings.

Education as Currency

This money metaphor must be explored further, for it sits at the heart of the banking concept of education. The terms "banking," "funds," and "currency" all relate to "wealth." Freire's decision to align education and wealth through the metaphor of banking was deliberate, though perhaps not for the reasons we might initially suspect. Freire's assertion—that oppressive education systems treat learners like empty bank accounts into which the teacher deposits funds—compels us to ask a simple question: Who is making "money" from these deposits?

In economic terms, which are the terms that Freire uses, the funds deposited into students' heads are a type of *currency*, a medium of transaction that facilitates the exchange of goods and services, like exchanging a few dollars for a cup of coffee. The buyer and the seller simply exchange one thing for the other. As long as the buyer and the seller agree to the exchange, everything works.

As a metaphor for learning, however, currency has some problems. For example, when the market of exchange becomes saturated with a particular currency, that currency begins to lose its value. It takes more and more currency to complete the exchange of goods. This is inflation. The cup of coffee that cost $3.00 yesterday costs $5.00 today. The currency that held so much value just a few days ago suddenly doesn't have nearly the *exchange value* that it used to have.

Exchange value is the key understanding here, because currency has no intrinsic value. That is, it has no value in and of itself. It's just a piece of paper or, more commonly, ones and zeroes in a bank's software system. Its value lies solely in what it can be exchanged for. If sellers will not accept your currency, and you are unable to exchange your money for the goods you need, then your currency has no value. It is worthless.

The banking concept treats education as currency. Funds are deposited into students in the form of facts and skills. Students then exchange those funds for a paycheck, a grade on a test, entrance into college, etc. As a unit of exchange, those funds are valuable *as long as the person or institution you're trying to exchange with will accept your currency*. But what happens when the deposited funds add up to a 4.0 GPA, and then, due to grade inflation from AP courses, universities begin expecting applicants to have at least a 4.2? What happens when the facts and skills that were deposited into you are no longer needed in the marketplace? What happens when there are 100 jobs that require skill-set X, but there are 100,000 graduates who have had skill-set X deposited into them? Will you be able to exchange your currency for a job? What is the value of your currency-based education if you can no longer exchange it for anything?

These questions call to mind the "company stores" that emerged in the late 19th century in Appalachia and other economically depressed regions where "extractive industries" (that is, mining) became common (Sawyer, 2013). Companies would hire local workers to work in the mines, but they wouldn't pay them in dollars. Instead, workers were paid in scrip, a currency developed by the company that could only be spent at the company store, which was a literal store erected on or near the job site. Workers could buy groceries, clothes, and other household basics. Many companies built cheap housing on site that workers and their families could rent (again, using the scrip they were paid in). Quite often, the company would ensure that the cost of rent and groceries exceeded the workers' paychecks, forcing workers to borrow scrip from the company bank to make ends meet. And thus did the worker become a prisoner of the company: He was paid in currency that had exchange value in only one place, meaning that he could not spend his wages anywhere else (such renting a house not owned by the company). Furthermore, because the company controlled the currency, they could manipulate the exchange value, ensuring that the workers remained indebted and insolvent. Even if a worker did somehow manage to live within his means and save scrip, his savings would be worthless the moment he stepped off company property.

In educational terms, these company stores are akin to schools teaching students a set of skills which have value in and only in academic and limited work settings. Imagine, for example, the high-school English teacher whose primary focus is ensuring that students can create properly formatted MLA citations because they will "need this in college," or imagine a university that closes down humanities programs while simultaneously investing in "market-driven" majors like business, engineering, and other STEM fields. Imagine an elementary school that cuts recess time in half so that third graders can have extra math instruction or one that devotes weeks of instructional time to improving students' test-taking skills in anticipation of the upcoming standardized assessment. In each of these scenarios—which are so unquestioningly normal in contemporary education as to be absurd—teachers are depositing into students' heads not a widely-accepted currency but a company scrip. This is knowledge with limited exchange-value, and the inevitable result is not freedom but captivity. A liberal arts education is one designed to create a free citizen (*liberal* sharing a root with *liberty*), and yet more and more education systems are "paying" learners with an increasingly narrow set of knowledge and skills, leaving them bound by corporate interests, serving masters they did not realize they had.

Education as currency is a fundamentally broken concept, which is precisely what Freire (1970) highlighted through the metaphor of banking:

> In the banking concept of education, knowledge is a gift bestowed by those who consider themselves knowledgeable upon those whom they consider to know nothing. Projecting an absolute ignorance onto others, a characteristic of the ideology of oppression, negates education and knowledge as processes of inquiry. . . . It is not surprising that the banking concept of education regards [people] as adaptable, manageable beings. The more students work at storing the deposits entrusted to them, the less they develop the critical consciousness which would result from their intervention in the world as transformers of that world. The more completely they accept the passive role imposed on them, the more they tend simply to adapt to the world as it is and to the fragmented view of reality deposited in them. The capability of banking education to minimize or annul the students' creative power and to stimulate their credulity serves the interests of the oppressors, who care neither to have the world revealed nor to see it transformed. The oppressors use their "humanitarianism" to preserve a profitable situation. (pp. 72–73)

If the knowledge and skills gained in education have only exchange value, then they do not have intrinsic value for the learner and the learner's community. An education devoted solely to the depositing of currency leaves the learner subject to the whims of the market. It renders them powerless, dependent on forces outside their control to determine what is and what is not of value, what does and does not *matter*. This education is dehumanizing, reducing education to transaction and forgoing all possibility of transformation. This is an education designed for servitude, not freedom, and it is, in many ways, the education that dominates American education today.

Education as Capital

Although Yoda does not use banking or money metaphors when talking about Luke's education, he *does* often refer to the importance of the learner being *passive*. He says it explicitly: Luke will understand the ways of the Force when he is "calm. At peace, passive" (Kirshner, 1980). And how should Luke achieve this passivity? He should "clear [his] mind of questions" (Kirshner, 1980). The emptier the vessel, the easier it is to fill.

So Yoda attempts to deposit the right kind of funds into Luke, all the while ensuring his student's unquestioning subservience. Although Yoda gives lip-service to an interdependent connection between the learner and the subject being learned—"[The Force is] a powerful ally . . . Life creates it, makes it grow. Its energy surrounds us and binds us. . . . You must feel the Force around you. Here, between you, me, the tree, the rock, everywhere" (Kirshner, 1980)—his pedagogical practices actually reinforce the opposite. Instead of relationship and mutual submission, Yoda regularly emphasizes isolation and dominance. He talks a good game, but his true feelings come out when he is angry or stressed. When Luke fails a task, Yoda begins yelling about "control." When Luke asks questions, Yoda yells "No! There is no why!" (Kirshner, 1980). He tells Luke that there is either "do, or do not," but there is "no try" (Kirshner, 1980), suggesting that learning can be reduced to a simple, mechanical binary ("you can do it, or you can't"), ignoring the fundamentally formative and often non-linear nature of human learning. Perhaps most importantly, when Luke's friends are in danger, Yoda tells Luke to let them die in order to prove his allegiance to a power structure that requires its followers to be passive and empty. When Luke finally dares to question Yoda's commands, Yoda tells him that he is becoming "an agent of evil" (Kirshner, 1980), because there is no other possible explanation for a student who does not unquestioningly accept what is being deposited into him and who dares to draw his own conclusions and invest in a different kind of future.

Invest is the appropriate word here, especially if we are looking for alternatives to the "knowledge-as-currency" metaphor inherent in the banking concept. To be clear, critical pedagogues are not necessarily opposed to the idea that the facts and skills acquired during education may be exchanged for goods such as jobs. Indeed, providing learners with the skills and knowledge to be gainfully employed *is* one of the primary purposes of contemporary education, both in K–12 and beyond. But, as detailed, knowledge-as-currency is problematic for a host of reasons.

If we are compelled to use an economic metaphor for education, we should perhaps use *capital* instead of currency. Though the terms *currency* and *capital* are often used synonymously, they actually represent fundamentally different, albeit related, concepts. Whereas currency has exchange value (and *only* exchange value), and whereas that exchange value is unstable and often manipulated by those in power to keep learners "in their place," capital refers to an accumulated, stable, often embodied wealth (Bourdieu, 2018). Though currency may be a form of capital, it is only one of many ways that wealth might be stored.

> Capital is accumulated labor . . . it is what makes the games of society—not least, the economic game—something other than the simple games of chance, offering at every moment the possibility of a miracle. Roulette . . . gives a fairly accurate image of this imaginary universe of perfect competition or perfect equality of opportunity, a world without inertia, without accumulation, without heredity or acquired properties, in which every moment is perfectly independent of the pervious one . . . and every prize can be attained, instantaneously, by everyone, so that at each moment anyone can become anything. [In contrast,] Capital . . . [which] takes time to accumulate . . . contains a tendency to persist in its being, is a force inscribed in the objectivity of things so that everything is not equally possible or impossible. (Bourdieu, 2018, p. 15)

Currency, according to Bourdieu, is a game of chance. We take risk, gambling that our education will "pay off" in the form of a high-paying job. We might get lucky, pick the "right" major, and score the six-figure income right out of college. Or we might strike out, having to put all our education chips into a field of study that suddenly isn't worth anything. The gods of chance are fickle, and, as Bourdieu reminds us, simple currency, by itself, has no lasting value. Today it might be worth a fortune; tomorrow, it might be worthless.

Capital, on the other hand, "contains a tendency to persist in its being," (p. 15). In perhaps more comprehensible terms, capital's value tends to last. It is much more stable than currency alone, and it tends to hold its worth. This stability, or, to use Bourdieu's term, *persistence of being*, can be ascribed in part to its *use value*.

Use Value vs. Exchange Value

As discussed above, the exchange value of an object is determined by what that object can be exchanged for. This exchange value may fluctuate a great deal, and, over a relatively short period of time, the exchange value of an object may decrease or increase dramatically, depending on any number of factors. In the late 1990s, when the general populace became aware of the Y2K problem, people across the country began preparing for a doomsday scenario. People hoarded canned food, stockpiled gasoline for generators, and gathered like-minded survivalist friends into compounds to wait out the inevitable societal collapse (Surman & Blake, 1999). One couple I knew began to stockpile toilet paper. They spent well over $100,000 on tens of thousands of rolls. Their rationale was that the dollar was going to be worthless once the banks collapsed, so there was no point in keeping their money. Toilet paper, they figured, would skyrocket in value. People wouldn't need debit cards, but they would always need toilet paper. And, because the factories and supply chains were about to fall apart, my friends quite earnestly believed that their warehouse full of double ply would become something akin to Fort Knox, holding the world's most valuable commodity.

My friends believed that the exchange value of toilet paper was about to skyrocket, and they bet accordingly. They lost. Big. The world did not collapse, the supply chains kept on trucking, and toilet paper never replaced the dollar as the de facto currency of the United States.

But, they didn't lose everything. Because, as it turns out, toilet paper has more than just exchange value. It also has *use value*.

As the name implies, the use value of an object lies not in what it can be exchanged for but rather in what one can *do* with it. Consider a pair of shoes. Their value most likely lies in the fact that they protect your feet, allowing you to go outside, run, etc. Yes, some people buy shoes for their exchange value (such as those who buy and sell vintage Air Jordans). An object can simultaneously have both exchange value and use value. However, when the market for vintage Jordans collapses, the shoes can still be worn. They retain their use value, even when their exchange value disappears.

One of the primary reasons that capital is a more stable form of investment than currency is that capital often has use value. In many Western countries, capital often takes the form of real estate. Yes, a house has exchange value, and many people, myself included, have profited by selling a house whose exchange value has increased dramatically. And many people, myself included, have seen the exchange value of their home fall below the price they originally paid for it. But the primary value of a house lies not in what you can exchange it for but rather in what you can use it for. That is, a house's primary value is that you can *live* in it. Though the exchange value of my current house has fluctuated in the decade I've owned it, its use value has remained steady. I have a place to sleep, to eat, to stay dry, to stay warm, to store my belongings, to commune with my family. Regardless of how the real estate market may rise or fall, the use value of my house does not waver.

My house does more than keep me warm, however. It also serves as a status symbol, for example, identifying me as a member of the "homeowner's club." In a society that privileges the private ownership of real estate, this is not insignificant. In this sense, my house provides me with *cultural capital*, signifying to those around me that I possess things that are valuable in our shared culture. My house is a form of *social capital*, providing me with a space to host neighborhood barbeques, allowing me to build and maintain relationships with the people of my community. I've planted a garden in the backyard, and every summer I sit and watch the hummingbirds dart to and fro between the flowers. It brings me joy, a joy that is not dependent on the exchange value of my property.

When applied to education, the differences between currency and capital, exchange value and use value, become all the more important. What would an education that attempted to increase the learners' capital look like? Imagine an education system that provides learners with skills and knowledge that are of use value, skills and knowledge that are recognizable as valuable by members of the learners' communities and that retain their value over time? Imagine a system of learning based not solely on depositing exchange-value knowledge into learners' heads but instead on investing in long-term, stable, funds of knowledge that are useful to learners and their communities *now*?

This notion of education as the creation of capital is not particularly new, but it does stand in stark contrast to the banking system described by Freire (1970). Currency has exchange value, but capital adds use value. Currency lacks stability, but capital is stable over time. Currency usually takes only one form, but capital can take many forms. Currency can be difficult to save, but capital can be passed down from generation to generation. Though currency can be one kind of capital, capital, as a category, far transcends the limitations of cash.

If education is the accumulation of intellectual wealth (which is admittedly a big "if"—see Chapter Four for alternatives), then we must be thinking of wealth in terms of capital, not in terms of currency. We do not want an education that devalues over time or that lacks intrinsic worth for the learner. Nor do we want an education that focuses solely on equipping learners with a limited set of skills that have no value outside an extremely limited setting. The art and practice of critical pedagogy lies, in part, in questioning assumptions that we have never thought to question. In this case, this means following Freire's lead and questioning our assumptions about education as a form of wealth. If we are to equate education and wealth (again, a rather enormous "if"), then what kind of wealth are we talking about? A wealth based on what others will give us for our knowledge, or a wealth determined by how we're able to use our knowledge in our own lives, and for our own benefit? There is a self-determining aspect to educational capital that is conspicuously absent in the banking model of education.

Conclusion

Yoda does not want Luke to be self-determining. He wants Luke to be passive to the point of sacrifice. However, as we discuss in Chapter Four, this kind of unthinking passivity does not necessarily have to be part of the Jedi training. Obi-Wan Kenobi offers a startling alternative to the banking system of Force education espoused by Yoda, focusing instead on education as the development of interdependent and mutually transformative relationships with the world around us. In fact, Obi-Wan never refers to capital or money or any other economics related metaphor. The entire idea of education as a form of wealth development is entirely absent from other *Star Wars* films (Lucas, 1977–present).

This absence makes it clear that Yoda's particular brand of Force education is a *choice*. It is not *the* way to train Jedi, despite Yoda's claims about his own pedagogical expertise. It is merely *a* way, one of many. One that is, I might add, spectacularly unsuccessful. Luke does, in fact, eventually become a Jedi, but only because he ignores Yoda's instructions in *The Empire Strikes Back* (Kirshner, 1980). Yoda tells Luke to sacrifice his friends. Luke refuses, choosing active relationship over passive obedience. In later films, Yoda tells Luke that he has to confront Vader in order to become a Jedi. Luke does meet Vader, but he ultimately refuses to fight him, throwing away his weapon, once again choosing relationship over the economically-driven power dynamics that Yoda is so intent on instilling in his pupil. Luke's future successes come *in spite of*, not because of, Yoda's instruction. To return to the claim made at the beginning of this chapter, the claim that "we should be teaching our students the way that Yoda taught Luke" (Phillips, 2015, n.p.), I say simply this: teach like Yoda, we should not.

Questions for Reflection

1. The rise of mandated standardized testing has corresponded to increased profits for testing companies. Pearson, for example, makes five *billion* dollars in profit each year. How might corporate interests conflict with an assessment's pedagogical purposes?

2. How much of the technology in our classrooms is pedagogically necessary? If it isn't necessary, why is it there? Whose interests are being served?

3. Which elements of our curricula are there not because of any immediate value to students but rather because they'll "need it someday?" *Will* they actually need it someday? If not, why is it still part of the curriculum?

4. What would a school day or year look like if students could "invest" their time in the areas they choose? How would things be different if we taught students to build meaningful capital instead of filling them with currency?

5. What do we teach that has no *use value* outside an academic setting? What are the functional equivalents of company scrip? How do we break that cycle?

Endnote

1. See Chapter Four for a more thorough description of Luke's initial introduction to the Force.

References

Bourdieu, P. (2018). The forms of capital. In *The sociology of economic life* (pp. 78–92). New York, NY: Routledge.

Colvin, S. (2024). *David is the Yoda of using rust with python.*[Post]. X. https://twitter.com/samuel_colvin/status/1750512231123472754

Constitutional Accountability Center. (2013). *"The Yoda of Constitutional Law" on PBS.* https://www.theusconstitution.org/blog/the-yoda-of-constitutional-law-on-pbs/

Davidson, J. & Orsini, M. (2013). *Worlds of autism: Across the spectrum of neurological difference.* Minneapolis, MN: University of Minnesota Press. https://doi.org/10.5749/minnesota/9780816688883.001.0001

Delamarter, J. (2023). Missing voices: Challenging the assumptions of an emerging framework by listening to pre-service teachers of color. *Journal of Negro Education, 92*(2), 184–197.

Dinishak, J. (2022). The deficit view and its critics. *Disability Studies Quarterly, 36*(4). https://doi.org/10.18061/dsq.v36i4.5236

Freire, P. (1970). *Pedagogy of the oppressed.* New York, NY: Continuum.

Harris, W. (1991). *Canonicity.* PMLA, 106(1), 110–121. https://doi.org/10.2307/462827

Juice Ranch. (2022). Yoda. https://juiceranch.com/products/yoda?variant=35124556497062

Kirshner, I. (1980). *The Empire Strikes Back.* [Film]. 20th Century Fox.

Ladson-Billings, G. (2007). Pushing past the achievement gap: An essay on the language of deficit. *The Journal of Negro Education, 76*(3), 316–323. http://www.jstor.org/stable/40034574

Locke, J. (1690). *An essay concerning human understanding.* https://www.gutenberg.org/files/10615/10615-h/10615-h.htm

Lucas, G. (Director). (1977). *Star wars episode IV: A new hope.* [Film]. Lucasfilm.

Lucas, G. (1977–present). The Star Wars Universe. Lucasfilm.

Mack, H. (2022). *Yoda of the Dark Streets – Harry Mack Freestyle.* [Video]. YouTube. https://youtu.be/iIN5Qwdh3yA?si=I93q4_m5GVozeWkh

Moll, L., Amanti, C., Neff, D., & Gonzalez, N. (1992). Funds of knowledge for teaching: Using a qualitative approach to connect homes and classrooms. *Theory into Practice, 31*(2), 132–141. http://doi:10.1080/00405849209543534

Phillips, V. (2015). *We should be teaching our students like Yoda taught Luke.* Wired. https://www.wired.com/2015/02/teaching-students-like-yoda-taught-luke/

Prizant, B.M., & Field-Meyers, T. (2015). *Uniquely human: A different way of seeing Autism.* New York, NY: Simon & Schuster.

Ramos, D., & Kiyama, J. M. (2021). Tying it all together: Defining the core tenets of funds of knowledge. *Educational Studies, 57*(4), 429–449. https://doi.org/10.1080/00131946.2021.1904932

Rios-Aguilar, C., Kiyama, J. M., Gravitt, M., & Moll, L. C. (2011). Funds of knowledge for the poor and forms of capital for the rich?: A capital approach to examining funds of knowledge. *Theory and Research in Education,* 9(2), 163–184. http://doi:10.1177/1477878511409776

Roberts, S. (2018). *The Yoda of Silicon Valley.* https://www.nytimes.com/2018/12/17/science/donald-knuth-computers-algorithms-programming.html

Sawyer, L. P. (2013). Contested meanings of freedom: Workingmen's wages, the company store system, and the Godcharles v. Wigeman Decision. *The Journal of the Gilded Age and Progressive Era,* 12(3), 285–319. https://doi.org/10.1017/S1537781413000182

Silberman, S. (2015). *Neurotribes: The legacy of Autism and the future of neurodiversity.* New York, NY: Penguin Random House.

Surman, M., & Blake, C. (1999). *Spending the day stockpiling for Y2K.* Los Angeles Times, December 21, 1999. https://www.latimes.com/archives/la-xpm-1999-dec-31-me-49410-story.html

Tip of the Spear. (2017). *The Leadership Challenge: The Yoda Process to meeting success – 4 tips!* https://tipofthespearventures.com/leadership-challenge-yoda-process-meeting-success-4-tips/

Velez-Ibanez, C. G. (1988). Networks of exchange among Mexicans in the US and Mexico: Local level mediating responses to national and international transformations. *Urban Anthropology and Studies of Cultural Systems and World Economic Development,* 17(1), 27–51. https://www.jstor.org/stable/40553124

Yale University (n.d.). *The Yoda Project – Forging a unified scientific community.* https://yoda.yale.edu/

CHAPTER SEVEN

War of the Words: Weaponization and Linguistic Justice in *Arrival*

The Text: *Arrival* (Villeneuve, 2016). Film.

Introduction

DO YOU REMEMBER THE children's rhyme "sticks and stones can break my bones, but words will never hurt me?" It's completely untrue. Sometimes, words are *meant* to hurt. We say unkind things, tell lies, spread rumors, swap insults. We sharpen our words and hurl them toward our targets.

Other times, our words may have no ill intent behind them, but they sting, nevertheless. A professor criticizes our work. A love interest politely but firmly says "no." A form letter politely rejects the manuscript we've been slaving over. Even when they're well intentioned, words can cause tremendous amounts of pain. Words *can* hurt, no matter what we said as kids.

If words are capable of causing so much pain, how much impact can an entire language have? If words are capable of cutting down a person, could a language be capable of cutting down a civilization? If someone tries to force us to learn a new language, should we consider it an act of war?

These questions are of great concern both to critical pedagogy and to the writers of and characters in the film *Arrival*. The movie, which was based on the short story, *Story of Your Life* (Chiang, 2010), explores the relationship between language and culture and the ways that changes to the former necessarily lead to changes in the latter. In particular, the film explores the weaponization of language, the dangers and promises inherent in adopting—or being compelled to adopt—entirely new ways of thinking.

This is not just the stuff of science fiction. As we'll discuss later in the chapter, questions of language in schools and classrooms are central both to critical pedagogues and to those who seek to maintain the status quo. Both "sides" ask very similar questions: Whose language should we use? What do we lose if we use language X instead of language Y? What do we gain? What will happen to "our" culture if we use "their" language? What will happen to our values? To our understandings of the world around us? Will we still be "us," or will we be someone or something else?

Before tackling these questions, let's take a deeper look at the film we're analyzing. *Arrival* hit American theaters on November 11, 2016, just three days after Donald Trump was elected President of the United States. Trump's presidential campaign had focused almost exclusively on building a wall between Mexico and the southern United States, and anti-immigrant rhetoric was rampant. In that sense, the film portrayed many of the tensions and fears that were, and are, consuming American society: Are the aliens a threat to us or not? How do we act when confronted with someone different, someone that we don't understand? Despite these interrogations into the American *zeitgeist*, or perhaps because of them, the film was a commercial and critical success. It was nominated for eight Academy Awards, and it won an Oscar for best sound editing, not to mention the Ray Bradbury award and a Hugo award. It was also labelled one of the top movies of the year by the American Film Institute.

The film became a subject of much academic analysis, particularly in relation to its portrayal of time (e.g., Buckley, 2024; Carruthers, 2018; Fleming & Brown, 2018; Gokhale et al., 2023; Molyneux-Dixon, 2020), linguistics (e.g., Coon, 2020; Kusumastuti, 2019; Seemungal, 2018; Sticchi, 2019), and, most interestingly, the combination of the two (e.g., Akter, 2020). In order to better understand just how the film explores both of these topics *and* highlights the power of language to build community, particularly in education settings, let's begin with the text. First, however, a warning: This is a difficult film to summarize and discuss, not because the subject matter is sensitive or controversial but, rather, because it's just plain difficult. The ideas are complex, and they defy simple and simplistic reduction. The qualities that make the film so difficult to summarize are the same qualities that make it such a rich source of analysis. Any weaknesses in the following summary are due to the limitations of my writing ability and not to the quality of the source material. On the contrary: *Arrival* (2016) is a rich, complicated, and deeply compassionate film that resists compression or simplification. For example, I cannot capture the way that the Oscar-winning sound design and Grammy-nominated soundtrack enhance and add to the overall meaning of the film, and it is beyond my capacity to write about non-linear time (a key component of the plot) in a linear fashion. Conclusion: *Arrival* is a film that must be experienced to be fully understood.

And now, with that grain of salt firmly in mind, and with our metaphors thoroughly mixed, let us press on.

The Story

The aliens have landed, but this doesn't seem to bother Dr. Louise Banks, professor of linguistics. She's content to teach by day and sit alone in her waterfront house by night. The film opens with a flashback montage in which Dr. Banks remembers key moments of her daughter's life: birth, walking for the first time, laughing over a silly joke, pre-teen angst, and, eventually, her death to cancer while still in her teens. Dr. Banks sits alone with these memories, and the arrival of 12 alien spacecraft spread out across the world doesn't appear to shake her out of her stupor. That is, until the military literally comes knocking on her door (Villeneuve, 2016).

At some point in the past, Dr. Banks had done translation work for the military. Although she is a hum drum academic, she still holds top secret security clearance, which is why the military reaches out to her first instead of reaching out to another expert at Berkeley. The military has made contact with the aliens, and they've brought a recording of the first ever human/alien "conversation." Colonel Weber is leading the team (Villeneuve, 2016).

> **Weber:** I have something I need you to translate for me. *He pulls a small recording device from his pocket and pushes 'play.'*
>
> **Unidentified Military Official** [*on the recording*]: Why are you here? Can you . . . can you understand us?
>
> **Alien** [*on the recording*]: *clicks and deep rumbling noises. Clearly a language, but completely incomprehensible.*
>
> **Unidentified Military Official** [*on the recording*]: Where did you come from?

Alien [*on the recording*]: *more extensive clicks and rumblings.*

Colonel Weber stops the recording.

Weber: Now you heard it. What do you make of it?

Banks [*shaken*]: . . . is that . . . ?

Weber: Yes . . . How would you approach translating this? Do you hear any words? Phrases?

Banks: I don't . . . I don't know . . .

Weber: So what can you tell me?

Banks: I can tell you that it's impossible to translate from an audio file. I would need to be there, to interact with them.

Colonel Weber says he cannot take her to the landing site, yet Dr. Banks insists that she cannot help without being there in person. The Colonel turns to leave.

Banks: Colonel. You mentioned Berkeley. Are you going to ask Danvers next?

Weber: Maybe.

Banks [*forcefully*]: Before you commit to him, ask him the Sanskrit word for 'war' and its translation.

The colonel nods and leaves her office, only to return a few hours later.

Weber: 'Gavisti.' He says it means 'an argument.' What do you say it means? (Villeneuve, 2016)

Banks: 'A desire for more cows.'

Weber: Pack your bags.

On her way to the landing site, Dr. Banks meets Ian Donnelly, a theoretical physicist who will be joining her in trying to establish communication with the aliens. He introduces himself by reading to her a passage from her own book.

Donnelly: 'Language is the foundation of civilization. It is the glue that holds people together. It is the first weapon drawn in a conflict.'

Banks: That's quite a greeting.

Donnelly: Yeah, well, you wrote it.

Banks: It's the kind of thing you write as a preface. Dazzle them with the basics.

Donnelly: Well, it's great, even if it's wrong.

Banks: It's wrong?

Donnelly: Well, the cornerstone of civilization isn't language. It's science.

Colonel Weber makes formal introductions for the team and establishes their goals as a working group.

Weber: Priority one: what do they want, and where are they from?

Donnelly: And beyond that, how did they get here? Are they capable of faster-than-light travel? I've prepared a list of questions to go over, starting with a series of 'handshake' binary sequences . . .

Banks [*interrupting*]**:** How about we just talk to them before we start throwing math problems at them?

Weber: This is why you're both here. (Villeneuve, 2016)

Upon their arrival at the landing site, Dr. Banks and Dr. Donnelly join a handful of military experts in establishing communications with the aliens. The alien ship resembles a giant seed pod, hovering roughly 20 feet above the Montana countryside. Every 18 hours, a "door" opens at the base of the ship. The translation team enters from the bottom, but as they "ascend," the orientation of gravity changes, and the up/down perspective from within the ship differs greatly from that of the outside world. The team waits in what they have dubbed the "anteroom." They have cameras and other recording devices set up. The aliens have adjusted the atmosphere to human breathability standards, but each member of the team wears something resembling a space-suit to protect them from radiation and other dangers, even though every indicator, including a literal canary in a cage, suggests that the atmosphere is safe (Villeneuve, 2016).

At the other end of the anteroom is something akin to a glass wall. On the other side of the wall, the atmosphere is visibly different. It's cloudy, swirling with unknown gasses. It's difficult to see the aliens clearly, given the limitations presented by the glass and the helmets the team is wearing. What they can see is unlike anything they've ever seen before. The aliens are fantastically tall. All that's visible through the screen are seven spindly legs. The torso, if there is one, is hidden by the mist and clouds of the aliens' atmosphere. The team decides to call the aliens "Heptapods," Greek for "seven feet."

Overall, the visits are not yielding meaningful results. It is impossible for humans to recreate the Heptapods' spoken language, and, after a week, the team is no closer to establishing communication. In a moment of frustration, Dr. Banks brings a small white board into the anteroom. She writes the word "human" on the board and holds it up for the Heptapods to see. "Human," she says, pointing to herself. "Human."

There is no response from the Heptapods. Dr. Banks walks closer to the glass partition, closer than she or anyone else has ever been. "Human," she says again. "I'm human. What are you?" She holds up the whiteboard.

The Heptapods rumble a response. One of them lifts an appendage to the partition and squirts what appears to be some sort of ink. The "ink" creates a circle with flourishes and embellishments on the top left. This is clearly a form of written communication.

The most important breakthrough takes place a few days later. Dr. Banks has decided to teach the Heptapods her name and Ian's name. If they can learn the Heptapods' names in response, they will finally know whether or not the Heptapods consider themselves individuals or are more of a collective species, like bees or ants. Dr. Banks holds a whiteboard with "Louise" written on it. She points to herself, but she is clearly not making the connection she wants to. The military advisors urge her to move on to the next vocabulary word, but she hesitates. She looks at the canary in the cage, chirping happily. In an instant, she makes a decision and removes the hazmat suit that hides her face and body. The military members of the team spring into action, trying to stop her. "They need to see me!" she cries, pushing them back (Villeneuve, 2016).

Free from the constraints of her suit, she walks toward the partition until she is face to "face" with the Heptapods. She places her hand against the partition, much like putting one's hand against the side of an aquarium. From the other side of the glass, one of the Heptapods places its "hand" against the glass. The image is of two beings, shaking hands in greeting. After a moment, Dr. Banks smiles. "Now that's a proper introduction," she says. She holds up the sign again. "Louise," she says, pointing once again at herself. She points at one Heptapod and then the other. "You. And you. Who are you?"

This time, the response is immediate and clear. Each of the two Heptapods "writes" a circle on the screen. Each circle is distinct and easily distinguishable from the other, with different embellishments and flourishes.

"I think these are their names," Dr. Banks whispers. "They have names."

Upon returning to base, Dr. Banks begins having intense flashbacks of her daughter. They're strong enough to force her to sit and catch her breath.

Now that the initial breakthrough has been made, linguistic discoveries start coming at a rapid pace. Over the next few weeks, Dr. Banks and her team learn that there is virtually no correlation between Heptapods' spoken and written languages. Dr. Donnelly explains it well:

> Unlike all human written languages, their writing is semasiographic. It conveys meaning; it doesn't represent sound. . . . Unlike speech, a logogram [the circular style of Heptapod 'writing'] is free of time. Like their ship, or their bodies, their written language has no forward or backward direction. Linguists call this 'non-linear orthography,' which raises the question: is this how they think? Imagine you wanted to write a sentence using two hands, starting from either side. You would have to know each word you wanted to use, as well as how much space that it would occupy. A Heptapod can write a complex sentence in two seconds, effortlessly. It's taken us a month to make the simplest reply. (Villeneuve, 2016)

As these discoveries are being made, and as the team is working around the clock, Dr. Banks' flashbacks are becoming both more frequent and more intense. *She sees her daughter, age 8, drawing pictures for a school project. She remembers reassuring her daughter that both mommy and daddy still love her, despite their divorce. She remembers holding her teenage daughter as she lay dying in the hospital.* Others have started noticing her staring off into space, and the flashbacks are occasionally interfering with her work. Dr. Donnelly, who can tell that something is wrong, asks her if everything is ok.

> **Banks:** I need some sleep, but, um, I'm fine.
>
> **Donnelly** [*sits down next to her*]: Yeah. He pauses. You know, I was doing some reading about this idea that if you immerse yourself into a foreign language . . . , you can actually rewire your brain.
>
> **Banks:** The Sapir-Whorf hypothesis. That's the theory that, uh, the language you speak determines how you think and . . . *her voice trails off*.
>
> **Donnelly:** Yeah. It affects how you see everything. It's, uh . . . I'm curious. Are you dreaming in their language?

Banks [*clearly struggling*]: I may have had a few dreams, but I don't . . . I don't think that makes me unfit to do this job.

She looks up. Dr. Donnelly has been replaced by one of the Heptapods. The entire conversation has been a dream.

Meanwhile, tensions among the various nations of Earth are growing. The Heptapod ships are scattered across the globe, and the nations of the 12 landing sites have, to this point, been sharing all of their research. However, cracks begin to emerge in the uneasy alliance between China and the rest of the world. Dr. Banks learns that the Chinese have been teaching the Heptapods to play Mahjong, a classic Chinese strategy game. The problem, as she sees it, is not that the Chinese are using games to converse with the Heptapods; the problem is that they are using zero-sum games. "Let's say that I taught them chess instead of English," she explains to Colonel Weber. "Every conversation would be a game. Every idea expressed through opposition, victory, defeat. You see the problem? If all I ever gave you was a hammer . . ." (Villeneuve, 2016).

"Everything's a nail," Colonel Weber finishes, nodding in agreement. "We need to ask the big question. Ready or not."

The "big question" is simply this: Why are you here? What is your purpose on Earth? The last few months of translation and communication have led to this point, because the U.S. military—indeed, humanity as a whole—needs to know if the strangers among them are to be feared or to be welcomed. And so, Dr. Banks, against her better judgement, asks the question. The Heptapods' response is not reassuring. They are here to "offer weapon."

The mention of a weapon throws the entire military command into a tailspin.

Captain Marks [*afraid*]: You saw what they wrote!

Banks: We don't know if they understand the difference between a weapon and a tool. Our language, like our culture, is messy, and sometimes, one can be both.

Donnelly: And it's quite possible they're asking us to offer them something, not the other way around. It's like the first part of a trade.

Weber: So how do we clarify their intentions beyond those two words?

Dr. Banks insists that she be allowed to re-enter the antechamber and speak to the Heptapods to clear up any potential misunderstanding.

> *Agent Halpern of the CIA, who sees everything through the lens of allies and enemies, disagrees. (Villeneuve, 2016)*
>
> **Halpern:** We need to sit on this information until we know what it means, so we aren't sharing it with our enemies. We have to consider the idea that our visitors are prodding us to fight among ourselves until only one faction prevails.
>
> **Banks:** There's no evidence of that.
>
> **Halpern:** Sure there is. Just grab a history book. (Villeneuve, 2016)

Because scientists from around the world are sharing information, news of the word *weapon* spreads like wildfire and, within minutes, the 12 nations that had been cooperating withdraw from their accord. Each goes "radio silent," keeping all new information and discoveries to themselves. The air is thick with distrust.

At this point, a small group of soldiers slips away unnoticed and plants explosives in the Heptapods' antechamber. They are afraid, convinced that a Heptapod attack is imminent, and they decide to strike first. Dr. Banks, unaware of the explosives, makes an unscheduled return to the antechamber. One of the Heptapods sacrifices itself to save her from the explosion.

The Earth is now on the brink of global war. The American government is convinced that the Heptapods will retaliate, and they begin to prepare an assault. China declares war on the Heptapods, giving them 24 hours to leave the Earth before being fired upon. In the midst of the chaos, Dr. Banks, who sustained a concussion during the explosion, is studying the last Heptapod message, written just before the bomb went off. It's a data dump, tens of thousands of logograms, almost like a dictionary of the entire Heptapod language. As she studies, her flashbacks grow more intense. *Her daughter, early high school age, is working on a school paper. She has forgotten a specific term, and she asks her mom for help. "What's this term, for that thing . . . like a technical term, where we make a deal, and we both get something out of it?"*

"A compromise," Dr. Banks replies, but that's not the right answer. Her daughter frowns (Villeneuve, 2016).

"No. Like, it's a competition, but both sides end up happy."

Dr. Banks thinks for a moment. "Like a win-win."

Her daughter shakes her head. "More science-y than that."

Her flashback is interrupted by Dr. Donnelly, who drags her back to the present. He has discovered something. The "data dump" from the Heptapods is mostly empty, but it's empty in an interesting way. The ratio of data (filled space) to non-data (blank space) is 1/12. One of twelve. Dr. Banks believes this means that each of the sites has been given 1/12th of the tool or weapon or whatever it is that the Heptapods are offering. She tries to convince Colonel Weber that they need to reopen their data sharing with the other nations from the other landing sites.

> **Banks:** What they're saying here is that this is one of twelve. We're part of a larger whole.
>
> **Halpern:** Or we're one of twelve contestants for the prize.
>
> *Colonel Weber tries to defuse the tension in the room. It is clear that Halpern and the government are intent on interpreting everything as an act of hostility.*
>
> **Banks:** [This] could just be their way of saying 'some assembly required.'
>
> **Halpern:** Why hand it out to us in pieces? Why not just give it all over?
>
> **Banks:** What better way to force us to work together for once?
>
> **Halpern:** Even if I did believe you, how in the world are you going to get anyone else to play along and give up their data?
>
> **Donnelly:** We offer ours in return.
>
> **Weber:** Yeah.
>
> **Halpern:** A trade?
>
> **Donnelly:** It's a non-zero-sum game.

The second that Donnelly says these words, Dr. Banks' flashback returns. *"A non-zero-sum game," she says.*

Her daughter smiles. "That's it. Yeah. Thanks." She heads upstairs to finish her homework (Villeneuve, 2016).

Dr. Banks snaps out of the flashback, although it is suddenly not clear whether she is experiencing flash*backs* or something else entirely. In the background, the colonel and other military personnel are debating how to reestablish contact with the other landing sites. Communications have been cut, and there's not enough time to fly there. China will be launching their weapons in hours, and the world is on the brink of war.

As the men argue in the background, Dr. Banks slips away and heads to the Heptapods' ship. She's in a daze, reeling from the power of the visions she has been having. She enters what used to be the antechamber, although, due to the explosion, the partition between her and the Heptapods is no more. She is standing face-to-face with them, seeing them fully for the first time.

> **Banks:** I need you to send a message to the other sites.
>
> **Heptapod** [*in logogram writing*]**:** Louise has weapon. Use weapon.
>
> **Banks:** I don't understand. What is your purpose here?
>
> **Heptapod:** We help humanity. In three thousand years, we need humanity help.
>
> **Banks:** How can you know the future?
>
> *The Heptapod rumbles, and Dr. Banks is suddenly overcome by an intense flashback/vision. She sees her daughter at various life stages. Snapshots, snippets of scenes from her life.*
>
> **Banks** [*on the verge of tears*]**:** I don't . . . I don't understand. Who is this child?
>
> *The Heptapod rumbles again, and Dr. Banks suddenly 'sees.' The child is her daughter, the daughter who has not yet been born. She has not been having flashbacks; they are flash<u>forwards</u>, visions of life yet to come.*
>
> **Heptapod:** Louise sees future.
>
> *Dr. Banks sees her daughter as an infant.*
>
> **Heptapod:** Weapon opens time.
>
> *Dr. Banks sees herself weeping by her daughter's death bed. She sees her daughter playing by a stream. She sees herself laughing, loving, grieving.* (Villeneuve, 2016)

The door or gateway or whatever metaphor is appropriate has been unlocked. The "weapon" is not a weapon at all, at least not in a militaristic sense. It is a language, a language that has a non-linear relationship to time. As humans learn the Heptapods' language, their brains will be rewired, changing our sense of past, present, and future, blurring the lines between *now* and *then*. All this comes to Dr. Banks in a flash, and she sees what she has to do, because she can now see what she will have already done in the future. So she uses the "weapon," drawing on her future experiences to inform her current actions, using information that she will have in the future to help her solve the problems of today.

The global crisis is averted, but the questions of relationship remain. How does one love, marry, bring a child into the world, all the while knowing—being able to see—the heartache and loss and death that will happen . . . ? That have already happened? That are happening now? These questions go unanswered, as they are, I suspect, unanswerable.

The Critical Analysis

One of the most impressive elements of *Arrival* (Villeneuve, 2016) is how deftly and creatively the film highlights the relationships between language and culture. A culture steeped in competition has a language that both reflects and reinforces its own cultural norms. For example, *zero-sum* competition, in which conflict is resolved strictly in terms of winning and losing, is embedded into Western culture. Consequently, zero-sum metaphors are embedded in our languages. In English, for example, we "win" friends and arguments. People from lower socio-economic strata are "disadvantaged," meaning that they lack the strategic advantage that others possess. In romance, we "win" someone's heart. When we put in extra work, we are working "overtime," the same term that we use for describing a competition that has gone longer than anticipated. We are "goal-oriented." At corporate "retreats" we plan how to "advance" our causes, both terms being drawn straight from the vocabulary of the battlefield. When we are down, we feel "defeated," and our friends try to help us "beat" the blues. When we are afraid, we strive to "conquer" our fears. Perhaps most telling, the generic term for an unsuccessful or undesirable person is simply this: "loser."

But what has this "loser" lost? What are they competing for? Do we really see competition embedded into every aspect of our personal, financial, social, and emotional lives? Consciously, maybe not. But linguistically? Yes. And language can reveal basic assumptions about the world that we didn't even know we had:

> Our conceptual system is not something we are normally aware of. In most of the little things we do every day, we simply act more or less automatically along certain lines. Just what these lines are is by no means obvious. One way to find out is by looking at language. Since communication is based on

> the same conceptual system that we use in thinking and acting, language is an important source of evidence for what the system is like. (Lakoff & Johnson, 1980, p. 3)

If I am in a conversation with a person, and we disagree, the zero-sum metaphors embedded in English compel me to frame the experience in adversarial terms. I must "defend" my position while the other person attacks. If the other person says something that makes me reconsider, I say, "good point," much like I would concede the point if I had been scored upon in a sporting match. Linguistically, the purpose of the conversation is not to inform or learn or grow or reconcile. It is to *win*. Regardless of my individual intentions and purposes, the only language I have to describe and conceive of this interaction is rooted in adversarial and zero-sum terms. In this way, language often has a self-fulfilling effect, both reflecting and reinforcing the ways that people see themselves in relation to the world around them (Ferraro et al., 2005).

Embedded linguistic metaphors of winning and losing are commonly and openly embraced in many contexts, including those that we might expect, such as international trade (e.g., Cai, 2023), economics (e.g., Perkins et al., 2022), and business (e.g., Prelipceanu, 2008). Interestingly, the prevalence of zero-sum metaphors is being increasingly recognized in a wide range of perhaps *un*expected contexts, including forest management (e.g., Carlson & Wilson, 2004), familial health (e.g., Halpern & Murphy, 2013), and, perhaps most interestingly, education (e.g., Shen & Xia, 2012).

The landmark governmental education report, *A Nation at Risk* (National Commission on Excellence in Education, 1983), used competitive metaphors to describe the state of American education, bemoaning the belief that "our once unchallenged preeminence in commerce, industry, science, and technological innovation is being overtaken by competitors throughout the world" (p. 113). President Obama's signature education policy was called *Race to the Top* (H.R. 1532, 2011). The current U.S. Department of Education explicitly states that its mission is to "promote student achievement and preparation for global competitiveness" (U.S. Department of Education, 2024).

If the language we use shapes the way we conceive of the world, it follows that changing our language can change the way we think. The weaponized relationship between the shaping of language and the shaping of thought is well-documented (Bolinger, 1980; Landry et al., 2022; Stanley, 2015; Stroińska, 2000), although a generalized accounting of language weaponization through propaganda, advertising, and other manipulative modes is beyond the scope of this chapter. Instead, we are focusing on the ways that the control and policing of language have been in educational contexts. Quite often, these policing activities take place under the general framework of essentialism.

Essentialism

Essentialism is, in essence, the belief that the purpose of education is to pass on the skills and knowledge that are "essential" for maintaining a functioning society. In this regard, essentialism is conservative. That is, it seeks to preserve a degree of existing order by ensuring that each generation is equipped with the tools necessary for the continued running of a cohesive society. Essentialism is *not* necessarily a politicly conservative movement, and we must be careful not to equate (in this context) "conservative" with the American Republican Party or other right-of-center movements. In its pure form, essentialism does not necessarily prescribe which skills should be considered essential or which knowledge is necessary for the preservation of society. Instead, it simply argues that there are such things as essentials, and that it is the job of our education system to ensure that those essentials are taught. The essentials may change over time, particularly as the needs of society change. The skills and knowledge necessary for preserving social cohesion today are not the same as they were 100 years ago. That's okay, to a pure essentialist, just as long as our schools are teaching the essentials.

The social cohesion that essentialists want to maintain relies, in part, on shared language. On the surface, shared language might be understood simply as people in a given society all speaking English or Spanish or any other language. And certainly there is some truth to this. Shared language does involve a shared tongue. Historically, one of the purposes of American public education has been to teach all students to read and write in English. As early as 1642, American colonists had passed a law requiring parents to teach their children "to read the English tongue" so they might have "knowledge of the Capital Laws" (Massachusetts Bay Colony, 1642, chapter XXII). In order to function in puritan society—that is, follow the law—citizens had to be able to read the laws, and this required knowledge of a shared language. In 1647, a mere five years later, the colony transferred the responsibility of teaching English fluency from the parents to teachers, establishing a school system that would teach English so that students would be able to read Christian scriptures for themselves (Massachusetts Bay Colony, 1647). In the Puritan colonies, in which all citizens were members of the same narrowly-defined Christian sect, being able to discuss and understand a very specific English translation of the Christian Bible was an essential part of social cohesion.

As our country became more pluralistic, and as people from all over the world immigrated to (or were forcibly brought to) America, the need for teaching a common language became more important. John Dewey (1916) summarized the role of public schools in promoting a shared language:

> Countries like the United States are composed of a combination of different groups with different traditional customs. It is this situation, which has perhaps more than any other cause, forced the demand for an educational institution which shall provide something like a homogeneous and balanced environment for the young. . . . The intermingling in the school of youth of different races, differing religions, and unlike customs creates for all a new and broader environment. Common subject matter accustoms all to a unity of outlook upon a broader horizon than is visible to the members of any group while it is isolated. (p. 21)

A full 100 years after Dewey, and 350 years after the Puritans, English is still taught in American public schools with the explicit intent of maintaining social cohesion and promoting social participation, although there is a great deal of disagreement about how English might best be taught, particularly to immigrant students (Gándara & Rumberger, 2009). Nevertheless, despite these differences over pedagogical strategies, there is little disagreement that a primary purpose of public education is to ensure that every student has fluency and facility in the historically shared language of the country, because speaking a shared language ensures access to and allows for participation in our social institutions.

At this point, I hope that you have some alarm bells going off in your head, because although what I have just described is true, it is only part of the story. As most critical pedagogues will point out, a shared language in and of itself does not, in fact, create equal access for all. Instead, requiring students to learn a standardized version of English can lead to further inequity and even reinforce existing social divisions. To illustrate this point, we need only ask one simple question: Whose version of English do we use?

Most essentialists answer this question with an equally simple answer: We should use "standard English." But what is "standard English?" To answer this question, Strevens (1981) argues that we must first consider what standard English is *not*:

- It is not "pure" or "untainted" English. That is, it is not the "best" form of English;
- It is not "upper-class" English, because it can be found at all social strata;
- It is not the most frequently occurring or most often heard from of English. In fact, most native English speakers in the world are native speakers of something other than standard English (Trudgill, 2002); and
- It is not the result of planning or design.

Standard English is not, in fact, a language, but rather just one English dialect among many (e.g., Trudgill, 2002). Instead, most definitions highlight that standard English is non-localized, lacks significant variation in either written or spoken form, and functions as a global currency.

The standardization of both written and spoken English was a by-product of (primarily British) colonialism. As the British empire spread, it soon became apparent that management of the various colonies and administration of widespread colonial interests would be well-served by consistency and standardization of written and spoken communication. The 18th century saw the rise of standardization efforts in both Britain and America, primarily in the form of dictionaries and other reference materials (Hickey, 2012).

Of course, standardization of something as complex and dynamic as a widely-spoken language borders on both the impossible and the absurd, as illustrated by the fact that linguists cannot even agree on whether or not the "s" in "standard English" should be capitalized (Trudgill, 2002). And although it may be the case that standardization of English is not inherently an issue of social class, it does not follow that standardization cannot be used to sort, stratify, and categorize people into a ranked class system. Unfortunately, standard English, which was (generously interpreted) originally intended to facilitate communication, *is* a class marker that has, in fact, been weaponized and used to maintain existing social hierarchies (Wiley & Lukes, 1996).

In American educational systems, the standardized English taught in the classrooms and accepted as currency in academic settings is often at odds with students' own English traditions. Put simply, the way that students speak English at home often differs from the way they're expected to speak it at school. Because language embodies and informs culture, compelling students to use a form of English that differs from that of their home culture might damage or devalue students' cultural values and practices (Bohn, 2003).

Whose English becomes the "standard?" I grew up in a highly educated, white household, and I never felt a tension between the language of my home and the language of my school or my workplace. I never had to actively *code-switch*, adapting my syntax, grammar, or vocabulary to match the contextual expectations of a standardized language. Due to the accident of birth, the linguistic traditions of my home culture aligned perfectly with the linguistic traditions embodied in standard English and regulated in academic settings. But my experience is far from universal. For too many students, the compulsory use of standardized English in academic settings is a painful, diminishing experience, because standard English is set *against* their own linguistic traditions. Critical pedagogue bell hooks (1994) writes about her own school experiences. For hooks, being forced to learn standard English was akin to

> learning to speak against black vernacular, against the ruptured and broken speech of a dispossessed and displaced people. Standard English is not the speech of exile. It is the language of conquest and domination; in the United States, it is the mask which hides the loss of so many tongues. . . . I know that it is not the English language that hurts me, but what the oppressors do with it, how they shape it to become a territory that limits and defines, how they make it a weapon that can shame, humiliate, colonize. (p. 168)

Although linguists may agree that standard English is not "better" than any other version and that it is simply one dialect among many, it is too often taught as if it *is*, in fact, an aesthetically and grammatically superior form of English. In higher education settings, standard English is often used to "gatekeep," excluding speakers of non-standard English from academic spaces (Jenkins & Leung, 2019). In K–12 settings, standard English has often been used as a means of *eradication*, requiring students to abandon alternative forms of English on moral or patriotic grounds (Clark, 2023). In one particularly egregious example, the American Speech Committee of the Chicago Women's Club, together with the National Council of Teachers of English (an organization that remains powerful today), promoted school curricula that urged K–12 students to take the following pledge as part of a national "Better Speech Week:"

> I love the United States of America. I love my country's flag. I love my country's language. I promise:
>
> 1. That I will not dishonor my country's speech by leaving off the last syllable of words.
> 2. That I will say a good American "yes" and "no" in place of an Indian grunt "urn-hum" and "nup-um" or a foreign "ya" or "yeh" and "nope."
> 3. That I will do my best to improve American speech by avoiding loud rough tones, by enunciating distinctly, and by speaking pleasantly, clearly and sincerely.
> 4. That I will learn to articulate correctly as many words as possible during the year. (Robbins, 1918, p. 175)

As this pledge insinuates, to speak any version of English other than standard English is dishonorable, and the pledge is quick to both name specific groups whose speech is particularly dishonorable and reduce that group's language to nothing more than "grunts." This pledge was promoted under the guise of essentialist values, because "a love and respect for language, *our own language*, can be made one of the great forces working toward the solidarity of the American people" (Robbins, 1918, p. 171, italics original). Hidden not-too-deeply within this essentialist appeal is the division of English into "ours" and, by extension, "theirs." To "safeguard" the English language and, therefore, American institutions, (p. 171), immigrants, native Americans, Jews, and other "outsiders"[1] must adapt themselves to "our" ways.

The use of standard English to diminish the language of others and to highlight divisions between "us" and "them" is generally referred to as *weaponization*, which is fully in line with the central tension in *Arrival* (Villeneuve, 2016): Is the Heptapods' gift a tool or a weapon? As Dr. Banks' own words make clear, language is often "the first weapon drawn in a conflict" (Villeneuve, 2016). And, as hooks (1994) notes, standard English is often used as a weapon against students of color whose own English traditions differ from standard usage. The way that "they" speak is wrong, meaning that the teacher's job is to rebuke the student, fix the mistakes, and eradicate the wrongness. But the assumption that non-standard English is "wrong" is, itself, wrong. As noted above, linguists agree that standard English is not "better" than other dialects, and the term "standard English" was originally meant to be descriptive, not prescriptive. School policies, then, that enforce rigid adherence to standard English are practicing a form of *linguistic injustice* by using the language of the dominant group to diminish and, in some cases, destroy the language of the "other," even though the former is not superior to the latter. They are working from the (sometimes) tacit assumption that non-standard English is "inferior, pathological, deviant, and unnatural" (Baker-Bell, 2020b, p. xiii).

So what is the solution to this injustice? Many essentialists will agree that standard English is not "better" than any other form. However, they might argue, students need to learn standard English in order to have access to institutions of power. E.D. Hirsch, an essentialist who grew to prominence during the 1990s, claims that learning standard English is actually one of the key strategies for reducing the wage gap between Black and white Americans. His logic is this: The wage gap is primarily a function of a gap in educational attainment. The quickest way to close the gap is to ensure that *all* students are able to get the same high-quality education, which requires all students to learn to read and write to the same standard. We discuss Hirsch in greater detail in Chapter Two, but it's important to note that Hirsch would be the first to admit that standard English is not better than the alternatives. He doesn't claim that it *should* be the language of power. He merely notes that it *is*. Therefore, if we want to provide students with equitable access to power, we need to make sure that all students learn standard English.

The Limitations of Code-Switching

Using the logic that mastering standard English is an essential part of promoting equity, many essentialists urge students to code-switch, becoming masters of the dialects of both home and school, recognizing the contexts in which it is appropriate to speak one versus the other. In mainstream (that is, non-ESL) classrooms, the issue of code-switching generally arises when talking about standard English and Black English (also known as African-American Vernacular English, or AAVE). Advocates of code-switching argue that this practice allows students to become fluent in the language of the majority without sacrificing or devaluing their home languages.

Opponents of code-switching, on the other hand, argue that white students are not required to engage in the mental and cognitive gymnastics necessary for maintaining constant awareness of which version of English it is appropriate to speak at any given moment.[2] Although both Black and white students monitor their vocabulary depending on whether or not the teacher is in earshot, for example, code-switching is more than simple vocabulary monitoring. It involves constant adjustment of syntax, pronunciation, volume, vocal register, grammatical constructions, and non-verbal cues. Consequently, expecting Black students to code-switch in academic settings while not expecting the same of white students is a form of *linguistic racism* involving structuralized linguistic bias against Black students (Johnson et al., 2022).

Code-switching is a tension-filled practice (Wei & Martin, 2009) that may impact students' sense of belonging in academic settings (Wright et al., 2022), sense of personal identity (Myers, 2020), and sense of community (Williams et al., 2022). These impacts are often (though not always) negative, serving to separate students from the place and people around them, creating an additional barrier to belonging or to a coherent sense of self. Expecting Black students to code-switch can contribute to a *double consciousness* (Dubois, 1994), the jarring psychological phenomenon of having two parallel selves, such as the "home" self and the "school" self. Certainly, Black students are not the only ones to experience a disconnect between home and school. However, the codification and explicit expectation that one's home language and one's school language are kept separate is not applied equally across the board, and such injunctions are almost always applied across racial and cultural lines (Young, 2009). Whereas white students are able to bring their full selves to the classroom space, some Black students (and other native speakers of non-standard English) are required to divide themselves. This divide implicitly reinforces the stereotype of school being, by default, a white space, as "academic language" so closely resembles the native English of the mainstream white students (Baker-Bell, 2020a).

In response, some Black students resist using standard English for fear of "sounding white," thereby alienating themselves from both self and community (Lyn, 2022). Still others develop a chronic usage of standard English out of an attempt to curry favor with white peers and teachers (Wei & Martin, 2009). In either case, neither resistance to nor blind acceptance of code-switching is about *learning*, per se. Students who have to negotiate the complexities of when to code-switch, how to maintain relationships in the midst of code-switching, worrying about what code-switching might imply about their personal identities or cultural values, or any other code-switching related topic or fear are employing their cognitive facilities on something other than the course material. In other words, students who code-switch have to think about a whole lot more than students who don't, and this extra cognitive duty comes at a cost. Social psychologist Claude Steele (2011) notes that schools are microcosms of our larger society and therefore subject to the same social organizations, histories, and biases as the culture at large. Unfortunately, much of American history and the organizational structures of contemporary American society combine to place Black students under what Steele calls "downward constituting pressure (p. 28). The combined forces of having to code-switch, feeling out of place in white-dominated courses, being tokenized, not being represented by the teaching workforce, and many more factors tend to push downward on students, meaning that they have to—or they feel they have to—work twice as hard just to make the same progress as their white peers. These downwardly constituting pressures, Steele (2011) claims, "have the power to interfere directly and indirectly with intellectual performance. That is, they might have the power to cause underperformance" (p. 28). There's a sort of grotesque irony in the fact that code-switching, which is so often touted as a pathway to academic success, might actually be partially responsible for academic underperformance. The student can't just worry about giving the right answer; they have to worry whether or not they sound the right way as they're giving it.

In addition to the potential fallout from mandated code-switching, there are legitimate questions about whether or not code-switching is a sufficient response to linguistic racism in the classroom. Baker-Bell (2020b) summarizes the problem with damning insight:

> If we, as teachers, truly believe that code-switching will dismantle white supremacy, we have a problem. If we honestly believe that code-switching

> will save Black people's lives, then we really ain't paying attention to what's happening in the world. Eric Garner was choked to death by a police officer while saying "I cannot breathe." Wouldn't you consider "I cannot breathe" 'standard English' syntax?[3] (p. 5)

Even if code-switching does, in fact, lead to fluency in standard English, and even if it does not interfere with the other cognitive processes necessary for academic performance, it is difficult to imagine how code-switching, by itself, can effectively combat all the legal, social, and other cultural structures that disadvantage those who are not in the white majority. The automatic assumptions of both individual bias and structural racism are at play long before a person opens their mouth or puts metaphorical pen to paper.

In *Arrival* (Villeneuve, 2016), Dr. Banks' entire framework for seeing the world is upended as she learns the Heptapods' language. To the film's credit, this new framework comes at a cost. Although Dr. Banks is able to see the future, and though that new skill helps her save the planet, it also means that she is experiencing the unimaginable heartbreak of losing her daughter *before her daughter is even born*. Burdened with her knowledge of the future, she tells her husband of the fate that their daughter will suffer, *and her husband leaves her*, saying that she made the wrong choice, that she should have chosen not to have children if she knew this would be the outcome. She becomes something of an outsider in her own family, living in the present and the future simultaneously. She experiences a sort of double consciousness, as if she is watching herself from the outside in. Yes, the Heptapods have given her a gift, and yet she has paid dearly for it. At one point in the film, she openly questions whether or not it has been or will be worth it.

The Heptapods explain their mission on Earth simply. They are here to "offer" their language. In American history, however, standard English has not always been an "offer." For much of U.S. history, the "tool" really was a "weapon."

Eradication of Culture and Language

Captain R.H. Pratt, who founded the Carlisle Indian School in 1879, was horrified by the slaughter of Native Americans. These were people. Uncivilized people, in his opinion, but people nevertheless. The solution to the problem of Native Americans was not murder, he said. It was civilization.

It was Native American *culture* that needed to be eradicated, not Native American people, which led him to utter these famous and chilling words: "Kill the Indian in him, and save the man" (Pratt, 1892, p. 46).

Pratt and those like him held to a *deficit model* of education when it came to Native Americans. A deficit model begins by assuming that student performance is primarily a function of what is *wrong*. For example, if a student fails a math test, that failure is due to an inherent weakness or problem either in the student or in the student's background/culture/whatever. Teachers who use a deficit model see education in terms of "fixing" students, of correcting bad habits, of compensating for deficiencies, of undoing damage. Something is broken in the student, and the teacher is here to fix it.

Most of the time, the deficit model is subtle. Consultants and their curricula use words like "solutions" and "at risk." Students are described as "*lacking* reading skills" or "*below* grade level." This language is common and, unfortunately, relatively uncontroversial. The assumption that the primary purpose or strategy of education is to "fix" students can be found embedded in such wide-ranging pedagogical topics as the five-paragraph essay (Brannon et al., 2008), science communication (Reincke et al., 2020; Grant, 2023), family dynamics (Minniear, 2023), and comparative international assessments of student performance (Anderson-Levitt, 2023). Even the notion of "grit," the incredibly popular and go-to term for persistence or "stick-to-it-iveness" is rooted in deficit model thinking, because it presumes that the fundamental explanation for poor academic performance is a lack of student effort, or at least a lack of the right kind of effort. Instead of questioning whether or not the task that was given to students was fair, well-communicated, or even achievable, the deficit model begins and ends with the assumption that the solution to poor performance is to teach students to try harder and not quit (Tewell, 2020).

There is nothing wrong with grit, and providing students with tools and strategies for overcoming obstacles is a necessary and vital part of teaching. But are the strategies important because students are inherently prone to giving up, or are the strategies necessary because the nature of the task is such that multiple attempts are just part of the process? If the task is difficult, is that due to a deficiency in the learner or simply due to the nature of the task itself? A deficit model points toward the former, whereas an *asset-based model* points to the latter. In the asset-based model, the differences that students bring to the classroom are strengths or, at the very least, the raw materials for future success. In a deficit-model approach, a student whose says "ain't" speaks a broken version of English, and their contraction needs to be corrected to the "proper" *isn't* or *aren't*. In the asset-based approach, however, "ain't" is a sign of grammatical and syntactical sophistication. It indicates that the student knows how and when to use contractions, and the teacher notes that the student follows the rules of "ain't" consistently. The student's use of "ain't" reveals a keen and clever use of language, which the teacher can build upon.

Pratt did *not* have an asset-based model of Native American education. His school, which became the flagship school under the administration of the Bureau of Indian Affairs and the model for hundreds of future boarding schools, sought to fix the so-called deficits of Native American culture by removing Native American children from their families, communities, and lands and forcing them to adopt and learn Western customs. Students were forced to wear suits and ties or dresses. They had to cut their hair according to mainstream American styles. They learned to play Western instruments so well that the Carlisle Band performed for the inauguration of President Theodore Roosevelt. They learned American sports like football and baseball, winning national championships and creating future Hall-of-Famers. Of course, the methods used to bring about this radical transformation were often appalling. Students were beaten, placed in solitary confinement, forced into hard labor, and, in some cases, outright killed. More than 180 students died at the Carlisle school during its 39 years of operation. They are buried on school grounds to this day (National Park Service, 2024, n.p,).

One of the primary ways that the school sought to "civilize" the Native American students was by forbidding them to speak their native languages and forcing them to learn English and English only. Interestingly, Pratt (1892) saw his work through an essentialist lens. Learning to speak English, he claimed, was the only way to bring the Native Americans into community with the general American populace. Pratt abhorred the reservations to which Native Americans had been condemned, and he believed that the public school system was the perfect place to bring *all* people together:

> We have established the public school system , where people of all races may become unified in every way, and loyal to the government; but we do not gather the people of one nation into schools by themselves, and the people of another nation into schools by themselves, but we invite the youth of all

> peoples into all schools. We shall not succeed in Americanizing the Indian unless we take him in in exactly the same way. (Pratt, 1892, p. 54)

The Carlisle school, which was a Native-American-only school, was supposed to be a temporary endeavor:

> Indian schools must, of necessity, be for a time, because the Indian cannot speak the language, and he knows nothing of the habits and forces he has to contend with; but the highest purpose of all Indian schools ought to be only to prepare the young Indian to enter the public and other schools of the country. (p. 58)

One primary method for preparing Native American students for entrance into public schools was to teach them English. However, because Pratt and his followers held Native American culture in such contempt, they did not allow code-switching. Instead, they sought to eradicate all traces of Native American language. Only by learning English and forgetting their old languages could the Native American students be made ready for citizenship. Citing some of his previous "successes," Pratt notes that his former students are now "English-speaking and civilized" (p. 51). He uses this particular combination of adjectives on more than one occasion, because language and civilization are inextricably linked.

A wide variety of still-existing records from the Carlisle school provide some graphic and disturbing details of the ways that students were forced to learn English. When new students arrived at the school, school officials assigned each student a new English name and forbid them to use their "old" names (National Park Service, 2024), kept students from the same tribe apart from one another so that they could not use their native languages (Townsend, 1880), prohibited them from singing Native songs unless the songs were translated to "stimulate proper English instruction" (Carlisle Arrow, 1913, p. 8), and compelled them to labor alongside native English speakers as factory workers, farmers, and/or housekeepers in order to practice their English (Commissioner of Indian Affairs, 1885). By all contemporary accounts, these strategies, combined with their regular classroom instruction, were effective at teaching students to master standard English.

The process in which one group is expected to adopt the language, patterns, customs, and values of the other group is called *assimilation.* This is not the great "melting pot" of American mythology, in which people from many cultures come together, meet in the middle, and become something new. This is, instead, a concept of unity based solely on erasing difference. Assimilation involves no give-and-take, no back-and-forth exchange of ideas, cultures, languages, or customs. Instead, it is a one-way street where the burden of change and adaptation rests solely on the shoulders of the "other." The Carlisle Indian School and all the other schools it inspired were based on an assimilationist version of essentialism: the best way to preserve our society and maintain our culture is to make "them" more like "us." Assimilation is often framed in noble language—that is, it is framed as a gift. For example, current-day efforts to promote standard English in classrooms are framed as "preparing students for the real world" (CCCC, 2020, n.p.). The underlying assumption, however, is that the world of standard English is the one that matters most, and the teacher's job is to bend the student to the expectations of that world, whether they like it or not. After all, it's for their own good, right?

Let us be clear: Pratt's attempts to "civilize" Native Americans were grotesque, vile, criminal, and morally wrong. What is also clear, however, both from Pratt's own writings and from general consensus, is that Pratt understood the relationship between language and culture very, very well. Because he believed that Native American cultures were deficient, it must follow that their languages were also deficient. In order to "fix" the deficiency, he had to start by "fixing" the language. To use Pratt's own highly disturbing metaphor, in order to kill the Indian (meaning the Indian culture), he had to start by killing the language. Or you could look at it this way: the English language was the weapon that Pratt (1892) used to "kill" the Indian culture (p. 46).

Of course, if you had asked Pratt, he would have said that he was doing good, that English was a gift, which brings us right back to the central question of *Arrival* (Villeneuve, 2016): Is language a gift or a weapon? Which, exactly, are the Heptapods offering?

The complex answer is "both." There is, unfortunately, a long history of English instruction being used as a weapon designed to destroy, eradicate, and erase. Some essentialists cite the preservation of culture as the reason for compelling the use of standard English. If we do not maintain our language, they claim, we will fail to preserve our culture. And they are right, to a degree, because language and culture are inextricably linked.

But what about the cultures whose languages are *not* the standard? If standard English is the language of the schools, of the marketplace, of the government halls, what happens to the cultures whose languages are not heard? Are those cultures not worth preserving, as well? Why does one culture's language take precedence over another's, particularly when both cultures are part of the same nation?

Linguistic Justice

What are the solutions to systems of English instruction based on the weaponization of language? If mandated code-switching and the promotion of standard English based on a deficit-model are examples of linguistic injustice, what would linguistic justice look like? These questions are neither idle nor rhetorical, and they are the same questions being asked by a growing number of educators, researchers, and policy makers. There is a growing recognition across the world that educational systems that require standard English as the *lingua franca* do so at the expense of local and regional language norms (Csata & Marácz, 2021). There is also a growing awareness that the solution to this problem will most likely be found through public policy (De Schutter, 2007). In other words, the solution, if there is one, is political, which may explain a rise in linguistic activism in educational settings.

In 2020, the Conference on College Composition and Communication (CCCC), which is a sub-organization of the National Council for Teachers of English (NCTE), released a document entitled "This Ain't Another Statement: This is a DEMAND for Black Linguistic Justice." This "non-statement" included a list of demands:

1. teachers stop using academic language and standard English as the accepted communicative norm, which reflects White Mainstream English!

2. teachers stop teaching Black students to code-switch! Instead, we must teach Black students about anti-Black linguistic racism and white linguistic supremacy!

3. political discussions and praxis center Black Language as teacher-researcher activism for classrooms and communities!

4. teachers develop and teach Black Linguistic Consciousness that works to decolonize the mind (and/or) language, unlearn white supremacy, and unravel anti-Black linguistic racism!

5. Black dispositions are centered in the research and teaching of Black Language! (CCCC, 2020).

The CCCC's demands are centered on the beliefs that 1) the normalization of standard English promotes white cultures to the detriment of Black cultures and Black students; and 2) multiple languages can exist side-by-side without the need to promote one over the other. The CCCC calls for the normalization of Black English in education spaces by adopting representative curricula, training teachers in linguistic justice and activism, discarding racist constructs such as "academic language," and reforming the research and publication process to not penalize Black English in academic spaces. This is, of course, a small and insufficient summary of their demands.

Policies that encourage monolingualism (such as allowing for standard English only) often enforce an asymmetric bilingualism, in which students from group A are forced to learn the language of group B, but group B does not learn the language of group A (Van Parijs, 2002). One potential step toward linguistic justice is to formally recognize the multilingualism that so many students bring to the classroom. This may involve rethinking the group names used for describing native speakers of other languages. The term "English Language Learners," for example, uses an assimilationist deficit model to define students' linguistic abilities. They are defined not by what they *do* know but rather by what they do not yet know. González-Howard & Suárez (2021) suggest that the simple act of using an asset-based name such as "multilingual students" or "emergent bilingual students" might decentralize standard English as the sole measure of linguistic ability, taking the first step toward a greater linguistic justice in the classroom.

Schools and universities are beginning to recognize and push back against their own legacies of exclusionary linguistic policies. The Writing Center at East Carolina University, for example, publishes a linguistic justice pamphlet for professors and students, reminding them that "a preoccupation with standard English is a gatekeeping mechanism" (East Carolina University, 2024, p. 2) and encouraging professors to keep in mind that while standard English grammar is not racist, the policies that weaponize it are (Inoue, 2017).

Conclusion

Weapon or tool? Blessing or curse? *Arrival* (Villeneuve, 2016) highlights the dual potentials of language education to broaden our horizons or trap us in solitude, to connect us to a larger world or to isolate us from ourselves and our communities. When language is used to destroy—that is, when it is weaponized and wielded against students to highlight their supposed deficiencies, or when it is used as a means of cultural erasure in the name of social cohesion and unity—it is poison. In *Arrival* (Villeneuve, 2016), the Heptapods' language fundamentally transforms Dr. Banks' interpersonal and temporal relationships, but we must remember this: she *chose* to learn. The gift was offered, and she said *yes*. Even then, the psychological, emotional, and relational costs were high. How much higher the cost for students who are compelled to check their own languages at the door and forced to learn a language that they never asked to learn? How much higher the cost for the students whose own languages have been deemed insufficient and lacking, whose ways of thinking and being, they are told, are simply not good enough? Gloria Anzaldúa (1987) tells us just how high: "So, if you want to really hurt me, talk badly about my language. Ethnic identity is twin skin to linguistic identity—I am my language. Until I can take pride in my language, I cannot take pride in myself" (p. 39).

Questions for Reflection

1. What would you have to learn before creating a linguistically diverse learning space? What would others need to learn about you?

2. Imagine a classroom in which all students learn about one another's linguistic norms. What would language instruction look like? How would you identify and respond to students' linguistic needs?

3. How do we avoid weaponizing language instruction while still preparing students for the norms of outside entities (e.g., universities, the corporate world, etc.)?

4. How can we normalize linguistic diversity when so many instructional materials assume a standard English norm?

5. How would you respond to parents who worry that your language instruction is not preparing students for the "real world?" How would you communicate the need for linguistic justice?

Endnotes

1. These are all groups specifically named by Robbins as having English deficiencies that must be "corrected" if we are to protect our language and way of life.
2. The Black/white divide in code-switching is overly simplified here. For example, white students from rural Appalachia, say, might find it necessary to code-switch in academic settings. Extreme regionalisms will be subject to code-switching, regardless of race or skin color. However, most school policies and legislative agendas around code-switching are based on a perceived Black/white divide.
3. As I typed this quote, Word underlined "ain't" in red, indicating that spellcheck algorithms are trained using the linguistic norms of standard English, even though "ain't" is common usage for many native English speakers. Does structural racism extend to spellcheck and other AI functions?

References

Akter, H. (2020). Semiotic and temporal relativity in Arrival. *Global Journal of Human-Social Science: Arts and Humanities – Psychology, 20*(13).

Anderson-Levitt, K. (2023). The deficit model in PISA assessments of competencies: counter-evidence from anthropology. *Globalisation, Societies and Education*, 1–17. https://doi.org/10.1080/14767724.2023.2223141

Anzaldúa, G. (1987). *Borderlands/La Frontera: The new mesitiza*. San Francisco, CA: Spinsters/Aunt Lute.

Baker-Bell, A. (2020a). Dismantling anti-black linguistic racism in English language arts classrooms: Toward an anti-racist black language pedagogy. *Theory Into Practice, 59*(1), 8–21. https://doi.org/10.1080/00405841.2019.1665415

Baker-Bell, A. (2020b). *Linguistic justice: Black language, literacy, identity, and pedagogy*. NCTE, New York.

Bohn, A. P. (2003). Familiar voices: Using Ebonics communication techniques in the primary classroom. *Urban Education, 38*(6), 688–707. https://doi.org/10.1177/0042085903257315

Bolinger, D. (1980). *The use and abuse of language today*. London, UK: Routledge. https://doi.org/10.4324/9781315842103

Brannon, L., Courtney, J. P., Urbanski, C. P., Woodward, S. V., Reynolds, J. M., Iannone, A. E., & Kendrick, M. (2008). EJ extra: The five-paragraph essay and the deficit model of education. *The English Journal, 98*(2), 16–21. https://www.jstor.org/stable/40503377

Buckley, N. E. (2024). Temporal journeys and human perception: Analyzing nonlinear narratives and scientific fantasy in the film Arrival. *Art and Society, 3*(1), 53–59. https://www.paradigmpress.org/as/article/view/978

Cai, D. (2023). Zero-sum or win-win Game? Comparative studies on sports/game metaphors and ideological framing in economic news on Sino, EU and US trade disputes. *Review of Cognitive Linguistics*. https://doi.org/10.1075/rcl.00164.cai

Carlisle Arrow. (1913). Navajo Indian song by Abbott children. *The Carlisle Arrow, 10*(15). December 12. https://carlisleindian.dickinson.edu/sites/default/files/docs-publications/CarlisleArrow_v10n15.pdf

Carlson, L. J., & Wilson, P. I. (2004). Beyond zero-sum: game theory and national forest management. *The Social Science Journal, 41*(4), 637–650. https://doi.org/10.1016/j.soscij.2004.08.007

Carruthers, A. (2018). Temporality, reproduction and the not-yet in Denis Villeneuve's Arrival. *Film-Philosophy, 22*(3), 321–339. https://doi.org/10.3366/film.2018.0083

CCCC. (2020). *This ain't another statement! This is a DEMAND for Black linguistic justice!* https://cccc.ncte.org/cccc/demand-for-black-linguistic-justice

Chiang, T. (2010). *Stories of your life and others.* New York, NY: Knopf Doubleday Publishing Group.

Clark, T. (2023). Destandardizing English: Seeking linguistic justice in the English Language Arts classroom. *Literacy Information and Computer Education Journal (LICEJ), 14*(1), 3748–3756. https://doi.irg/10.20533/licej.2040.2589.2023.0493

Commissioner of Indian Affairs. (1885). *Annual Report of the Commissioner of Indian Affairs to the Secretary of The Interior for the year 1885.* Washington: Government Printing Office. https://carlisleindian.dickinson.edu/sites/default/files/docs-publications/BIA-Annual-Report_1885_Narrative_OCR.pdf

Coon, J. (2020). The linguistics of Arrival Heptapods, field linguistics, and universal grammar. *Language Invention in Linguistics Pedagogy,* 32–48.

Csata, Z., & Marácz, L. (2021). Social inclusion and multilingualism: Linguistic justice and language policy. *Social Inclusion, 9*(1), 1–4. https://doi.org/10.17645/si.v9i1.3941

De Schutter, H. (2007). Language policy and political philosophy: On the emerging linguistic justice debate. *Language problems and language planning, 31*(1), 1–23. https://doi.org/10.1075/lplp.31.1.02des

Dewey, J. (1916). *Democracy and education.* New York, NY: Macmillan.

DuBois, W.E.B. (1994). *The souls of black folk.* New York, NY: Dover Thrift Edition.

East Carolina University. (2024). *What is linguistic justice?* https://criminal-justice.ecu.edu/wp-content/pv-uploads/sites/72/2023/03/Linguistic-Justice.pdf

Ferraro, F., Pfeffer, J., & Sutton, R. I. (2005). Economics language and assumptions: How theories can become self-fulfilling. *Academy of Management Review, 30*(1), 8–24. https://doi.org/10.5465/amr.2005.15281412

Fleming, D. H., & Brown, W. (2018). Through a (first) contact lens darkly: Arrival, Unreal Time and Chthulucinema. *Film-Philosophy, 22*(3), 340–363.

Gándara, P., & Rumberger, R. W. (2009). Immigration, language, and education: How does language policy structure opportunity? *Teachers College Record, 111*(3), 750–782. https://doi.org/10.1177/016146810911100303

Gokhale, S., Basu, D., Mokashi-Punekar, R. (2023). The TIME IS A CIRCLE/CYCLE Metaphor in Denis Villeneuve's Film '*Arrival*' (2016). In: Chakrabarti, A., Singh, V. (Eds.), *Design in the Era of Industry 4.0, Volume 3. ICORD 2023.* Smart Innovation, Systems and Technologies, vol 346. Singapore: Springer. https://doi.org/10.1007/978-981-99-0428-0_8

González-Howard, M., & Suárez, E. (2021). Retiring the term English language learners: Moving toward linguistic justice through asset-oriented framing. *Journal of Research in Science Teaching, 58*(5). https://doi.org/10.1002/tea.21684

Grant, W. J. (2023). The Knowledge Deficit Model and science communication. In *Oxford Research Encyclopedia of Communication*. https://doi.org/10.1093/acrefore/9780190228613.013.1396

Halpern, D. F., & Murphy, S. E. (2013). From balance to interaction: Why the metaphor is important. In D. Halpern & S.E. Murphy (Eds.), *From work-family balance to work-family interaction* (pp. 3–9). New York, NY: Routledge.

Hickey, R. (2012). Standard English and standards of English. In R. Hickey (Ed.), *Standards of English: Codified varieties around the world*, 1–33. Cambridge, UK: Cambridge University Press.

hooks, b. (1994). *Teaching to transgress: Education as the practice of freedom*. New York, NY: Routledge.

H.R. 1532. (2011). *Race to the Top Act of 2011*. [Government]. U.S. Government Printing Office

Inoue, A. (2017). Is grammar racist? A response. *Asao B. Inoue's Infrequent Words*, 27 Feb. 2017, http://asaobinoue.blogspot.com/2017/02/is-grammar-racist-response.html.

Jenkins, J., & Leung, C. (2019). From mythical 'standard' to standard reality: The need for alternatives to standardized English language tests. *Language Teaching*, *52*(1), 86–110. https://doi.org/10.1017/S0261444818000307

Johnson, D. G., Mattan, B. D., Flores, N., Lauharatanahirun, N., & Falk, E. B. (2022). Social-cognitive and affective antecedents of code switching and the consequences of linguistic racism for Black people and people of color. *Affective science*, *3*(1), 5–13. https://doi.org/10.1007/s42761-021-00072-8

Kusumastuti, F. (2019). Polysemy in and of the science fiction film Arrival (2016). *Research in Social Sciences and Technology*, 4(1), 73–91. https://www.learntechlib.org/p/209834/.

Lakoff, G. & Johnson, M. (1980). *Metaphors we live by*. Chicago, IL: University of Chicago Press.

Landry, A. P., Orr, R. I., & Mere, K. (2022). Dehumanization and mass violence: A study of mental state language in Nazi propaganda (1927–1945). *PLoS one*, *17*(11), e0274957. https://doi.org/10.1371/journal.pone.0274957

Lyn, K. O. (2022). Negotiating African American language, identity, and culture in the urban classroom. *Journal of Black Studies*, *53*(8), 780–795. https://doi.org/10.1177/00219347221115

Massachusetts Bay Colony. (1642). *Acts respecting children and youth*. https://ia601202.us.archive.org/18/items/chartersgeneralloomass/chartersgeneralloomass.pdf

Massachusetts Bay Colony. (1647). *The Old Deluder Satan Law*. https://www.mass.gov/doc/old-deluder-satan-law/download

Minniear, M. J. (2023). The role of counter-narratives in resisting the Deficit Model of Families for BIPOC families. *Journal of Social and Personal Relationships*, 40(3), 976–995. https://doi.org/10.1177/02654075221123095

Molyneux-Dixon, L. (2020). Adapting complex time: 'Story of Your Life'(1998) and Arrival (2016). *ECAH*.

Myers, T. K. (2020). Can you hear me now? An autoethnographic analysis of code-switching. *Cultural Studies↔Critical Methodologies*, 20(2), 113–123. https://doi.org/10.1177/1532708619879208

National Commission on Excellence in Education. (1983). A nation at risk: The imperative for educational reform. *The Elementary School Journal,* 84(2), 113–130.

National Park Service. (2024). *The Carlisle Indian Industrial School: Assimilation with education after the Indian Wars (Teaching with historic places).* https://www.nps.gov/articles/the-carlisle-indian-industrial-school-assimilation-with-education-after-the-indian-wars-teaching-with-historic-places.htm

Perkins, K. M., Toskos Dils, A., & Flusberg, S. J. (2022). The perceived threat of demographic shifts depends on how you think the economy works. *Group Processes & Intergroup Relations, 25*(1), 227–246. https://doi.org/10.1177/13684302209516 21

Pratt, R.H. (1892). The advantage of mingling Indians with whites. *Proceedings of the National Conference of Charities and Correction.* Boston, MA: Press of G.H. Ellis. https://carlisleindian.dickinson.edu/sites/default/files/docs-resources/CIS-Resources_1892-PrattSpeech.pdf

Prelipceanu, C. (2008). Military metaphors in business. *Synergy,* (2), 219–227.

Reincke, C. M., Bredenoord, A. L., & van Mil, M. H. (2020). From deficit to dialogue in science communication: The dialogue communication model requires additional roles from scientists. *EMBO reports, 21*(9), e51278. https://doi.org/10.15252/embr.202051278

Robbins, K. (1918). The work of the American Speech Committee of the Chicago Woman's Club, and notes upon its School Survey. *The English Journal,* 7(3), 163–176. https://doi.org/10.2307/801681

Seemungal, A. B. (2018). Logograms and Linguistics: An Analysis of the Figure of the Translator in Arrival. *WL 404W: Literature and Translation, 3.*

Shen, J., & Xia, J. (2012). The relationship between teachers' and principals' decision-making power: Is it a win-win situation or a zero-sum game?. *International Journal of Leadership in Education, 15*(2), 153–174. https://doi.org/10.1080/13603124.2011.624643

Stanley, J. (2015). *How propaganda works.* Princeton, NJ: Princeton University Press.

Steele, C. (2011). *Whistling Vivaldi: How stereotypes affect us and what we can do.* United Kingdom: W. W. Norton.

Strevens, P. (1981). What Is 'Standard English'?. *Relc Journal, 12*(2), 1–9. https://doi.org/10.1177/003368828101200201

Stroińska, M. (2000). Forbidden reality: The language and function of propaganda. In F. Lloyd & C. O'Brien (Eds.), *Secret spaces forbidden places: Rethinking culture,* 121–32. New York, NY: Berghahn Books.

Sticchi, F. (2019). From Spinoza to contemporary linguistics: Pragmatic ethics in Denis Villeneuve's Arrival. *Canadian Journal of Film Studies,* 27(2), 48–65. https://doi.org/10.3138/cjfs.27.2.2018-0003

Tewell, E. (2020). The problem with grit: Dismantling deficit thinking in library instruction. *Portal: Libraries and the Academy,* 20(1), 137–159. https://doi.org/10.1353/pla.2020.0007

Townsend, S. (1880). Editorial. *School News, 1*(7). December. https://carlisleindian.dickinson.edu/sites/default/files/docs-publications/SchoolNews_v01n07_0.pdf

Trudgill, P. (2002). Standard English: What it isn't. In T. Bex & R.J. Watts (Eds.), *Standard English: The widening debate* (pp. 117–128). London, United Kingdom: Routledge. https://doi.org/10.4324/9780203054062

U.S. Department of Education. (2024). *Mission Statement.* ed.gov.

Van Parijs, P. (2002). Linguistic justice. *Politics, Philosophy & Economics, 1*(1), 59–74. https://doi.org/10.1177/1470594X02001001003

Villeneuve, D. (2016). *Arrival.* [Film]. Paramount Pictures

Wei, L., & Martin, P. (2009). Conflicts and tensions in classroom codeswitching: An introduction. *International Journal of Bilingual Education and Bilingualism, 12*(2), 117–122. https://doi.org/10.1080/13670050802153111

Wiley, T. G., & Lukes, M. (1996). English-only and standard English ideologies in the US. *Tesol Quarterly, 30*(3), 511–535. https://doi.org/10.2307/3587696

Williams, Q., Williams, B. M., & Brown, L. C. (2022). Exploring Black girl magic: Identity development of Black first-gen college women. *Journal of Diversity in Higher Education, 15*(4), 466–479. https://doi.org/10.1037/dhe0000294

Wright, N. L., Longerbeam, S. D., & Alagaraja, M. (2022). Chronic codeswitching: Shaping Black/white multiracial student sense of belonging. *Genealogy, 6*(3), 75. https://doi.org/10.3390/genealogy6030075

Young, V. A. (2009). "Nah, we straight": An argument against code switching. *Jac, 29*(1/2), 49–76. https://www.jstor.org/stable/20866886

AFTERWORD

WORLDBUILDING USUALLY REFERS TO the construction of a fictional universe, but we must also remember our roles in the ongoing, collective construction of the real world. Here, I consider some implications of this work for policy. I encourage you, the reader, to expand these thoughts and consider how they might apply to your educational context—whether that's a small rural elementary school, a mid-sized urban liberal arts college, or anywhere else that people are engaged in the difficult work of learning.

First, it is clear that schools and classrooms must be organized in ways that promote critical reflection. By *organized*, I not only mean the physical layout of these spaces—although that is certainly important—but also their social and cultural landscapes. But how can this be achieved? Should individual student desks be eliminated in favor of flexible workspaces? Should teachers use discussion-based exercises in lieu of lectures? Perhaps. These logistical considerations are crucial, and are best decided locally. More broadly, educators need to be aware that fostering critical consciousness is a perpetual project. No one way of organizing a classroom or designing a learning activity will ensure that learners develop an awareness of power relations or resist oppressive structures. Educators committed to critical pedagogy should expect, and welcome, uncomfortable encounters with their students, peers, and/or other observers (e.g., administrators, parents). For example, activities that encourage learners to share knowledge they've gained outside the formal learning space can appear disorganized, drawing ire from those who value orderliness and predictability. Such activities can also cause conflict among learners if their externally-gained knowledge conflicts with one another's. Anticipating and planning for disruptions, conflict, and misunderstandings are crucial tasks for pedagogues committed to critical inquiry.

Legislators, school and district leaders, and teachers all create and enact policies—both formal and informal. It is my belief that policies cannot be counted on to cultivate critical consciousness. Certain policies, such as those that seek to restrict learners' access to particular content or those that emphasize order above exploration, are anathema to critical inquiry. Yet identifying policies that are conducive to it is more difficult. This is because learning is an unstable process, and generating an awareness of power structures that are both transformative and durable necessarily entails extensive adaptation and responsiveness to learners' needs. *Policy* may not be able to promote critical reflection, but *practitioners* can.

Second, it is essential that pedagogues help learners achieve algorithmic awareness, as discussed in Chapter Three. The use of algorithms in education is not new (after all, long division is a mathematical algorithm). It is also not avoidable, and not inherently "good" or "bad." Given their omnipresence, it is essential that learners understand what algorithms they're encountering, how they operate, and what they mean for how the world works. I believe that schools should feature curriculum explicitly intended to promote data literacy. As with other "core" subjects, I think that such instruction should occur across all ages and grade levels. At all stages, learners should be equipped to identify the origins of different types of data, the assumptions baked into it, the ways it is or can be used, and the consequences of those uses.

Lastly, I think that the insights shared in this book underscore the importance of crafting education policies that leave room for flexibility—for both learners and teachers. The rapid pace of technological development; changing demands of workplaces; escalating and compounding crises of capitalism, climate, democracy, and more; and the global expansion of formal education all demand educational systems that can be responsive to novel conditions. Practices like standardized testing can offer important insights into educational inequities, but an emphasis on tests alone can contribute to restrictive learning environments that prioritize testing skills and rote learning above flexible thinking and critical analysis. Similarly, rigid curricula can provide support and structure for teachers and learners, and this can be especially important in contexts with less-experienced, less-trained, and/or less-supported teachers. Yet such curricula come at the expense of responsiveness to teachers' and learners' interests and needs, and can be alienating for both parties. While prescriptive policies can appear as solutions to educational shortcomings, policymakers should be mindful of how these approaches trade off with flexibility.

Ultimately, as the Introduction to this book makes clear, questions of policy depend on questions of intent. What is the purpose of education?

What does it mean to learn? Is education meant to preserve existing systems or to bring about new ones? Is there a difference between education and learning? Chapter Two emphasizes the stakes in these conversations—cultural identity, community, and the threat of societal demise. While the delightful nerdiness of this book may obscure the weight of these questions, readers should consider their implications for daily practice, as well as how they may change over time. As Spock reminds us, it is logical to cultivate multiple options. Good luck.

Dr. Karlyn J. Gorski
Assistant Instructional Professor of Public Policy
University of Chicago

ABOUT THE AUTHOR

DR. JEREMY DELAMARTER is an associate professor and chair of the education department at Saint Martin's University in Lacey, WA, an hour south of Seattle. His research to-date has focused primarily on the ways that pop culture representations of teaching influence, shape, and sometimes distort pre-service teachers' expectations of teaching. His "Inspiration/Content Dichotomy" (ICD) framework, which measures the extent to which pre-service teachers expect to foster affective or academic outcomes in their future students, is used around the world to help teacher educators, education programs, and future teachers develop healthy, realistic, and sustainable teaching practices. Dr. Delamarter's current research interests are increasingly focused on helping education programs develop learning spaces that are, first and foremost, human. Given the mounting pressure to mechanize teaching and learning in the name of speed and algorithmic efficiency, Dr. Delamarter's work seeks to highlight the ways that human learning processes are, in fact, bound in relationship to time, space, and other people. Delamarter's model of a sustainable educational ecology sees the limitations of human scalability not as a liability but as an asset, highlighting the crucial differences between a statistical and a relational understanding of the world, because, unlike statistical knowledge, relational knowledge begets mutual obligation and interdependence. This research has led Dr. Delamarter to be an in-demand consultant with Seattle-area tech companies working with AI in education. In addition to his work at Saint Martin's, Dr. Delamarter holds teaching privileges at Roma Tre University in Italy, and he serves on the executive board of the Washington Association of Colleges of Teacher Education. He is the author of *Proactive Images for Pre-Service Teachers* (Palgrave Macmillan) as well as numerous academic articles and other publications.

INDEX

D